D0812731

THE MISSION

THE MISSION

JOURNALISM, ETHICS
AND THE WORLD

JOSEPH B. ATKINS

EDITOR

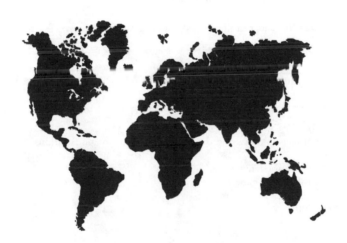

INTERNATIONAL TOPICS IN MEDIA

Iowa State Press
A Blackwell Publishing Company

JOSEPH B. ATKINS is Associate Professor of Journalism at the University of Mississippi, where he teaches courses in reporting, media ethics, and international journalism. Since 1977, he has served as reporter, editor, writer, and columnist for several newspapers, including five-years as congressional correspondent for Gannett News Service.

© 2002 Iowa State University Press
A Blackwell Publishing Company
All rights reserved

Iowa State Press
2121 State Avenue, Ames, Iowa 50014

Orders: 1-800-862-6657
Office: 1-515-292-0140
Fax: 1-515-292-3348
Web site: www.iowastatepress.com

Authorization to photocopy items for internal or personal use, or the internal or personal use of specific clients, is granted by Iowa State Press, provided that the base fee of $.10 per copy is paid directly to the Copyright Clearance Center, 222 Rosewood Drive, Danvers, MA 01923. For those organizations that have been granted a photocopy license by CCC, a separate system of payments has been arranged. The fee code for users of the Transactional Reporting Service is 0-8138-2188-6/2001 $.10.

♾ Printed on acid-free paper in the United States of America

First edition, 2002

International Standard Book Number: 0-8138-2188-6

Library of Congress Cataloging-in-Publication Data

Atkins, Joseph B.
The mission : journalism, ethics and the world / edited by Joseph B. Atkins.
    p. cm.
Includes bibliographical references and index.
ISBN 0-8138-2188-6 (alk. paper)
1. Journalistic ethics. I. Atkins, Joseph B.
PN4756 .M57 2001
174'.9097—dc21
                          2001004640

The last digit is the print number: 9 8 7 6 5 4 3 2

The Mission: Journalism, Ethics and the World is dedicated to my children, Rachel Marie Atkins and Joseph Michael Atkins, and to the memory of their mother and my late wife, Marilyn Tapscott Atkins, and to my late father, Roger Burton Atkins.

Contents

Contributors

Maria Henson is deputy editorial page editor at the *Austin American-Statesman* in Austin, Texas, and a former editorial writer with *The Charlotte Observer*. As editorial writer for the *Lexington Herald-Leader* in Lexington, Ky., in 1992, she won the Pulitzer Prize for her editorials on battered women in Kentucky. A Nieman Fellow at Harvard University and Burns Fellow in Bonn, Germany, Henson served as a Pulitzer juror in 1994, 1995, 1999, and 2000, and has been appointed to the ASNE writing awards committee.

Joseph B. Atkins is an associate professor of journalism at the University of Mississippi, a statewide syndicated columnist, and a former congressional correspondent with Gannett News Service. His writings have appeared in such newspapers as *USA Today, Detroit News, Baltimore Sun, Honolulu Star-Bulletin*, and *The Cincinnati Enquirer*, and in such journals and magazines as *Journalism & Mass Communication Educator, International Communication Bulletin, Quill, Oxford American*, and *Christianity Today*.

John Merrill is professor emeritus at the University of Missouri-Columbia School of Journalism and author of more than twenty books on international journalism and media ethics, including *Existential Journalism, The Foreign Press, The Imperative of Freedom, The Dialectic in Journalism, International Communication, The Elite Press*, and *Legacy of Wisdom*. Merrill wrote the first textbook in English that compared world press systems. He was a distinguished visiting professor at the American University in Cairo.

Jerry Mitchell is an investigative reporter with *The Clarion-Ledger* in Jackson, Mississippi, and winner of the Sigma Delta Chi Award for Public Service, Heywood Broun Award, the Sidney Hillman Award, and the NAACP Community Service Award. He was one of four journalists honored by the Anti-Defamation League at the Kennedy Center in Washington, D.C., in October 1998. Portrayed in the movie, *Ghosts of Mississippi*, Mitchell has spent years investigating unsolved civil rights–era murders. His work led to the convictions of white supremacist Byron De La Beckwith and former Imperial Wizard Sam Bowers.

Michael Snodgrass is an assistant professor of history at Indiana University at Indianapolis who has investigated and written on the media in Latin America, the Mexican Revolution, and labor relations and the working class in twentieth century Mexico and Argentina. His work has appeared in the *Latin American Research Review, International Labor and Working Class History*, and in several anthologies on Latin American History.

Stephen F. Jackson is associate editor and publisher of the *Latin American Post* in Bogota, Colombia, and associate professor of journalism at Stillman College in Tuscaloosa, Alabama. A Freedom Forum fellow and Knight Journalism Foundation International fellow, Jackson has produced radio and television documentaries as well as numerous articles on the Colombian drug wars and the plight of journalists in that country. His work on those issues has been praised by top Gannett newspaper executive Ken Stickney as "well ahead of other journalists in North America."

Georg Ruhrmann is chair of media science at the University of Jena in Jena, Germany, and an expert in risk communication, new media, and television. Ruhrmann has done extensive studies of media coverage of immigrants in Germany, media aspects of the relationship between East and West in the reunited Germany, and media coverage of issues in biotechnology. He is coauthor of the book *Interactive Television* and is widely published in media and communication anthologies and journals in Europe.

Ildikó Kaposi is a doctoral student at the Central European University, and she holds degrees from Kossuth Lajos University and Goldsmiths College, University of London. Her work on the mass media in post-communist Hungary has been published in journals and magazines in Europe and the United States. She also is an editor with *Médiakutató*, a Hungarian media studies quarterly.

Eva Vajda is a top investigative reporter in Hungary and works as home affairs editor of *Népszabadság Online*. She teaches courses on investigative reporting and basic journalism skills at Eotvos Lorand University in Budapest. A former reporter with the independent weekly *Élet és Irodalom*, she recently coauthored a book of collected investigative stories with Attila Oszabo. She also is an editor with *Médiakutató*, a Hungarian media studies quarterly.

Pavol Mudry is editor-in-chief and general manager of the SITA Slovak News Agency, the first private, independent news agency in Slovakia. A former professor at the Economic University in Bratislava, Mudry helped found SITA in 1997 after working as a correspondent for the Austrian Press Agency and as deputy editor-in-chief at the state-supported TASR news agency in Bratislava. He established and headed the English language desk at that agency.

Bernard Nezmah is an award-winning author and journalist in Slovenia who also serves as an assistant professor of sociology on the Faculty of Philosophy at the University of Ljubljana. He is the author of the best-selling book, *Cursing and Swearing*, and his writings on politics, the media, censorship, and other issues have been published in a variety of anthologies and in such Balkan magazines as *Mladlina*, *Problemi*, and *Tribuna*. A frequent foreign correspondent for journals throughout the Balkans and Eastern Europe, he covered the political crises in Russia in 1991 and 1993, and the rise of Russian leader Vladimir Putin.

Nabil Dajani is professor of communication and chairman of the Department of Social and Behavioral Sciences at the American University of Beirut, Lebanon. A specialist in the role of the Lebanese and Arab media in the Arab world, Dajani completed the essay for this book while serving as a Fulbright Visiting Scholar at the Center for Contemporary Arab Studies, School of Foreign Service, Georgetown University. From 1971 to 1975, he served as a member of UNESCO's International Panel of Experts on Communication Research and worked with other leading scholars in initiating the international debate for a new world communication order. He has also served with the International Association for Mass Communication Research and with its 21st Century Task Force.

Regina Jere-Malanda is a Zambian and London-based journalist. She is an associate editor of *New African* magazine and a former Zambian correspondent for Agence France-Presse. She is also a former Africa researcher with the Index on Censorship, an organization that monitors free speech and related issues around the world. She has written extensively about free speech, women's rights, and other issues in Zambia and across southern Africa.

Minabere Ibelema is a native of Nigeria and an assistant professor of communication studies at the University of Alabama-Birmingham. His research interests are in communication policies and media coverage of Africa. He wrote about media and the colonial legacy in Congo for the 1997 anthology, *Press Freedom and Communication in Africa*. He recently completed a major study of the Nigerian press performance during the country's political crisis in the mid-to-late 1990s.

Jayanti Ram-Chandran is a native of Calcutta, India, and a freelance writer now living in Vancouver in British Columbia, Canada. Her writings on the press in India have been published in such journals as the *International Communication Bulletin*. She has worked with CNN and CNN Headline News in Atlanta, Ga., and as a correspondent in the United States for several South Asian newspapers. She recently returned from a four-month tour of India, where she conducted research for her essay for this book.

xii

Contributors |

Akhilesh Upadhyay is U.S. correspondent for Kantipur Publications, Nepal's leading media organization and publisher of the Nepali-language newspapers, *Kantipur* and *The Katmandu Post*. Upadhyay is also a Fulbright scholar now pursuing graduate studies at New York University. His articles have appeared in such publications as *The Baltimore Sun* and *The New York Daily News*. His major areas of reporting are foreign policy, national politics, human rights, and the environment.

Takehiko Nomura is a freelance writer based in Tokyo, Japan, who has worked with JapanToday.com, a newly established online news service in Tokyo, and as a correspondent with Bloomberg Television in Tokyo. His writings have appeared in such publications as the *Christian Science Monitor* and *The Washington Times*. He was a 1996 fellow at the Washington Center for Politics and Journalism in Washington, D.C.

Neil W. White III is the creative director and publisher of *Life 101* magazine and is president of The Nautilus Publishing Company in Oxford, Mississippi. He is the former publisher of *New Orleans*, *Coast* and *Louisiana Life* magazines. He also served as publisher and editor of the *Coast Business Journal* and *The Oxford Times* newspaper. He is a playwright whose produced works include *Paper* and *Lepers & Cons*.

Chuck Trapkus illustrated, edited, and published *The Catholic Radical*, a quarterly journal of issues and ideas related to the Catholic Worker Movement. He helped start the Dorothy Day Catholic Worker House of Hospitality in Rock Island, Ill., in 1983. He was a former editorial artist with the *Daily Dispatch* in Moline, Illinois, whose writings and illustrations have been published in *The New York Times*, *Philadelphia Inquirer*, *The Other Side*, *Plains Magazine*, and numerous other periodicals and books. Trapkus tragically was killed in a car accident during the Christmas holidays of 2000.

Foreword

by Douglas A. Boyd
University of Kentucky
and
Joseph D. Straubhaar
University of Texas at Austin

We are pleased to introduce you to the second book in our international communication series published by Iowa State University Press. When you examine the table of contents and list of contributors you will understand how impressed we were when Professor Joseph Atkins originally proposed this book for our series. Our initial positive evaluation was based on Professor Atkins' accomplishments and professional experience, the comprehensive and contemporary nature of the chapters, the experience and writing ability of contributors, and most importantly the importance of the subject matter itself.

Joseph Atkins does an excellent job of introducing his book, especially in providing a context for his treatment of the courage shown by both print and electronic media journalists around the world. Of course, this publication focuses to a large extent on journalism ethics and philosophy, largely within an international framework. Immediately following Atkins' introduction, we see the important contribution of John Merrill, Professor Emeritus at the University of Missouri-Columbia. No other American journalism academic has written more extensively and eloquently than John Merrill about international journalism and journalism ethics. Professor Merrill sets the tone for the chapters that follow.

Many readers will immediately recognize the names of the chapter contributors that follow Maria Henson's preface and Joseph Atkins' and John Merrill's introductory chapters—Jerry Mitchell, Michael Snodgrass, Stephen Jackson, Georg Ruhrmann, Ildikó Kaposi and Eva Vajda, Pavol Mudry, Bernard Nezmah, Regina Jere-Malanda, Minabere Ibelema, Jayanti Ram-Chandran, Takehiko Nomura, Neil White, Chuck Trapkus, Nabil Dajani, and Akhilesh Upadhyay. There is, of course, documentation using secondary sources. However, all contributors bring on-the-scene experience and insight to the various countries, including the United States, covered in this book. While it may be unfair to highlight a particular part of this comprehensive publication, we do want to point to Akhilesh Upadhyay's contribution regarding coverage of the terrible situation involving the murder of the Nepalese king and many royal family members in June 2001.

Finally, we believe that readers will find this publication a helpful resource in general for examining the ethics of global journalism and more specifically a valuable resource for the journalism and communication classroom.

Preface

by Maria Henson
Deputy Editorial Page Editor
Austin American-Statesman
Austin, Texas

As an English major with a background in art history, I might have become a high school teacher or a public relations executive or a press agent for an art museum. In my first year out of college in 1982, I might have earned a lot more than $13,300 as a general assignments reporter in the Arkansas state capital. But I had a fever for what my friend and former colleague, Joe Atkins, so aptly calls "the mission," and, to this day, I can't shake it. I wouldn't want to.

Journalists know this code. The mission is a sense of purpose that compels us to define our work as more than gathering facts, interviewing sources for stories, reciting what happened and why. Joe understands that journalists share a common bond no matter where they live. There is a character to what we do, and "the mission" describes it.

"Journalism is storytelling with a purpose," says the Committee of Concerned Journalists, a group of journalists who examined the profession and its core principles at the end of the twentieth century. I think that definition is on target. In U.S. society, as I see it, the purpose is to serve citizens first, providing them with the information they need to make the best decisions for a self-governing society. Our allegiance as journalists is to our fellow citizens: we serve them by giving them reliable, accurate information, acting as their watchdog over those who hold power, and speaking for the forgotten ones and for the voiceless.

I am well aware that U.S. journalists often have an easier road to travel in gathering and verifying facts than our counterparts elsewhere around the globe. In this book, *The Mission: Journalism, Ethics and the World*, Joe has written, collected, and edited essays that will help the reader understand the difficulties that journalists face in emerging democracies and in oppressive regimes. In the United States, our First Amendment grants us the freedom to speak and publish even when the words afflict the powerful and the comfortable. The courts have reinforced our role in helping democracy work. No better example comes to mind than the U.S. Supreme Court ruling in 1971 that upheld the right of *The New York Times* to publish secret documents about the Vietnam War. In the Pentagon Papers case, the Supreme Court said, "In the First Amendment, the Founding Fathers gave the free press the protection it must have to fulfill its essential role in our democracy. The press was to serve the governed, not the governors."

In other parts of the world, journalists' publications have been shut down for offending the governors, and journalists themselves are in peril. The Committee to Protect Journalists, a nonprofit organization dedicated to fighting for global press freedom, reports that in 2000 alone, twenty-four journalists were killed; they either were killed in the line of duty or were deliberately targeted for assassination because of their reporting or affiliation with their news organization. By the end of the year 2000, eighty-one journalists were in prison around the world, from China to Burma, from Turkey to Ethiopia. Their crime? They had done their jobs.

In Germany in the first half of the twentieth century, we saw a press eventually put into service solely to promote the government's interests. The press became both a lap dog and a propaganda machine. Still, the yearning for people to know the truth could not be stifled. Joe recounts in this book the genesis of the underground revolution, the White Rose movement, whose novice journalists had "a ragtag collection of typewriters, stencils, paper, and a mimeograph machine" with which to publish their leaflets decrying Hitler. They stepped in where professional journalists would not go. They did it for their neighbors, their countrymen, the whole of humanity. In the end, they were executed for their deeds and their words.

As a Nieman Fellow at Harvard University in 1993–1994, I began to understand on a deeper level the advantages that U.S. journalists have in fulfilling the mission. Our class of fellows consisted of twelve U.S. journalists and twelve foreign journalists. Within our group, one journalist said she had to write her stories as allegories to dodge government censorship of her newspaper in Indonesia. One journalist, a Palestinian, had dodged bullets time and again on the West Bank. Another was a black journalist toiling to make journalistic inroads among white journalists in a newly democratic South Africa. He was navigating a new system that finally counted him a full citizen and finally gave him the right to vote in multiracial elections that spring of 1994. I was humbled by their service and the obstacles these foreign journalists confronted daily in practicing their profession. I also grew more committed to upholding the journalistic values in this country, especially at a time when market forces were changing the industry and technological changes were forcing journalists to deliver news and commentary ever faster.

Call it old-fashioned idealism, but journalists share a common bond. At their best, they follow their conscience to be independent and probing and satisfied with nothing less than bearing witness to the truth as they best can discern it. At their best, they serve the public good, sometimes revealing more truth than society can bear at a given moment, but always fueled by a fundamental belief that to do anything less than pursue and publish the truth would be failing the public. *The Mission* shows readers the best and the worst that can happen in the profession and why we should all hope future journalists will embody the strengths as a testament to liberty.

Acknowledgments

I am grateful to so many people who helped make *The Mission: Journalism,* xvii
Ethics and the World a reality. No one worked harder than Rita Moraes, who
kept faith in this project from the very beginning. I also want to thank my
mother, Maria Stoller Atkins, who helped plant the seed long ago.

Also, I would like to thank the following in no certain order: Stuart Bul-
lion, Xu Yan, Wlodek and Ala Kopycki, Chantal Vassaux, Janusz Amanowicz,
John Merrill, Maria Henson, Pavol Mudry, Linda Trapkus, Stephen F. Jackson,
the Tamm family, Bill Day, Brian Wiulff, Karl Meyer, Wieslaw Oleksy, Elzbi-
eta H. Oleksy, Dan and Ann Searcy, Kevin Bales, Michael Metcalf and the
Croft Institute for International Studies at the University of Mississippi, Laird
Anderson, Juana Suarez, Greg Crofton, Suzanne Byrd, Robin Street, Tom
Lozar, Kathleen Wickham, Robert Oakley, Adrian Aumen, Michael Griffin,
David Hall, Jürgen Hendrich, Evi Womble, John Atkins, Rachel Marie
Atkins, Joseph Michael Atkins, and many, many more.

PART ONE

Introduction

The first two chapters in *The Mission* set the stage for the subsequent essays that take the reader on a journalistic tour from the United States to Latin America, Europe, the Middle East, Africa, and south and east Asia before concluding with three case examples of very different journalists and their own individual journeys and missions.

In Chapter 1, Joseph B. Atkins, associate professor of journalism at the University of Mississippi and editor of *The Mission*, provides an overview of this book with its special focus on the crucial role and responsibilities of the journalist, particularly in societies undergoing profound change.

In Chapter 2, John C. Merrill, professor emeritus at the University of Missouri-Columbia and one of the world's leading writers on international journalism and media ethics, warns of a media world that will increasingly prefer order, harmony, and conformity to what it views as the chaos of freedom and individuality.

Both chapters look at the world as a whole rather than focusing on one particular country. Atkins sees the individual journalist and his or her sense of purpose or mission as central to the health and survival of society as well as journalism. He finds reasons for hope in the examples of journalists such as the late *Catholic Radical* editor Chuck Trapkus and Polish writer Ryszard Kapuscinski, who combine individualism with a strong sense of compassion for others. Merrill is more pessimistic and sees forces at play in the world that ultimately threaten to overwhelm and even destroy individuality.

Chapter one

Journalism as a Mission

Ethics and Purpose from an International Perspective

by Joseph B. Atkins
Associate Professor of Journalism
University of Mississippi

The streets of Belgrade were alive with democracy in late 1996. Hundreds of thousands of protesters marched, shouted, banged pots, tossed eggs, and blew whistles at the regime of strongman Slobodan Milosevic and the state-run television that had tried to portray the antigovernment demonstrations as minor events caused by a few troublemakers.

Journalist Lawrence Weschler described the scene for *The New Yorker* magazine: "It was decreed…that the entire town should endeavor to drown out the noxious bleatings of the TV news. Night after night…all Belgrade seemed to let loose full throttle…. People carried placards that taunted the authorities—especially the resolutely oblivious state-television newscasters."[1]

To get to the truth of what was actually taking place in the streets, the people of Belgrade had to turn off their televisions and turn to alternative, independent media such as Radio B92, which broadcast the demonstrations directly over its weak but persistent signal.

Within this story—an especially poignant one considering the subsequent NATO bombing of Belgrade and the Milosevic government's crackdown on Radio B92 and other independent media—are the essential questions of journalism: What is its purpose? What is its relationship to the public? To government? What do people expect from journalists? What are their responsibilities?

The questions are the same for all journalists, whether they are in Belgrade, Tokyo, Bogota, or New Orleans. The answers may be as different as the cultures and histories of each of those cities. However (and this is the central theme of this book), good journalists everywhere share a common bond: the

3

sense of purpose, of mission, that they carry with them in their work. It is a mission larger than their current story, larger than their news organizations, larger than themselves. And how they define their mission determines to a great extent how they deal with the many ethical dilemmas that all journalists face.

Journalists today work in a world that is more interconnected than ever in history, a world of global politics, global economy, and global media. Within that world, the challenge to journalists to define their purpose or mission and to find and adhere to a personal ethical center has never been greater.

That challenge goes to eastern European journalists still emerging from the legacy of authoritarian governments as well as to Western journalists wrestling with what University of Texas media scholar Mercedes Lynn de Uriarte calls "corporate authoritarianism."[2] The ongoing debate in the United States between the journalistic advocates of traditional, libertarian individualism and those of the more socially conscious public or civic journalism movement could be greatly enriched by incorporating the experiences of reporters and editors in nations such as Hungary or Slovenia. There the ideals of individualism, egalitarianism, and the vision of journalism as a kind of public square where ideas and issues are discussed openly in a common search for truth—ideals that helped bring down communism—now struggle with modern-day corporate pressures that often mimic the communist-era view of media as message bearer for those in power.

This book confronts these matters by probing the hearts of the journalists themselves as well as by considering the systems under which those journalists operate. You will find essays by reporters and editors on the front lines of the news around the world: Stephen Jackson, editor of the only English-language newspaper in the capital of Colombia, one of the world's most dangerous countries for journalists; Takehiko Nomura, a freelance writer and former reporter with an online news service in high-tech yet highly traditional Japan; Pavol Mudry, the courageous editor of the first independent news agency in post-communist Slovakia; and Bernard Nezmah, one of Slovenia's top political writers and a correspondent who has followed stories from Moscow to Paris.

Here are the stories of those who have covered the drama of great political change in their countries—such as Hungarian writers Ildikó Kaposi and Eva Vajda—and those who faced life-changing personal dramas in dealing with the ethical challenges and temptations that journalists encounter even in rich, stable nations such as the United States. One is the late Chuck Trapkus, a political artist whose sense of journalistic integrity led him to leave a mainstream newspaper to follow the self-described "radical" path of journalist Dorothy Day, founder of the Catholic Worker Movement. Trapkus died tragically in an automobile accident during the Christmas holidays in 2000, and his essay here is one of the last he wrote. Another is newspaper and magazine publisher Neil White, who began his career as an idealistic crusader but soon found himself in bankruptcy court after challenging the powers that be in a small Southern town.

This is not a book of communication or ethical theory, but it does address some of the broader issues that affect journalism as a whole, such as fairness and prejudice—as in Georg Ruhrmann's essay about the German media's treatment of minorities—and the relationship between individual freedom and social responsibility. For decades, John Merrill, who wrote the first textbook on international journalism and who is one of the world's most prolific writers on media ethics, has challenged journalists to "exit the stultifying cocoon of conformity, to break ranks and take the existential plunge into the swirling waters...."[3] In a wide-ranging essay that helps provide context for the major concerns of this book, Merrill concedes that the lonely individualism he has long extolled is being superceded today by the more community-oriented ideals envisioned by such media thinkers as Clifford Christians, who wants a journalism that holds the reporter's "feet to the fires of injustice and suffering" and makes the press "a megaphone for those who cry for fairness, relief, and recognition."[4] Yet, this book ultimately belies Merrill's pessimism about the future of freedom and individuality by showing how mission-driven journalists are as individualistic as they are committed to their fellow human beings. One example is the Polish foreign correspondent Ryszard Kapuscinski, fiercely independent yet driven by a profound sense of empathy for the marginalized and oppressed. Another is the aforementioned Chuck Trapkus, who carried on the communitarianism of one of Clifford Christians' heroes, Dorothy Day, yet who was every bit as iconoclastic and courageous as Merrill's existentialist hero.

Another media philosopher, James Carey, once called the ragtag, rough-hewn, "itinerant scribblers" whence all journalists come nothing less than the very root and foundation of democracy itself.[5] Carey, the descendant of Irish working-class immigrants, views the reporter as "the archetypal figure of journalism," and so does this book.[6] Media systems and theories are very important, but the fundamental question, "What kind of journalist am I going to be?", has to be answered by the one who is getting the story. With all the restraints and obstacles inside and outside the newsroom that plague journalists, their job is still to try to make sense of the world. How do they meet such a challenge? What motivates them? What gives them the courage, strength, and persistence to do the hard work and take the risks that journalism often requires?

"Once we establish who we are and why we are, all the rest follows," Chuck Trapkus once wrote.[7] "All the rest" includes some resolution perhaps to those endless newsroom and classroom discussions about invasions of privacy, bribe-taking, undercover reporting, and conflicts of interest.

BORDERS

The bigger questions often get sidetracked in debates about journalism ethics in the United States. And rarely do these debates consider journalists from other countries. In the journalism ethics courses of most U.S. universities, the only significant international elements are the requisite discussions of the classical ethical theories of European philosophers such as Aristotle, Immanuel Kant, and John Stuart Mill, which are used for theoretical underpinnings in assessing the ethical dilemmas of the domestic media. Except for the more recently added debates about the Internet and global media ownership, the world beyond U.S. borders barely exists in these discussions.

In a study of media ethics education at seventy-three U.S. universities in the 1990s, University of Mississippi graduate student Heidrun Kempt found that "the areas that seem to be most neglected are questions dealing with international reporting."[8] This lack of interest is reflective of the apathy in the United States about world news in general, an apathy that, as a Columbia School of Journalism panel once observed, serves to rend the "connective tissue [binding] us to the rest of the world."[9]

Yet, until recent years, discussion of media ethics in other parts of the world was even more restricted. "In Europe, outside of periods like the post-Gulf War crisis of 1991, little attention is paid to media ethics and few media accountability systems are in operation," French scholar Claude-Jean Bertrand said in 1992.[10]

With the fall of communism in much of central and eastern Europe only a year away, the 1987–1988 curriculum of the Moscow State University College of Journalism included as many as ten courses about various aspects of Marxist-Leninist thinking but not a single course devoted to media ethics.[11]

According to Bulgarian media scholar Ekaterina Ognianova, "the textbook on journalistic ethics used in the Department of Journalism in Sofia University until 1989 [framed] the professional morality of journalists…in the Marxist-Leninist ideology."[12]

Under the old regimes of eastern Europe, journalism was ideological work, directly linked with the mission of the state and communism. Foreign correspondents in particular were judged by their ideological purity and their ability to work as spies—not by their ability to gather information and convey it to the public accurately and effectively. Journalists with a simple commitment to truth and justice were demoted, fired, imprisoned, or killed.

The revolutions of 1989 and 1991 showed how things can change, however. Ognianova writes that after 1989, "broad cultural experiences, good writing, and professional competence were viewed as the most important features of journalism"—and, she adds, "knowledge of the West, and of the market economy, and nonpartisan media were in demand."[13]

Today, according to Yassen Zassoursky, longtime dean of the Moscow State University School of Journalism, media ethics is offered in many journalism departments across Russia. "We pay more attention now to ethical problems," Zassoursky says.[14]

Ognianova says concern for media ethics is growing in all of the eastern European countries. Journalists are asking whether they should pay for information, whether it is right to do undercover reporting, how long a promise of confidentiality should be kept, and other questions. The adoption of new codes of ethics in Bulgaria, Russia, Hungary, Croatia, the Czech Republic, and other former communist countries in the region reflects these concerns.

Growing concern isn't necessarily resulting in more ethical journalism, however. "Many journalists simply are missing the fundamentals," write Oleg Stakhanov and Chris Bowman in *Nieman Reports*. "They often fail to independently research or check for accuracy or evaluate the quality of information and sources. Reporters' bylines are attached to unedited news releases from industry and activists. They generally pick up only what is easy and obvious."[15]

Are the challenges facing these journalists really so different from the challenges facing journalists in the United States or other countries?

DIFFERENCES AND SIMILARITIES

Two regions receive special attention in this book—the U.S. South and central/eastern Europe. Beyond being areas of long-held interest to the editor, they are key here in that they show how people vastly separated by geography, history, and culture can have much in common. These regions also show the potential for change. As in post-communist eastern Europe, Mississippi and the rest of the Deep South underwent a revolution during the civil rights movement that deeply affected all aspects of society, including media. The reverberations from those changes continue today, as writers in this book demonstrate.

In Mississippi, scene of so much racial turmoil during the civil rights movement, prominent journalists and news organizations virulently defended the status quo by planting articles, suppressing others, and spying on people challenging the status quo. Later these journalists faced the dilemma of reconciling their past both to themselves and to others.

In Mississippi, the director of the state's own pro-segregationist spy agency, the Sovereignty Commission, was newspaper editor Erle Johnston. Mississippi's most powerful newspapers, the Hederman-owned *Clarion-Ledger* and *Jackson Daily News*, worked with the commission in its war against civil rights workers. Later, under the new ownership of Gannett, the two newspapers published a joint Sunday edition editorial that proclaimed, "We were wrong, wrong, wrong."[16] *The Clarion-Ledger* went on to win a Pulitzer Prize in 1983 for its education reform campaign, a racially charged issue that put the newspapers firmly in the camp of the racial progressives it once opposed.

Bulgaria's Ognianova believes real change is impossible without remembering the past. She cites the philosophy of existential responsibility espoused by media ethicist Merrill (a native Mississippian) in making the case that pre-1989 journalistic spies for the communist regime in Bulgaria should not be forgiven their betrayals of the public and of journalism, that they had choices even under authoritarian rule. She doesn't trust the rehabilitation efforts of these journalists.

In the midst of all the journalist-collaborators, however, we find heroes as well. Bulgarian journalist Georgi Markov paid for his commitment to truth with his life, dying as a London expatriate from the poisoned tip of a communist agent's umbrella. In Mississippi, newspaper editor Hazel Brannon Smith suffered financial ruin for her support of civil rights. Cross burnings, threats, and official condemnation from the state legislature were the lot of editor Hodding Carter Jr., yet he persisted. Mississippi investigative reporter Jerry Mitchell, a contributor to this book, continues today the legacy of these crusading journalists.

Journalists around the world continue to risk their careers and their lives to pursue their calling. They do it in countries as far flung as Mexico, Algeria, Cyprus, Ireland, and Cambodia. According to Mark I. Pinsky in *Quill* magazine, more than one hundred journalists have been killed in Mexico alone since 1970.[17] In his essay for this book, Latin American specialist Michael Snodgrass describes how self-censorship among most journalists in Mexico worked to uphold one-party rule there for seven decades, but how journalistic courage also helped to bring about an end to that rule. Self-censorship is another word for fear, and it is a fear that can kill journalism.

Lamenting the death of nearly two hundred journalists throughout Latin America in just the past decade, syndicated columnist Anthony Lewis wrote: "The purpose of the murders is to send a message—to the press and to all citizens. The message is: Do not disagree with the powerful; do not speak out against evil. Unchallenged, the result would be a silent society, and that is a terrible price to pay."[18]

These modern-day martyrs to journalism are part of a long tradition. Ernie Pyle, Elijah Lovejoy, and Dickey Chappelle are just a few of the many journalists in the United States who have lost their lives doing their jobs. Another is French reporter Paul Guihard, who was shot to death while covering the 1962 race-related riot at the University of Mississippi. In their essays for this book, Nigerian-born media specialist Minabere Ibelema and Zambian journalist Regina Jere-Malanda show how the same spirit that drove these courageous journalists has inspired journalists in their own countries despite great risks.

"The journalist—certainly in the best traditions of the term—is...obsessed with the truth," John Merrill wrote in *Philosophy and Journalism.* "Truth must certainly be the key word in the journalist's lexicon, however it may be conceived."[19]

The journalist knows that this persistent ideal is what makes his work more than just a job, and he knows how vulnerable it makes him. Even erstwhile champions can turn against him. Czech president Vaclav Havel and former Polish president Lech Walesa are examples.

Havel has been calling for a code of "journalistic responsibility" ever since a team of television reporters filmed him in a hospital bed during treatment of lung cancer.[20] The films were secretly made from a nearby building with a view into the window of his hospital room.

The underground or "samizdat" press that challenged the official versions of the truth in Poland during the 1970s and 1980s "played a tremendous role" in the ultimate success of the Solidarity movement, Walesa once told the Freedom Forum in Arlington, Va. "Media shape views and behavior. They affect moods and popularity of politicians. They can turn an unknown person into a famous one, but they can also deprive a respectable person of his good name."

So Walesa asked: "Who do the press, radio, and television answer to? ... Free competition on the media market has become a reality. Not all of us, however, are able to find ourselves in this new reality. Not all the politicians are able to live with the Open Curtain. ... We are pondering the best way for the media to assist the construction of democracy and wonder how to organize this important aspect of life."[21]

Journalists get nervous, and rightly so, when politicians talk about codes of responsibility and assume the task of organizing the media. Consider the proliferation of so-called "insult" laws that work to protect political leaders from an overly critical press in the former Soviet bloc nations.

Veteran Hong Kong politician Martin Lee once offered journalists this advice: "Write the truth as you see it—for every sensitive truth that you report today can only give all of us a little more protection tomorrow. And if everyone reports fearlessly, we will kill self-censorship, because we will kill fear."[22]

Fear, self-censorship, truth—these are the real ethical issues that face every journalist, and at the heart of each is the question of freedom.

"Human society cannot improve, cannot function properly, may not even be able to survive, if the media do not do their job well," Claude-Jean Bertrand writes. "The media's purpose should be to help cure human society of its ailments: to make it free for all and more happy."[23]

Intrinsic to this purpose is a profound commitment—to oneself, to others. How do we view this in an international context? Christians, Ferré, and Fackler, in their book *Good News,* call for a journalism that "joins the outrage against the evils of transnational corporations, the abject failure of five-year economic plans, and the obscenity of regimes maintained only by military might."[24]

In order to write the truth, to rage against evil, to make society "free for all," journalists themselves must have freedom—something that is not, as John Merrill reminds us later in this book, universally valued. Yet in the existentialist tradition that Merrill extols, freedom can exist even in the most authoritarian societies where forces seek to control every thought. Witness Hans and Sophie Scholl, the young, idealistic students at the University of Munich who, in the midst of the most vile and outrageous totalitarian regime of the twentieth century, had the courage to be free. "Freedom" was the last word on Hans Scholl's lips as his Nazi executioner beheaded him. It was the word he and other members of the "White Rose" resistance movement repeatedly wrote in their leaflets and scrawled across the university walls for the world to see.

GLOBAL MEDIA

As for the world today, Merrill isn't particularly optimistic. He sees a retreat from freedom and a growing love of order—be it governmental or corporate. He sees these tendencies in the communitarians and public journalism advocates whose distrust for the intensely individualistic can all too easily be appropriated by mass market–minded corporations.

Working journalists today get their paychecks from corporate media owners whose influence and power extend around the world. Australian-born U.S. citizen Rupert Murdoch oversees a media empire that stretches from New York to Hong Kong. Within four years after the fall of communism, nearly 80 percent of the Hungarian press was foreign-owned.[25] More than 85 percent of the newspapers in the former East Germany are now owned by twelve West German publishers.[26] Even in the world's largest and most diverse democracy, India, the press is largely owned by just a handful of business groups, as Indian-born journalist Jayanti Ram-Chandran tells us in her essay for this book.

Ben Bagdikian has long tracked the trend toward media concentration in the United States. In the latest edition of his *The Media Monopoly*, he writes that just twenty-three corporations control most of the twenty-five thousand media outlets in the country, including daily newspapers, magazines, television, books, and motion pictures.[27] A 1997 study by *Southern Exposure* magazine showed that 84 percent of all daily newspapers in the American South are owned by corporate chains.[28] The club of media owners is becoming more exclusive everywhere. Media scholar Robert W. McChesney says that fewer than ten corporations now dominate the world media market.[29]

The implications of this media globalization and concentration are profound. The globalization of the world's economy—a development accelerated by NAFTA, GATT, and similar agreements—leaves the public "with a corporate protectionism that does not act to protect jobs, communities, democracy, or the natural world," Jerry Mander writes in *The Nation*. "It works to protect and expand business freedoms, to circumvent democratic control and to establish effective transnational corporate governance."[30] John H. McManus puts it this way: Journalists are "bounded by three universal commands: Do whatever it takes to maximize audience; minimize cost; don't embarrass big advertisers or the owners' other interests. ... Content (is) designed more to sell than inform."[31]

Conglomeratization is rife with potential conflicts of interest. Eric Alterman of *The Nation* asks: "Could ABC do a better job of covering Disney-owned sweatshops in Haiti? Could NBC and CBS do a better job of reporting on GE and Westinghouse plants making nuclear weaponry and providing nuclear power?"[32] ABC and Walt Disney are now part of the same conglomerate, as are NBC and General Electric, and CBS and Westinghouse.

The University of Texas's de Uriarte sums up the challenge facing journalists in this global economy: "Obviously, today there are some similarities between the role of a press constricted by an authoritarian government and that of a press constrained by a profit-driven corporation. In both cases, content and participation are narrowly constructed, albeit more by thought-manipulation than by daily brutality. Regardless, such systems both serve the ends of those who control. Corporate authoritarianism is no more appealing than any other form of tyranny."[33]

GLOBAL TECHNOLOGY

In the Beijing Spring of 1989, students and dissidents used the ancient media of posters, leaflets, street corner speeches, and *xiaodao xiaxi*, or "alley talk," to communicate the news and ideas of the ill-fated democracy movement that met its end in Tiananmen Square.[34] Even Beijing journalists waved banners that proclaimed "Don't Believe Us: We Print Lies."[35]

But also key to the movement were the newer media of television, radio, faxes, VCRs, and computers. In the time preceding the spring of 1989, these media had opened the doors to nonofficial perspectives about issues and events, creating questions in the minds of the public from Shanghai to Beijing.

After the tanks rolled through Tiananmen Square, hundreds of journalists were arrested, fired, or forced to write *mea culpas*.[36] But the Chinese government may find it increasingly difficult to enforce its control over the minds of the Chinese people, particularly in and near the more media-savvy big cities such as Beijing, Shanghai, Guangzhou, and now Hong Kong.[37] Indeed, China's reappropriation of Hong Kong may ultimately lead to greater media access in the mainland even as Beijing tries to rein in press freedom in the former British colony.

"Despite the daunting array of challenges facing the developing world, progress is slowly being made," Philip Gaunt writes. "Transborder information flows and the spread of such technologies as videocassettes and fax are making it increasingly difficult to impose tight press controls."[38]

Yet the power of the most basic and simple human means of communication should not be overlooked in our awe of modern technology. The *xiaodao xiaxi* that proved so important in Beijing in 1989 exists in dynamic form in other parts of the world. Philip Gourevitch, author and writer for *The New Yorker* magazine, has written of the importance of the *radio trottoire*, or word on the street, that enlivens political and social discussions in the rapidly changing Congo and other countries in central Africa.[39] Rap, the street poetry and musical lyrics of inner-city African-Americans, could be considered a similar form of communication.

The Colombian novelist and journalist Gabriel Garcia Marquez has warned against an excessive love affair with technology. Stressing that journalism is "a literary art" that should involve reflection and creativity, he once told the Inter-American Press Association that "the profession did not evolve as quickly as its instruments of work" and that many journalists have become "lost in a labyrinth of technology that is madly rushing the profession into the future without any control."[40]

Some worry that commercial forces may ultimately betray the egalitarian promises of the new technology. "Computer technology, rather than empowering people, may actually end up contributing to rising social inequality; the gap between rich and poor further exacerbated by a growing rift between the information haves and have-nots," says Frank Owen of the *Village Voice*.[41] University of Maryland media scholar Mike Dorsher notes that "the information superhighway is fast becoming lined with garish billboards and cybermalls. ... In other words, the Internet increasingly looks and acts like the traditional, business-dominated, consumption-oriented mass media that helped deflate the public sphere."[42]

Marquez calls for a return to timeworn truths, "the old mechanisms of participation," and a commitment to ethics. "Ethics must accompany journalism always, just as the buzz comes with the horsefly."[43]

A JOURNALISM WITHOUT BORDERS

The great Polish journalist Ryszard Kapuscinski writes eloquently in his book *Imperium* about the concept of borders, both political and psychological.

> At the approach to every border, tension rises within us; emotions heighten. People are not made to live in borderline situations; they avoid them or try to flee from them as quickly as possible. ... How

many victims, how much blood and suffering, are connected with this business of borders! ... Be careful that you don't go too far, for you will overstep the mark!

That is why (the gods) try to win adherents by promising people that as a reward that they will enter the divine kingdom—which will have no borders. ... In short, that which is most desired, awaited, and longed for by everyone is precisely this unconditional, total, absolute boundlessness.[44]

Many kinds of borders exist today: Balkan wars, tribal conflicts in Africa, the gaps between rich and poor, North and South. Yet this is a world, too, of global media, global technology, global politics. It is a world that needs a global perspective, not just from political leaders and CEOs but from everyone, particularly journalists charged with the great responsibility of trying to make sense of the modern world.

Is modern journalism the birthright solely of Rupert Murdoch and Time/Warner/Turner-like megacorporations? Do journalists in post-1989 Poland and other former communist countries truly want the kind of journalism wherein "the media treat corporate figures mainly as glorious celebrities and speak respectfully in the new language of consolidation—efficiency, structural engineering, and downsizing—rarely attempting to present such activities within their economic and social context," as Jerry Mander of *The Nation* accuses the Western media of doing?[45]

"Regional and international assistance programs will gradually raise the level of communication in the developing world," Philip Gaunt has written optimistically. "As this occurs, press philosophies, communication systems, and training needs will grow closer together, and the homogenization of journalism already apparent in the countries of the West will spread to the developing countries."[46]

Homogenization simply for the sake of corporate profits isn't a particularly admirable goal, but a common recognition of and respect for our basic humanity and human rights and needs certainly is. So is a journalism that works to uphold such recognition and respect.

So how do individual journalists find their way through this brave new world? Communitarians Christians, Ferré, and Fackler, who place themselves in the intellectual tradition that includes St. Augustine, Martin Buber, and Wendell Berry, say that the alienation of the traditionally detached, aloof, "lone wolf" journalist often helped allow political and corporate forces to circumvent society's best interests. These writers would replace the deep-seated suspicion of community ties that they see as characteristic of journalists, especially foreign correspondents, with "an ethics of universal solidarity, one grounded in our being as humans."[47]

John Merrill is also critical of journalistic detachment or aloofness. However, he believes "universal solidarity" ultimately would mean the end of individualism. Poland's Kapuscinski is one who rises above this dichotomy, for he has already cleared a path that embraces both individualism and solidarity. In many ways the quintessential "lone wolf" journalist, Kapuscinski nevertheless strongly identifies with the defeated, downtrodden, and colonized of the world, people whose experiences remind him of his own long-embattled homeland. "Empathy is perhaps the most important quality for a foreign correspondent," Kapuscinski once said, using a word that also is key in Merrill's essay for this book. "If you have it, other deficiencies are forgivable; if you don't, nothing much can help."[48]

Another great writer from eastern Europe, an early exponent of existential thinking, said as much in the last century. "In our age, all of mankind has split up into units; they all keep apart...each one holds aloof from the rest, hides himself," Fyodor Dostoevsky wrote in *The Brothers Karamazov.* "Sometimes, even if he has to do it alone and his conduct seems to be crazy, a man must set an example and so draw men's souls out of their solitude and spur them to some act of brotherly love, so that the great idea may not die."[49]

Isn't Dostoevsky's challenge to keep the great idea alive the same that faces every good journalist? That, in a sense, is the mission of this book: to keep the great idea of good journalism alive. The writers and scholars here are part of this mission, from the United States to Colombia, Hungary, Lebanon, and Nepal, from the hard-nosed investigative reporters and authority-defying editors to the young idealist who lost his way yet hoped to find it again. As do all missionaries, journalists carry with them the baggage of their own cultures and histories, and they sometimes commit the blunders that this baggage makes inevitable. They often are strangers among strangers, even in their own land, and yet the bond of their common humanity and the nobility inherent in the search for truth that is their work make it a worthy mission, not only for them but for us all.

NOTES

1. Lawrence Weschler, "Aristotle in Belgrade," *The New Yorker*, 10 February 1997, 33.
2. Mercedes Lynn De Uriarte, "Where has the free press gone?" *Quill*, December 1996, 21.
3. John C. Merrill, *Existential Journalism* (Ames: Iowa State University Press, 1996), 124.
4. Clifford G. Christians, John P. Ferré, and P. Mark Fackler, *Good News: Social Ethics & The Press* (NY: Oxford University Press, 1993), 92.
5. James W. Carey, "Where Journalism Education Went Wrong," *Journalism Education, The First Amendment Imperative, and the Changing Media Marketplace*, Middle Tennessee State University, April 1996: 5.
6. Carey, "Where Journalism Education Went Wrong," 5.
7. Chuck Trapkus, "Reclaiming Responsibility: A Catholic Worker Take on Art," *The Catholic Radical* of Rock Island, IL, Winter 1999, p. 7.
8. Heidrun Kempt, *Media Ethics Education in the '90s: Status and Trends* (Master's Thesis, University of Mississippi, 1994), 67.

9. William A. Hachten, *The World News Prism* (Ames: Iowa State University Press, 1996), 127–128.

10. Claude-Jean Bertrand, "Foreword" to *Good News: Social Ethics & the Press,* Christians, Ferré, and Fackler (NY: Oxford University Press, 1993), vi–vii.

11. Elisabeth Schillinger, "Journalism at Moscow State: The Impact of Glasnost," *Journalism Educator* 43 (summer 1988): 52–56.

12. Ekaterina Ognianova, "The Transitional Media System of Post-Communist Bulgaria," *Journalism & Mass Communication Monographs* 162 (June 1997): 27.

13. Ekaterina V. Ognianova, "On Forgiving Bulgarian Journalists/Spies,*" Journal of Mass Media Ethics* 8 (1993): 156–157.

14. Joy Morrison, "The Changing Model of Russian Media and Journalism Education," *Journalism & Mass Communication Educator* 52 (Autumn 1997): 31.

15. Oleg Stakhanov and Chris Bowman, "Russia at the Crossroads," *Nieman Reports* 4 (winter 1996): 50.

16. "Finally, we're moving beyond our lost causes," *The Clarion-Ledger/Jackson Daily News* of Jackson, Miss., 26 September 1982, sec. E, p. 10.

17. Mark I. Pinsky, "Living Dangerously: Journalism in Mexico can be a deadly business," *Quill,* May 1997, 18.

18. Anthony Lewis (columnist for *The New York Times*), "Rally for Latin Journalists," *Commercial-Appeal* of Memphis, TN, 6 August 1997, sec. A, p.10.

19. John C. Merrill and S. Jack Odell, *Philosophy and Journalism* (NY: Longman Inc., 1983), 172.

20. Dean A. Murphy, "A Slow Transition In Eastern Europe," *IPI Report,* first quarter 1997, 13.

21. "President of Poland Praises a Free Press," *Editor & Publisher,* 22 May 1993, 52, 43.

22. *The Freedom Forum International 1996 Annual Report,* 18.

23. Bertrand, "Foreword," vi.

24. Christians, Ferré, and Fackler, *Good News: Social Ethics & the Press,* 104.

25. Ognianova, "The Transitional Media System of Post-Communist Bulgaria," 8.

26. Terhi Rantanen, "What Is to Be Done? Media in Postsocialist Countries," *Journal of Communication* 46 (Autumn 1996): 171.

27. Ben H. Bagdikian, *The Media Monopoly* (Boston: Beacon Press, 2000), p. 4.

28. Ron Nixon and Jordan Green, "Who owns the Southern Media?" *Southern Exposure,* XXV/1 & 2 (spring/summer 1997): 12.

29. Robert W. McChesney, *Rich Media, Poor Democracy* (Urbana and Chicago: University of Illinois Press, 1999), 79.

30. Jerry Mander, "The Dark Side of Globalization," *The Nation,* 15/22 July 1996, 10.

31. John H. McManus, "Who's Responsible for Journalism?" *Journal of Mass Media Ethics* 12/1 (1997): 5.

32. Eric Alterman, "Lionizing Journalism," *The Nation,* 24 March 1997, 6.

33. De Uriarte, "Where has the free press gone?" 21.

34. Lewis A. Friedland & Zhong Mengbai, "International Television Coverage of Beijing Spring 1989: A Comparative Approach," *Journalism & Mass Communication Monographs* 156 (April 1996): 11.

35. Philip Gaunt, *Making the Newsmakers: International Handbook on Journalism Training* (Westport, CT: Greenwood Press, 1992), 113.

36. Jon Vanden Heuvel and Everette E. Dennis, *The Unfolding Lotus: East Asia's Changing Media* (NY: The Freedom Forum Media Studies Center, 1993), 31.

37. Friedland & Mengbai, "International Television Coverage of Beijing Spring 1989: A Comparative Approach," 12.

38. Gaunt, *Making the Newsmakers: International Handbook on Journalism Training,* 159.

39. Philip Gourevitch, "Letter from the Congo: Continental Shift," *The New Yorker,* 4 August 1997, 42.

40. Gabriel Garcia Marquez, "Out of the Labyrinth; Back to Creativity," *IPI Report*, first quarter 1997, 26.
41. Frank Owen, "Let Them Eat Software," *Village Voice*, 6 February 1996, 30.
42. Mike Dorsher, "Whither the Public Sphere: Prospects for Cybersphere" (paper presented at the spring conference of the Mass Communication & Society Division of AEJMC, University of North Dakota, Grand Forks, ND, 1996).
43. Marquez, "Out of the Labyrinth; Back to Creativity," 27–28.
44. Ryszard Kapuscinski, *Imperium* (NY: Vintage International, 1995), 19–21.
45. Mander, "The Dark Side of Globalization," 13.
46. Gaunt, *Making the Newsmakers: International Handbook on Journalism Training*, 161.
47. Christians, Ferré, and Fackler, *Good News: Social Ethics & the Press,* 176.
48. Judith Graham, ed., 1992 *Current Biography Yearbook* (NY: The H.W. Wilson Company, 1992), 307.
49. The Bruderhof, eds., *The Gospel In Dostoevsky* (Farmington, PA: The Plough Publishing House, 1988), 193–194.

Chapter two

Chaos and Order

Sacrificing the Individual for the Sake of Social Harmony

by John C. Merrill
Professor Emeritus
University of Missouri-Columbia

(A version of this essay appeared as "Social Stability and Harmony: A New   17
Mission for the Press?" in the *Asian Journal of Communication*, Vol. 10, No. 2,
2000.)

*The world appears to be ready for a new journalism paradigm, one that stresses or-
der and social harmony. Western media dominance is still a fact of life as the
twenty-first century dawns. But the social forces, pulling ever more complex popu-
lations toward order, cooperation, and a need for authority, are thrusting media
systems into a new and more harmonious communitarianism. The harbinger of
such a drift away from the older libertarianism is found even in the United States,
where "public journalism" is being heralded by many as an antidote to harmful effects of eighteenth century Enlightenment liberalism that is accused of pushing
journalism increasingly toward social irresponsibility and even chaos.*

Trite as it may sound, a shift is occurring in the mass media paradigm
throughout the world, a shift that is aimed at bringing about order and social
harmony. Governments, journalists, and (perhaps) even the public seem to
welcome, for various reasons, such a change. The shift is basically from *the
press* to *the people* (or to national rulers)—from press libertarianism to press responsibility. It began, perhaps, at mid-century and is gaining renewed momentum at century's end. A harbinger of this is the recent appearance of *public journalism* in the United States. The old freedom paradigm based on the
European Enlightenment, however, is still the dominant one in the West.

For example, American communications scholars of press-government relations begin most of their studies with a basic premise: *that Western-style libertarian press theory is what the rest of the world should accept*. And, quite often with missionary zeal, they build their capitalistic and press-centered structure upon such a theoretical foundation. Many of their hypotheses (and conclusions) defend and solidify such assumptions as these:

• Only under capitalism can a press system be diversified, thus furnishing the public with a realistic, helpful, and socially responsible view of the culture and the society.
• The libertarian theory of the press (of communication) is rational *per se* and is therefore a universal objective.
• Democracy, as the West understands it, will (and should) triumph.
• The truth will win out in a free marketplace of ideas and information.

THE ENLIGHTENMENT BIAS

The concepts listed previously as well as many other Western-oriented foundational concepts still guide our study of communication, culture, and the symbiosis between media and government.[1] They are powerful principles—better, *assumptions*—and their proponents have fortified them well against any enemies that have the audacity to challenge them. Of course, these assumptions have been challenged from time to time and by some noteworthy persons.[2] But the challengers are generally pushed over into an ideological corner and, when possible, ignored. Naturally, such criticisms of the Western communication paradigm take on a kind of Marxian dimension, and Marx in Western capitalistic culture is associated with thought control and enslaved media systems.[3] The Marxian label is enough to discredit many socialist and quasi-socialist endeavors to build a state media system that could serve a society or a culture well.

The fact that many so-called libertarian media systems are suspect even by their own societies (such as the United States) and are believed to be socially harmful do little to dissipate the constant barrage of procapitalist media information flooding the world. Western—especially American—academics and practicing journalists travel increasingly to the Third World, preaching the benefits of capitalistic and pluralistic media structures, insisting that every country's media system should conform to such media structures. This perspective is, of course, not only an arrogant and ethnocentric one but also betrays a stultified, intellectual view of reality. Cultures are different. The values that shore up such cultures are different. Stages of national development are different. Citizen expectations are different. When Country A is at one development stage, it would seem obvious that its information system would differ from its system at another stage. When Country A's citizens are tribalized, fragmented, and basically orally conditioned, it should be obvious that its communication system will be different from that of Country B's, which is a highly literate, economically prosperous, and nationally solidified society.

Academic researchers and scholars, and their Western journalistic counterparts, should build their rhetorical and study designs on the realization that Country A is not Country B, and that even Country A at one time is not Country A at another.[4] All nations are *becoming* something else; all nations are developing or changing constantly. It may well be that as one country becomes more economically developed, it is generally becoming less developed in other ways—for example, morally, artistically, or humanistically. A culture's state of development is, indeed, very important when one tries to lower a net of theory or ideology upon it. The communication scholar or researcher is largely defined by ethnocentric forces that push away conflicting assumptions and articulate even basic hypotheses in the familiar and confining ethnocentric formulations.

THE FREEDOM PRINCIPLE

These confines can, with great effort, be broken. It is not easy, and it is often culturally and psychologically threatening and traumatic. But it can be done, and conscientious scholars and researchers, who espouse neutrality and objectivity, should make every effort to do it. People are biased, of course. The good researcher, however, should try to sublimate cultural bias and break out of a natural ethnocentric determinism. Empathy is a key factor in this effort. Scholars who can submerge themselves in another culture, attempting to understand basic values and traditions, are those whose research and pronouncements hold the greatest promise for edification. For a moment, let us look at one concept—*freedom*—and note the difficulty that scholars may have when dealing with it interculturally. The following five propositions (Enlightenment derived) serve to point out underlying problems with cross-cultural dialogue:

1. Freedom is good for a media system and a people.
2. Freedom is necessary for national or cultural development.
3. Freedom is needed for maximum news coverage.
4. Freedom is needed for the discovery of truth.
5. Freedom is necessary for information pluralism or diversity.

The American scholar in communications would probably agree with all five of the preceding statements. Ditto for the scholar from Europe, and maybe Japan and a few other countries. But one shouldn't expect such statements to be warmly embraced in most of Africa and the Middle East. Or, for that matter, in most of Asia and Latin America. For the thrust of these five tenets posits basic values in Western mass communication. These values come from the eighteenth century European Enlightenment, and such libertarian ideas are still very much alive in the Anglo-American political and journalistic cultures.

As valuable to the American culture as this Enlightenment ideology has been, it should not be the dynamo that drives American scholarship. In fact, the best perspective to take in challenging each of these five propositions would be thus: Not necessarily.

Of course, in the case of some of them, the reaction of the largely culture-free scholar might better be more absolute: No. Freedom is not necessary for the good for a people or a press. Freedom is not necessary for national development. Freedom is not necessary for maximum news coverage. Freedom is not needed for the discovery of truth. And freedom is not necessary for informational pluralism or diversity.

Such theorizing does little to satisfy the closed-minded ethnocentrist. It does, however, open the doors of research and scholarship to the wider fields of global and cultural reality. Current media criticism would tend to support a case against Western communication hegemony. For example, mounting criticism of the American press (even from American critics) states that the media are destructive to moral standards, the mental health of children, and national stability and security. Any number of references can be cited to bear this out.[5] Many of these references are critical of American media for their delinquent activities (such as the whole Clinton sex story, the O.J. Simpson trial story, or the Princess Diana death story). And all this in free press systems. But what really do we know about the particulars of any one of these stories? Where is the truth that is supposed to emerge from such a diversity of information? Where is the moral tenor of any one of these stories? Why, it might be asked, should people in the United States and Britain be proud of such journalism?

ETHNICITY AND INDIVIDUALISM

Another assumption among communication scholars in the West today is that ethnicity, although natural throughout the world, is a kind of negative concept that leads to ethnocentrism and thus to intracultural friction and international wars. The advice seems to be this: shed your ethnicity as much as possible, get out of your culture and be acultural, cooperating with those who are designing a more inclusive culture or even a "world culture" in which friction is diminished and harmony is enhanced. Many suggest that similar microcultures should be merged into larger and larger cultural communities.

In spite of the surface appeal of this trend toward eradicating or merging ethnicity and working toward broader communities, it has some questionable aspects. Do not ethnic differences make the world more interesting? Do not ethnic differences lead to group loyalty and pride? Do not ethnic differences simply reflect the cultural personality in the same way that individual differences reflect the human personality? Does not a great variety of cultures provide individuals a better chance to find a comfortable home in which to live with compatible colleagues?

Such questions are interesting, but for many new scholars they are but rationalizations for an old pluralistic paradigm that is now becoming suspect. Ethnocentrism grows naturally out of ethnic differences, and ethnocentrism leads to social or cross-cultural friction, envy, and competition. What we need, for instance, say many new Western communications scholars, is an international or world code of journalism ethics. The plethora of cultural and institutional codes simply does not suffice. Relativism and subjectivity in ethics is no more than a sign of the failed ideas of pluralism spawned by eighteenth century Enlightenment liberalism. This old paradigm simply has not worked, they say, and should be abandoned.[6] Nationalism and ethnocentrism militate against the establishment of such global codes of ethics. But as nationalism and ethnocentrism shrink at the dawn of this new century, as the new communications scholars want and predict, a universal or global Code of Journalistic Ethics will be spawned by some version of the United Nations.[7]

Although the new civic/public journalism advocates, working under the umbrella of communitarianism, want a new paradigm for America, they are generally still tied to the capitalistic media system.[8] Although the people would have more of a say in journalism, the basic private ownership and control structure, though weakened, is still there. So it can be said that civic journalists are still tucked into a traditional paradigm in which the government is locked out. Media-people symbiosis may be gaining ground, but the old concept of libertarianism is still present in the Western media-government relationship. In de-emphasizing journalistic competition, individualism, and editorial self-determination, public/civic journalism shows a basic suspicion and distrust of libertarianism and does move American journalism in the direction of order and harmony.

A small step forward, say the public journalists. At last, communitarianism is replacing individualism in journalism in the West.[9] The journalistic culture is being overlaid by a public culture, and a kind of democratization process is taking place. No longer, it is said (or hoped), will irresponsible editors be able to produce socially harmful journalism. At last the public will serve as a check on press excesses. Egocentric editors will lose much of their power to the people, just as ethnocentric groups will lose much of their power to the people, just as ethnocentric groups will lose much of their power to the more inclusive communities and, ultimately, to the global society. This, at least, is the theory.

So we can see that even civic journalism, little more than a restatement of the mid-twentieth century propositions of the Hutchins Commission, does not really break with the Western paradigm.[10] In fact, its critics believe that it is little more than a new attempt to maximize audiences and profits. But undoubtedly civic journalism is more people oriented and does move a step away from libertarianism, while retaining—for the time being, at least—a basic suspicion of government involvement in the media systems. And, in due time (if it is not already true), its proponents will see it as a new Western paradigm (antilibertarianism in many respects) that is superior to all others and should, if possible, be implemented in other countries—especially in the so-called Third World.

FROM CHAOS TO ORDER: A PARADIGM SHIFT?

Many Third World countries at present simply do not want a Western model for their communication systems.[11] They do not worship the concept of freedom as do Westerners of the more highly advanced (economically) countries. They do not readily accept the assumptions of traditional first principles ingrained in the West. They do not think that government direction (even control) is necessarily bad. In fact, some among them realize that freedom is a danger to their society at its particular stage of development. They trust the government more than they do individual media owners, who are often seen as greedy elitists. They see Western libertarian journalism as harmful to social stability and national development. And they see the Western journalism model as arrogant and based too solidly on economic or profit-making motivations. In short, they want more control of the media for their country, not less. They want order, not chaos. They want more of a monolithic press, not a pluralistic one. They believe that government should have more power over communication. They feel closer to government (a kind of tribal legacy) than they do to independent media owners.

Many of these Third World countries (and even some that are not Third World, such as Singapore, Saudi Arabia, Iraq, and Iran) respect authority and really want a monolithic press. They feel that social order is more important than individual pluralism. They feel that Western journalism is irresponsible, biased, greedy, imperialistic, and harmful to nation building. They are repelled by the chaotic inclination of Western journalism. They gravitate toward a paradigm based on order.

Let us consider the two basic paradigms of the press in the world—first, the Western freedom-centered one that clings to its past; and second, the non-Western, authority-centered one that prevails in most of the world and seems to be getting stronger. There is nothing really new here, but this will serve to show that the slow movement that is occurring away from media autonomy and toward more monolithic media systems (neoauthoritarianism). Simultaneously, a renewed attack on traditional libertarianism is taking place. Let me call these two media paradigms Order and Chaos. These labels reflect a Third World dichotomy and may not fit neatly into Western thinking. From the

Third World perspective, the neo-authoritarian system is mainly designed for social order, whereas the Western libertarian system brings about some degree of social and moral chaos.

Table 2.1. Order and Chaos: Two Paradigms

Authoritarian leaning	Libertarian leaning
O — Organization/autocracy	C — Competition
R — Regimentation	H — Heterogeneity
D — Discipline/direction/dependability	A — Autonomy
E — Egalitarianism	O — Openness
R — Responsibility	S — Selfishness

The Order paradigm, although perhaps not popular in advanced Western countries, is popular in more underdeveloped cultures in which tribalism and respect for authority have a long history. In such countries, centralization of power is important and some form of Machiavellianism is accepted—even expected—from the leadership.[12] There is a desire for homogeneity of the national culture, projected over from the micro-ethnic or tribal cultures. Puritanism is implicit in the Order paradigm. Cooperation is very important, and the certainty principle is enthroned. Harmony, predictability, and socialization are considered very important.

A kind of equality (even if it is an equality of poverty and powerlessness) is reified. Authority and discipline are necessary to social order. And social responsibility is considered far more important than individualism and freedom. Those countries espousing the Order paradigm are not looking for atomistic, journalistic or media activities that may lead to social friction and agitation. Rather they seek social harmony and centralized control that really can come about with orderly and predictable media control. In short, such societies basically find freedom traumatic and psychologically and socially disruptive. So they naturally have a deep aversion to the Western paradigm, which they might well characterize as leading to social disintegration and even to cultural chaos.

The Chaos paradigm is a liberal communications structure that permits great diversity in public messages and in mass media. At least this is the theory.[13] In addition, its pluralism (stemming from freedom) does not permit the accumulation of centralized power. It is a Western theory predicated largely on the ideas of eighteenth century Enlightenment thought that enthrone individualism and freedom. Also, it is theoretically a power-dispersal construct, designed to permit as many voices as possible, with the ultimate aim of allowing the truth to come out. Its faith in media competition (the market place) to bring about good journalism and to eliminate media monopoly is significant. Its critics see its so-called diversity as nothing more than a chaotic cauldron of babble where clarity cannot be found. "Chaos," a term heard often in the Third World describing this libertarian perspective, of course seems excessive to Western ears, but it seems to indicate adequately the extreme reaches of the Western paradigm.

It is this author's contention that, in spite of the harshness of the term "chaos," such a Third World label does have some merit. Few critics of the media would disagree that increasingly there seems to be a drift toward anarchy and lack of direction (legal or moral) to excesses that are observed on every hand. Although it is quite true that there are editors and publishers, news directors and managers, who produce responsible and salutary messages for the public of a libertarian society, their production is increasingly drowned out in a din of shallow and superficial "news," uninformed speculation, vulgar humor, flamboyant advertising, large doses of crime and sex, and repetitious gossip.

As sad as it is for libertarians to acknowledge the drift toward order, toward social harmony, and increasingly toward social control of the media, it is understandable that such a paradigm shift is in the talking stage and, here and there, even taking place. The diagram shown in Figure 2-1 ("Paradigm Shift to Order") provides some of the main characteristics of the neo-authoritarians and of the libertarians, and also gives exemplar countries for each. The diagram also provides a few examples of countries caught in a transitional stage between the two main paradigms. Such countries (for example, Egypt and South Africa) might even come up with their own media paradigms that could avoid the excesses of the main two.

In a recent trip to the West Bank (to Birzeit University near Ramallah), I was asked by a student what type of media system (vis-à-vis government) I thought would be a good one for his evolving country. I surely could not answer specifically but said that I thought it ought to spring from the country itself, from its traditions, values, religion, and so forth. He replied that, if that were the case, it would be mainly a highly controlled, puritanical system. His guess seemed to me to be about as good as any. As a libertarian myself, I am far from optimistic about the spread of free-press theory in the twenty-first century world.

What this neo-authoritarianism (Order) will likely be is a kind of old-time authoritarianism (that has always dominated the world) but with a more humane demeanor. Humanistic values will overlay the authoritarian tendencies more than in the past. For example, the public will be consulted increasingly so that the media powers can ascertain at least what the people want. Such a trend will take place (and is to some degree already taking place) in all countries. In the United States, the new communitarianism (with its subgenre of public journalism) has already begun a campaign for more people-oriented and socially helpful journalism.

Neo Authoritarians   Libertarians

Groupists, Egalitarians   Individualists, Egocentrists,
Altrists, Democrats   Enlightenment Liberals

Order ◄───────────────────────── Chaos

Traits   Traits

Restrained freedom   Maximum freedom
Civic transformation   Self-transformation
Normative ethics codes   Personal ethical codes
Selflessness   Self-concern
Cooperation   Self-enhancement
Social influence on policy   Personal influence
Bonding/Conformity   Autonomy/Diversity
Group progress   Competition/Meritocracy
Like-minded worldview   Diverse worldviews
Positive cohesive news   Total spectrum news
Social guidance   social information
Universal solidarity   Universal diversity
Agreement on common ethics   Disagreement on ethics
Universal-Legalistic ethics   Relative-Situation ethics
Reliance on many laws   Favor of very few laws
Media professionalism   Anti-media professionalism

NEW-AUTHORITARIAN   TRANSITIONAL   LIBERTARIAN
(Exemplars)   (Exemplars)   (Exemplars)

Saudi Arabia, Iran, Iraq, China   Sweden   U.S.A., Britain, France,
North Korea, Cuba, Singapore,   Finland   Japan, Canada, Australia,
Libya, Indonesia, Laos, Syria,   Norway   Germany, Switzerland,
Pakistan, Nigeria, Cambodia,   Egypt   India, Spain, Italy, Costa
Vietnam, Paraguay, Sudan,   South Africa   Rica.
Afghanistan, Bolivia, Kuwait

Order   ◄───────────────────────── Chaos

Figure 2.1. Paradigm Shift to Order

AROUND THE CIRCLE

Think of a circle that runs from libertarianism at the top to authoritarianism
at the bottom. And one can go around the circle either way—through socialism at the left and capitalism at the right. As one leaves the top of the circle

(libertarianism) and proceeds in either direction, the concern with the group (community) increases and the concern with freedom and individualism decreases. In the area of the circle diagram called "Democratic Socialism" (on the left) or "Democratic Capitalism" (on the right), we see the appearance of the Western concept of communitarianism, a fresh concern with establishing "a community" that participates in the communication process of the country.

Under this broad concept of communitarianism, we find a subtype that has not totally abandoned individualism and has been called "responsive communitarianism." It appears on both sides of the circle. Growing out of communitarianism is public or civic journalism, developing on both the left and the right. It is the thesis of this essay that most of the world is following this top-to-bottom route, often skipping some of the intermediary stages and moving slowly into the area of authoritarianism and order (into social conservatism on the right and neo-Marxism on the left) and retreating from what is increasingly considered to be the chaos of extreme libertarianism.

The diagram shown in Figure 2-2 (The Political-Press Circle) depicts this new developing paradigm in the context of the circular political model. If we were diagramming the trend in the old way—as a spectrum—Chaos (libertar-

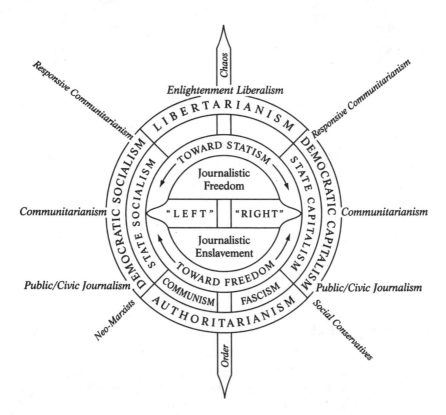

Figure 2.2. The Political-Press Circle (The Trend Toward Social Order)

ianism) would be on the far right end of the line and Order (authoritarianism) would be on the far left end of the line. The various intermediary points would be interspersed between the two extremes. The circular model that follows seems more realistic, however, and it is presented here to indicate how societies are moving up or down around the circle, depending on whether they are going toward order or toward chaotic libertarianism. In the new Order paradigm, the emphasis is on bringing the community together, or national stability, and personal and institutional cooperation. Let us proceed to look at this developing political-press paradigm.

A new paradigm is materializing that might be called moderately libertarian or moderately authoritarian. This paradigm puts people, not the press, at the center of social concern. This is what is often called *communitarianism*—cousin of social democracy—in the West and neo-authoritarianism in the Third World. Although it is nothing new, really, it has taken on a more positive connotation since about 1990. Regardless of its label, it is basically a paradigm of order, not freedom, and (as Figure 2-2 shows), the shift is a movement away from Enlightenment liberalism and toward the authoritarian or Order end (bottom) of the political-press circle. There is, of course, always the possibility, although seemingly not a great one—that the trend will reverse itself and develop in the direction of freedom.

TOWARD A PEOPLE'S PRESS

In America, one contemporary trend away from the Chaos paradigm and toward a communication system that moves toward the deindividualizing of society is the emphasis on what is termed "public" or "civic" journalism, as mentioned earlier. It is a further retreat from the Enlightenment concept of individual (thus, pluralistic) power centers, and without a doubt it is a step toward a more disciplined, ordered, and harmonious media system. The Western intellectual tradition has, as some have said, been mired in the eighteenth and nineteenth century Enlightenment philosophy for far too long.[14] Such a philosophy is still dominant in the West, however, and the new concept of civic/public journalism is having a rather difficult time (perhaps only temporarily) attacking the walls of American tradition. One important and populist proposition of the civic journalists is this: Civic journalism is a step away from media-centered, autonomous journalism and a step toward a kind of people's journalism that brings the public into the act.[15]

The new theme is this: Let the journalism sphere and the public sphere overlap. Let there be a real symbiosis between journalists and the people. Let people power increase and press power decrease. Let there be focus groups and more conversations between journalists and the public. Let there be more surveys and polls to guide the direction of journalism. In many ways, this new trend toward "people's journalism" is in keeping with the democratization principle of earlier days, but in other ways it flies in the face of the traditional

American principle of journalist-centered journalism and owner-controlled journalism stemming from Enlightenment liberalism. Therein lies the problematic aspects of the new civic/public journalism. What is yet not known is just how it will reflect American journalistic values. Civic journalists are saying, in effect, that the people can provide better journalism (more reflective of national values) than can the journalists. Or, at least many journalists feel that they need much more help from the public in ushering in a better, more socially responsible media system. Presumably out of this people-centered journalism will come a more responsive and therefore a more responsible press. This is a step toward order in the West, and it is being taken without throwing out, at least for the time being, many of the vestiges of libertarianism.

THIRD WORLD STIRRINGS

Certainly most countries of the world are not any more ready for public/civic journalism than they are for libertarian (press-centered) journalism. But the new emphasis in the West does show, at least, that the West is cognizant of the problems with traditional libertarianism and is trying slowly to change the paradigm—at least in some of its aspects. If the West can come up with such ideas as public/civic journalism, it is surely possible for many Third World nations to develop their own mode of public communication. And this probably would not, in major aspects, be the same as the Western paradigm.

Malaysia, for example, is trying to develop its communication system in its own mode. As one Malaysian editor has said, "We do not want to be like any of the nineteen countries that are generally to be regarded as developed countries. ... We should be developed in our own mold"[16]. Will new "molds" (paradigms) of communication around the world be market driven and profit inspired? Perhaps many will be. But the problematic aspects of the shift from socialism to capitalism in Russian and other East European nations points to further and continuing trauma associated with free-wheeling and advertising-driven journalism. It might just be that a more realistic and helpful communication policy in many parts of the world would repel the Western media model, preferring a more authoritarian system closer to a socialistic (even Marxist) model leading to national and cultural solidarity and a greater chance for social harmony.

SYSTEMS IN FLUX

National media systems around the world are in flux.[17] None, even at any single moment, is static. All are *becoming*. They are all seeding, adapting, grafting onto foreign elements. As we have seen, even in the United States, with the advent of social responsibility and public/civic journalism, a notable change is taking place. The emphasis since World War II has been changing over from press power to people's rights.[18] To some degree, this sort of thing is happening everywhere, and as the communications systems change, so do the cultures. Public communication is a barometer not only of social change but also of traditional cultural disintegration. In Indonesia, for example, culture circa 1950 is not culture circa 2000. Perhaps a better example would be China, where basic authoritarianism has held sway while many capitalistic adaptations have made the country into an economic powerhouse. China circa 1950 certainly is not China circa 2000. And such a General Semantics principle of change can be applied to the many cultures and subcultures existing around the world.[19] A national culture can be broken down into many of these subcultures—tribal, family, religious, age, sex, occupation, value-oriented, race, corporate, elite, economic, aristocratic, political elite, and so forth. It is indeed difficult, if not impossible, for the communication system of a nation to adequately serve all these cultures. The libertarian would say that a free-press system could best do it. But many countries don't agree, saying that the "class" or economic or elite nature of private ownership of the media militates against a basic concern for the inequities in a society. What the Order paradigm proponents want, among other things, is a kind of social egalitarianism—even if it often is an equality of poverty.

DEMOCRACY: GOOD FOR ALL?

Western analysts too often see Third World nations as "little Americas" and proceed to propose a Western-style media system for them. What they need, say the analysts, first of all, is *democracy*. And with democracy, of course, will come capitalism and media libertarianism. These analysts often overlook the country's stage of development, its governmental traditions, its autocratic government stemming from tribalism, its economic status, its literacy, and its cultural and ethnic propensity toward authoritarianism and paternalism. Elections might harm, not help, many countries. So also might a Western-style journalism.

Robert Kaplan, writing in *The Atlantic Monthly*, points out that if a country's population is not in reasonable health, democracy can be not only risky but also dangerous.[20] And, he says, the rate of employment is very important. Tunisia, for example, has a 25 percent unemployment rate. If elections were held in such circumstances, according to Kaplan, the result would be a fundamentalist government and violence such as in Algeria. A nation must first create a stable and healthy economy and a good infrastructure and communication system; then it can worry about elections. Tunisia, Kaplan points out, has been a peaceful nation without democracy, and neighboring Algeria has been engaged in violence with elections.

Kaplan refers to Kurdistan and Afghanistan, two societies where the United States encouraged democracy in the 1990s.[21] Their attempts at elections caused chaos, and in Bosnia, democracy legitimized the worst war crimes in Europe since the Nazi period.

Other countries have done well without democracy—at least without the libertarian version we value in the West. Peru is an example. In the early 1990s, parts of its democracy were dismantled for a while. Congress was disbanded and the president assumed total power, using it to weaken the Shining Path guerrilla movement, reduce inflation, and bring foreign investment back to Peru. The president, Fujimori, used Machiavellian methods to give the country stability, harmony, and a measure of prosperity. Authoritarianism, perhaps. But what is important is not the label given a system, but how the system actually works.

Perhaps a better example is Singapore, no Western-style democracy but a thriving and lawful country. Lee Kuan Yew's new authoritarianism produced a state that acts like a corporation—paternalistic, meritocratic, and decidedly undemocratic. Kaplan notes that from its status as a poor, crime-ridden, illiterate, mosquito-infested bog filled with slum quarters more than thirty years ago, Lee led the country to a point at which its per capita wealth is equal to that of Canada.[22] Its law and order are envied throughout Asia, and the health conditions there are among the best in the world.

On the other hand, look at South Africa. According to Kaplan, this democratic country has become one of the most violent places on earth. The murder rate is six times that of the United States. It has ten private security guards for every policeman, educated people are fleeing the country, and the currency has substantially declined.[23] Indeed, more stability and prosperity existed under the earlier semiauthoritarian apartheid regime.

THE FUTURE: ESCAPE FROM FREEDOM?

It seems quite natural that many Third World observers look at the American press and see chaos. Even many Americans see the same thing: sensation and prurience taking over the news programs. Gossip, speculation, lies, and half-truths prevailing over objective reporting. Soft news rooting out hard news. A cacophony of voices whining and shouting contradictory versions of events. Personalities and their private lives, the more eccentric and degraded the better, filling our press and TV screens. Sex-oriented advertising pumping its repetitious themes into our homes. It is little wonder that thoughtful critics in Third World countries want none of it, and look at media libertarianism as an intellectual absurdity and a moral disaster.

They prefer another paradigm, one stemming from their own cultural values and stage of development. They see order as more important than freedom in their media. They see social integration, public harmony, value retention, ethnocentrism, and social solidarity—in short, *community*—far more to be desired than journalistic and communication individualism and autonomy. National development does not necessarily stem from Western democracy or Enlightenment liberalism. History confirms this. Many parts of the world do not offer the simple choice between dictators and democrats, between authoritarianism and libertarianism. Perhaps the choice is between bad dictators and better ones, between some freedom and much freedom. Many nations have learned that evil and corrupt leadership resides in so-called democratic systems as well as in authoritarian ones. Democracy is no shield against corrupt, bickering, ineffectual politicians or libertinism in journalism.

It would appear to the global observer that the Western paradigm, tied as it is to freedom of expression, is being seriously challenged in spite of the collapse of the Soviet Union and the temporary setback to Marxism. More and more societies want security, stability, and social accountability. Increasingly, these societies show a tendency to "escape from freedom."[24] Fewer and fewer are satisfied with the splintering of cultures that they see as being brought about by individualism and egocentrism. Ethnocentrism, perhaps. Egocentrism, no. The old Western freedom paradigm of the Enlightenment, say many critics the world over, may have worked well enough in the United States and a few other countries in the past, but no longer.

The goal of a free state (and by extension, a free press) as defined by Locke and Montesquieu was this: to grant members of the society (or the media system) as much autonomy as could be compatible with the effective management of public affairs (or public communication). According to Jean-Francois Revel, such an Enlightenment aspiration "is thwarted by the growing demands of groups and individuals" so that the state must "intervene to protect and rescue them from all manner of difficulties."[25] As to the press, it would seem that such growing paternalistic tendencies would naturally tempt media managers to expand their community-related, social harmony journalistic emphasis. The underlying concepts in such an emphasis are social concern, the democratization of decision making, and thus a disintegrating of traditional concerns for autonomy and freedom.

Autonomy and freedom are fading internationally also. With ever more complex and populous societies and cultures mushrooming around the globe (where is the new World Culture?), the operative word is "order," not "freedom." The new paradigm of media structure is gravitating toward neo-authoritarianism in an increasingly pluralistic world that will need stability or order. The new feature here is the injection of the concept of social harmony. This *neo*-authoritarianism might well be called social responsibility or humanistic authoritarianism. In short, some kind of semiordered society built on a reformist and social democratic foundation will likely come into being, lessening the individualistic spirit and bringing about more social stability.

The libertarian looking at this Order paradigm that is considered socially responsible by its proponents might well ask this question: Does a paradigm that consists of control have moral justification? The answer, which has been expressed by the German philosophers Fichte and Hegel, is yes, of course, and it goes something like this: A person is morally the property of others—of those it is his or her duty to serve. As such, a person has no moral right to refuse to make the requisite sacrifices for others. If he attempts it, he is depriving people of what is properly theirs. He is violating their rights—their right to his or her service. It is therefore quite moral to intervene forcibly and compel the person to fulfill social obligations. Social justice in this view not only allows but demands that others put a stop to the evil of individual rights over social responsibility.[26]

Even John Stuart Mill wrote that large segments of the world were not ready for freedom and that they needed guidance, authority, and supervision. But as a product of the Enlightenment and a champion of libertarianism (albeit "restricted"), Mill saw the general advantages of liberty to most societies. But Mill was certainly not an absolutist, believing, as do the new Order advocates, that freedom cannot be absolute and there are simply many things that society cannot tolerate.[27] And it seems that in a world that increasingly venerates a monolithic concept of social responsibility, more and more things cannot be tolerated.

Some countries, such as the United States, are likely to try to hold on to Enlightenment concepts for a while. But the individualism of early America is fast being rooted out (from the outside) by new immigrants steeped in a co-operationist and inbred groupist philosophy that does not appreciate the concept of freedom, and (from the inside) by more organized subgroups (such as women, gays, African and Native Americans, and the new communitarians). Paternalism, stability, conformity, and harmony will dictate the new paradigm of media systems in the new century. And those who think that the United States will escape this move into the new paradigm are quite likely due for a great disappointment. Individuals, like this writer, who perhaps are mired in past times and who still have great respect for Enlightenment liberal ideas are sad to see the libertarian paradigm being replaced. But *c'est la vie*, as the French say.

NOTES

1. The exception to this is, of course, the many Marxist and socialist (and even social democratic) scholars—mainly from Europe, Africa, and Latin America—who, especially during the 1960s through the 1980s, consistently criticized the capitalist paradigm and insisted on non-Western media principles for vast parts of the world. Such critics are still with us, but their voices have faded somewhat since 1990 and the breakup of the Soviet Union. An excellent book that chronicles such communist and socialist apologists and warns against the new authoritarianism that is bewitching so many minds is Jean-Francois Revel's *The Totalitarian Temptation* (New York: Penguin Books, 1978).

2. A few of the critics pointing out the excesses of American journalism and weakness of a capitalist press are the following: Herbert Schiller, Michael Parenti, Edward Said, Noam Chomsky, Robert Cirano, Edward Herman, Christopher Hitchins, James Aronson, Todd Gitlin, David Paletz, Keenan Peck, Ben Bagdikian, Benjamin Compaine, Peter Dreier, George Krimsky, Steve Weinberg, R.C. Harwood, Yassen Zassoursky, Kaarle Nordenstreng, and Robert Picard. Many others, generally in the camp of civic/public journalism, have added their voices to those who think American journalism needs a new paradigm. Some of them are Davis "Buzz" Merritt, Robert M. Steele, Clifford Christians, Theodore Glasser, Ed Lambert, Lee Wilkins, Herbert Gans, Arthur Charity, Jay Rosen, and Cole Campbell.

3. Many of the critics of Western capitalistic journalism and its Enlightenment-derived liberalism, although sympathetic to some of the concepts elucidated by Karl Marx, are not Marxists at all. Rather, they see in Marx a strain of humanism and idealism that they feel can be beneficial to capitalistic and libertarian journalism. When one is criticizing capitalism and free-market journalism, it is only natural for such criticism often to be couched in terms that can be traced to Marx.

4. The concept of flux (of countries, in this case), along with the concept of differences among entities, is discussed at great length by Alfred Korzybski and his followers. See A. Korzybski, *Science and Sanity* (Lancaster, PA: Science Press, 1933). Korzybski drew on a number of fields, and his general semantics has a very eclectic orientation, centering on the meaning of language, the effect of thought on thought, and the effect of thought on action.

5. A plethora of articles, books, and even radio and television programs have hurled strong criticism at the American mass media in recent years: Too much sex, sensation, gossip, speculation, bias stories, negativity. Too little serious news. Too much entertainment. Too many instances of invasion of privacy. The demise of good taste. On and on goes the criticism. No doubt exists that the public faith in and respect for the media has diminished during the second half of the twentieth century.

6. Many new communitarian (and public/civic) journalists and journalism educators believe that libertarianism must be abandoned so that, as Clifford Christians, John P. Ferré, and P. Mark Fackler write, "citizens are empowered for social transformation, not merely freed from external constraint, as classical liberalism insisted." They go on to say, regarding ethics, that journalists should not fall into the trap of embracing situational or relativistic ethics. See *Good News* (Urbana, IL: University of Illinois Press, 1993, 54–55). The "concept of solidarity" is a key concept held by the communitarians, exemplified by Christians, Ferré, and Fackler. They write (p. 14), that journalists should realize that "universal solidarity is the nominative core of the social and moral order." And they go on to say (p. 185) that journalists should reject "the Enlightenment's individualistic rationalism."

7. Not many American journalists (perhaps many more educators) think that a global ethics code is realistic, at least not in the multi-ideological and multicultural world that emerges from the twentieth century. Some people (usually found in the news of the United Nations orthodoxy) believe that universal ethical principles exist that are appropriate for journalism, and for several years they have been talking and writing about them. In the United States, two academic researchers have been enthusiastic supporters of an international code of ethics: Thomas Cooper of Emerson College (Boston) and Hamid Mowlaw of American University (Washington, D.C.).

8. For a good summary of the general ideas of the civic/public journalism advocates, see Jay Black (ed.), *Mixed News: The Public/Civic Communitarian Journalism Debate* (Mahwah, NJ: Lawrence Erlbaum Associates, Publishers, 1997). See especially the chapters by Theodore Glasser and Stephanie Craft, Robert M. Steele, David "Buzz" Merritt, and Lee Wilkins. Opponents of public/civic journalism also give their opinions in the book.

9. Probably the most articulate spokesman for communitarianism has been the American sociologist Amitai Etzioni, professor at George Washington University. His book *The New Golden Rule: Community and Morality in a Democratic Society* (New York: Harper-Collins–Basic Books, 1996) gives a good overview of communitarianism and paints a com-

pelling picture of society's declining moral structure (including our media system) and of the need to introduce a moral voice in our public discourse. Related to the present paper is Etzioni's "The Need for a New Paradigm," in *Responsive Community 5*, no. I (1995). Also of interest to the reader of this paper would be Etzioni's Chapter 2 ("Order and Autonomy") in *The New Golden Rule* (1996).

10. The Hutchins Commission (named for University of Chicago Chancellor Robert Hutchins) was set up largely by Henry Luce to study the American press, especially looking at its state of freedom. The formal name of the thirteen-person commission was the Commission on Freedom of the Press. It published its report in 1947 in the form of a book, *A Free and Responsible Press*, published by the University of Chicago Press. The book dealt with commission-perceived press responsibilities and had little to say about freedom. The commission found the press seriously lacking in responsible journalism, gave some specific criticism, and provided some recommendations for improvement, such as a press council and more mutual press criticism. An excellent book that criticized the Hutchins Commission's report is Frank Hughes' *Prejudice and the Press* (New York: Devin-Adair Company, 1950).

11. The often misunderstood and disputed term "The Third World" usually applies (from a Western perspective) to the poor, undeveloped countries of the world, those lacking in economic development, infrastructure, literacy, health services, and a stable political system. This would include the majority of the countries of Africa and Asia, and to a lesser degree the countries of Latin America and the Middle East. Intellectuals in the Third World do not like the term and look upon it as another Western-inspired term to belittle the poor nations. The First World would be the highly industrialized, rich countries of North American and Europe, with a few other countries (such as Japan, Taiwan, Singapore, and Australia) thrown in. The Second World label has nearly disappeared. It has been associated mainly with the socialist nations of China and the Soviet Union (when it was intact).

12. Third World countries have a basic propensity for Machiavellian leadership, respecting the skillful, cunning, and brave leader. Most of these countries are still close to tribalism, and the strongman president or leader takes the place of the tribal chief. Machiavellianism in government and, by projection, in the mass media is not a negative but a positive concept. For a long time, critics have noted Machiavellianism in the Western, privately owned media system, but it is generally considered bad—at least in public pronouncements. Third World countries simply accept it as natural. For a discussion of what constitutes Machiavellianism in journalism, see John.C. Merrill, *The Princely Press: Machiavelli on American Journalism* (Lanharn, MD.: University Press of America, 1998). It is interesting to note that at least one university, New York University, had a course in 1998 called "Mass Communications and Machiavelli," taught in the Gallatin School of Individualized Study.

13. See the chapter on libertarian theory in Sierbert, Peterson, and Schramm, *Four Theories of the Press* (Urbana: University of Illinois Press, 1956). This chapter draws on works by John Milton, J.S. Mill, John Locke, Voltaire, and others. Many more recent books discussing libertarianism, such as William Emest Hocking *Freedom of the Press* (Chicago: University of Chicago Press, 1947); Leonard W. Levy, *Legacy of Suppression* (Cambridge: Harvard University Press, 1960); Gabriel Marquez, *Man Against Mass Society* (Chicago: Henry Regnery Co., 1962); Derrick Sington, *Freedom of Communication* (Oxford: Holywell Press, Ltd., 1963); Peter Radcliff (ed.), *Limits of Liberty: Studies of Mill's on Liberty* (Belmont, CA: Wadsworth 1966); J. Herbert Altschull, *Agents of Power* (White Plains, NY: Longman 1984); J. C. Merrill, *The Imperative of Freedom* (New York: Hastings House, 1974) and *Existential Journalism* (Ames: Iowa State University Press, 1996); Charles Murray, *What It Means to be a Libertarian* (New York: Broadway Books, 1997).

14. Some of the books that have taken up this critical theme are the following: Jerome A. Barron, *Freedom of the press: For whom?* (Bloomington: University of Indiana Press, 1973; James W. Carey, *Communication in Culture* (Winchester, MA: Unwin Hyman, 1988); Paul Chilton, *Orwellian Language and the Media* (Winchester, MA: Unwin Hyman, 1988); Commission on Freedom of the Press, *A Free and Responsible Press* (Chicago: University of

Chicago Press, 1947); Herbert Schiller, *Mass Communication and American Empire* New York: Augustus M. Kelly, 1969; Robert Cirino, *Don't Blame the People* (NewYork:Vintage,1972); Ben Bagdikian, *The Media Monopoly* (Boston: Beacon Press, 1983); Tom Goldstein, *The News at Any Cost* (New York: Simon and Schuster, 1985); Robert G. Picard, *The Press and the Decline of Democracy* (Westport, CT: Greenwood Press, 1985); Neil Postman, *Amusing Ourselves to Death* (New York: Penguin Books, 1985).

15. If nothing else can be said of it, civic or public journalism is critical of traditional libertarian insistence on editorial self-determination or media centeredness. This is why public journalism in this essay is contrasted with libertarian journalism or Enlightenment liberalism. The civic journalists want to see a more monolithic press, one that they believe will be more responsible. This is why I am suggesting that public journalism is a step along the authoritarian road to order and away from what the public journalists see as libertarian media chaos.

16. Donna McLean, "Development Redefined: An examination of Malaysian politicians' rhetorical efforts to explain full development to citizens" (paper presented at the 15th annual Intercultural Communication Conference, Miami, FL, Feb 6, 1998).

17. A general semantics principle, propounded by A. Korzybski, borrowing largely from the pre-Socratic philosopher Heraclitus, which says that nothing is static; all is in flux. No person, said Heraclitus, steps in the same river twice.

18. The watershed event, just after the end of World War II, was the publication of the Hutchins Commission Report as a book, *A Free and Responsible Press*, in 1947. This book, and many others that came along during the next few decades, restated the commission's call for a more socially responsible press, shifting the emphasis away from press freedom to press responsibility. This is believed by this writer to have been the impetus for a paradigm shift to a more monolithic press, configured under a philosophy of responsibility—not press directed but public directed. Communitarians and public/civic journalists picked up the Hutchins Commission mantle and continued the trend toward order and social harmony.

19. The General Semantics principle of change. China may have the same name in 2000, but its essence—its reality behind the name—is quite different from the way it was in 1950.

20. Robert Kaplan, "Was Democracy Just a Moment?" *The Atlantic Monthly*, December 1997, 55–80.

21. Kaplan, "Was Democracy Just a Moment?" 68.

22. Kaplan, "Was Democracy Just a Moment?" 68–69.

23. Kaplan, "Was Democracy Just a Moment?" 69.

24. Erich Fromm, *Escape from Freedom* (New York: Holt, Rinehart & Winston, 1941; Avon Books, 1965). The author discusses the basic inclination of people to "escape from freedom" to some kind of collective situation in which they will not feel isolated, anxious, and lonely. The flight from individuality and freedom to some form of authoritarianism and control is seen to be an extremely powerful inclination.

25. Jean-Francois Revel, *The Totalitarian Temptation* (New York: Penguin Books, 1977), p. 213. Cf. Friedrich A. Hayek, *The Road to Selfdom* (Chicago: University of Chicago Press, 1944). Hayek, a libertarian, admits (p. 56) that "our present society lacks conscious direction toward a single aim" and "that its activities are guided by the whims and fancies of irresponsible individuals."

26. Leonard Peikoff, *Ominous Parallels* (New York: New American Library, 1983), 91.

27. Maurice Cranston, *Political Dialogues* (New York: Basic Books, 1968), 148–49.

PART TWO

In the United States and Latin America

In this section of *The Mission* you will journey from the Deep South of the United States to Latin America, from societies still wrestling with the legacy of sins of the past to countries where journalists continue to be threatened and even killed for practicing their craft.

In Chapter 3, investigative reporter Jerry Mitchell tells of the methods he used to relentlessly track down civil rights-era murderers in Mississippi, which earned him the Heywood Broun Award, Sigma Delta Chi Award, and numerous other honors. He sees himself in the tradition of the muckrakers who deeply changed American society a century ago.

In Chapter 4, editor Joseph B. Atkins shows how journalists in very disparate societies   such as the U.S. South and central and eastern Europe—can face strikingly similar challenges dealing with a dark past whose legacy remains very much alive.

In Chapter 5, Latin American expert Michael Snodgrass assesses the role of the journalist vis-à-vis government in Mexico today and during the just-ended 71-year rule of the Institutional Revolutionary Party (PRI).

In Chapter 6, Stephen F. Jackson, associate editor and publisher of the *Latin American Post* in Bogota, Colombia, and also an associate professor of journalism at Stillman College in Tuscaloosa, Ala., reports from the frontlines on the life of the journalist in Colombia during the civil and drug wars that have long plagued that country, one of the world's most dangerous for journalists.

Chapter three

Ways of a Muckraker

by Jerry Mitchell
Investigative Reporter
The Clarion-Ledger
Jackson, Mississippi

Following is an essay by a top investigative reporter explaining his sense of purpose,   39
*his methods as a journalist, and his sense of lineage with the great muckrakers of a
century ago whose work changed American society for the better. His own work in
the 1980s and 1990s led to the long-overdue arrests and convictions of white supremacist Byron De La Beckwith and Ku Klux Klan Imperial Wizard Sam Bowers for civil rights–era murders in Mississippi. He has been called the South's Simon Wiesenthal for his relentless pursuit of violent racists and white supremacists
in the U.S. South who never paid for their crimes during the 1960s. He is a winner of the Sigma Delta Chi Award for Public Service, the Heywood Broun Award,
the Sidney Hillman Award, and the NAACP Community Service Award, and he
was one of four journalists honored by the Anti-Defamation League at the
Kennedy Center in Washington, D.C., in 1998.*

I am a muckraker.

I know. I know. It is not fashionable to be a muckraker anymore. Or at least
that is what I heard.

Mind you, plenty of people misunderstand what muckraking is. They think
it is the press peeping through the windows of celebrities. Or they think it is
paparazzi snapping pictures of celebrities in sinful moments.

I detest those acts as much as, and maybe more than, many of my fellow
Americans. I certainly detest what many of the media have become as they replace real reporting with high-tech graphics, hoping that viewers will never notice the loss in substance.

The philosophy behind muckraking is best summed up by the notion that journalism's role is to comfort the afflicted and afflict the comfortable. It is a philosophy sadly lacking in this age of Monica, in which notoriety and fame are hardly distinguishable.

For much of my journalism career, I have felt like a dinosaur, hopelessly out of step with the times. Lately, however, I sense that I am not alone. I sense that journalists of a new generation are waking up and wondering how they, too, can use the tools of muckraking to effect change in a society sorely in need of it.

And so I share whatever advice I have learned on the trail toward becoming a muckraker. None of it is new, but I hope that what I do share will help you join me.

And now, on with the advice.

BE WILLING TO LISTEN TO THE LUNATICS

It's amazing what information people will give you if you'll just sit and listen to them.

Much of my reporting over the past decade has centered on the radical right and the lunatic fringe. The truth is that if you want to truly cover these lunatics, you have to spend a lot of time with them and, more important, you have to listen to them. An occasional head-nodding won't cut it. As crazy as it sounds, you have to be interested in them.

For instance, my best source on the anti-abortion front is someone I believe may commit violence one day. He certainly condones violence against abortion doctors, which is back in the news again. He's the one who introduced me to Paul Hill, who later killed an abortion-performing physician in Florida. When that happened, it wasn't necessary to collect a lot of background because I'd already interviewed Hill, who started his anti-abortion efforts in Jackson, Mississippi.

We spend too much time prejudging our sources instead of seeing them as conduits of information. Just because someone is nuts, just because he has no credibility, just because he has a personality so offensive that you feel a need to shower later doesn't mean that the person can't be a valuable source. He may be crazy enough to get you those sealed documents you've been coveting for months.

For example, I spent seven hours interviewing white supremacist Byron De La Beckwith in Signal Mountain, Tennessee. What made the interview so valuable was Beckwith fully explaining his white supremacist philosophy to me. Even more valuable was his sharing the names of leaders on the radical right that he was close to, thereby beginning my education about this group.

In dealing with sources that you may indeed consider lunatic, you need to understand that their motives often are very different from yours. Perhaps they like having their egos stroked. Perhaps they like to see their rivals taken down a notch or two. Or perhaps their motives are much more complex and bizarre than that and are even motives you despise.

The bottom line for you in collecting information is to find ways to appeal to those motives. For instance, in obtaining the sealed records of a state segregationist spy agency known as the Mississippi Sovereignty Commission, I used a variety of sources, all with different motives.

BE WILLING TO TALK AT LENGTH WITH TARGETS OF YOUR REPORTING

I became furious after watching the film, *Absence of Malice*, but not because journalism was portrayed in a negative light. Heaven knows that journalism has plenty of sins. What upset me was that the reporter didn't bother to talk with the target of the apparent investigation. Incredible.

Some of the best quotes I've ever gotten have come from those whose exploits may have been highlighted by stories, sometimes even after initial stories were printed. What may be one of my best-read stories came about in 1995 when I reported: "On Valentine's Day, Michael Everett Martin received a present from the taxpayers: a penile implant to aid his impotence, despite the fact he is a convicted child molester."

When I spoke with Martin, he was more than willing to explain why he needed the operation. "It's real difficult to take a young lady out to dinner and dancing and she suggests something else, and all you can do is hold her hand," he said. "That takes a whole lot away from making me feel like a man." The story made national headlines, *Dear Abby*, Rush Limbaugh, you name it. I told my colleagues then and say it to this day: "Why would anyone want to write fiction when you have this kind of material?"

BE WILLING TO DIAL THE WRONG NUMBER

Once I was searching for one of two policemen in Greenwood, Mississippi, who gave Beckwith an alibi in the 1963 assassination of Mississippi NAACP leader Medgar Evers. No one seemed to know where the policeman was these days. Finally, I picked up the Greenwood phone directory and saw that several Cresswells were listed in the directory. I picked one that looked promising and dialed. "Is Hollis Cresswell there?" I asked in my most polite Southern accent.

"No," the man replied, "you want my brother. He's living over there near Maben. I got his number."

Hollis Cresswell ended up giving me the only interview he ever gave—to the media or to the authorities.

And that story showed the inconsistencies in Cresswell's alibi, helping lead to Beckwith's indictment.

BE WILLING TO HARASS

Yes, you read that right, harass. I'm not talking about the Mike Wallace in-your-face-so-that-you-automatically-look-guilty approach. I prefer an approach I call "polite harassment." Polite harassment is a continual, perpetual persistence that shows you're not going to give up until you get what you want.

An example: One day, I needed a quote from a lawyer. I called in the morning and reached his secretary, who was very polite. I explained to her the entire situation and why I needed the quote. Soon she began to turn into my ally. I called every hour, asking for him. By mid-afternoon, she said, "Hold on a minute. I'm going to get him on the phone right now."

He talked to me.

BE WILLING TO BE HARASSED

That is, be willing to write stories that are unpopular. Bob Woodward once said that great journalism stories are done in defiance of management. He's right. With luck, you have the kind of management that will embrace your efforts, but if you don't, you have to be willing to stick your own neck out.

BE WILLING TO PURSUE A STORY, EVEN WHEN YOU'RE SICK OF IT

This is perhaps one of the most important rules of journalism but is one that isn't taught in journalism school. I confess that I learned this early and, frankly, by accident when I was an investigative reporter in Hot Springs, Arkansas. I had written a story almost every day on how city leaders bailed out a theme park losing $1 million a year that not so coincidentally happened to have much of its stock owned by those same city leaders. I even learned that the park had violated its own bond agreement by using bond money to improperly pay off stockholders' loans.

A local motel owner finally sued the city. When I talked with him and asked him why, he replied, "Because I got tired of reading about it in the paper."

NEVER FAIL TO MAKE FRIENDS

Learn to make friends with everyone from the janitor on up. I always try to connect with secretaries. They can be your greatest allies. In fact, I always write down secretaries' names and put them in my Rolodex so that I won't forget. As someone once remarked, the sweetest sound to a person is his or her name. I think it's true.

NEVER FORGET THAT PHONE NUMBERS ARE GOLD

If you get a phone number, write it down. You never know when that number might come in handy. On the night that Mississippi's onetime segregationist governor Ross Barnett died, someone at the *Arkansas Gazette* in Little Rock graciously shared the phone number of Arksansas's own notorious segregationist, Orval Faubus. I later called him for a story on segregation in the South.

I'm getting ready to start filling a sixth Rolodex. I'm amazed when I see others who have been in the business for as long as I have who have only a few numbers filed away.

And never forget: "Comfort the afflicted and afflict the comfortable."

Chapter four

A Sinister Zone of Likeness

Journalists as Heroes and Villains in the U.S. South and in Central and Eastern Europe

by Joseph B. Atkins
Associate Professor of Journalism
University of Mississippi

Katrin Tamm and Sabine Lembke met in prison.

It is the bond that overcomes all their differences. Tamm, short, gruff, intense, her voice a permanent scratch from the long chain of cigarettes in her forty-four-year-old life, works with handicapped children. Lembke, thirty-three, is more soft spoken, quick to smile, thin, and freckled, with short dark hair slicked back like a man's. A doctoral student in communication science, she favors black—black jeans, black leather jacket, and black undershirt under a gray vest.

They walk me down Berlin's most famous boulevard, Unter den Linden, past the elegantly restored Hotel Adlon to the giant gate that once stood between them and the rest of the world. "You know, when there was a wall, I lived near it, and at night I could hear the screams and the shooting," Tamm says, her eyes moving across the empty space along the western side of the Brandenburg Gate where the wall once stood. "I don't want hate to consume me. But I don't want to forget, either."

Three years before the wall fell, in 1986, Tamm was arrested for trying to contact relatives in the West. She spent much of the next year in various prison camps. In one of those camps, she met Lembke, who had been imprisoned for alleged Western sympathies. Tamm remembers her guards. "They fed us soup with cockroaches in it, and when we complained, they'd say, 'What's wrong? You capitalists never get enough, do you?' They treated us like animals."

Tamm and Lembke watch the people walking past us, a mix of locals and tourists, crossing the once-forbidden zone as though the wall had never existed. Lembke remarks how the crowds might easily include the guards who once taunted and abused them, who today are free to enjoy new lives in the now-united, capitalist Germany. Some in the crowd, perhaps, were informers, people like the lifelong friend who doubled as a spy and betrayed Tamm to the Stasi, East Germany's secret police.

"They'd been spying on me since I was sixteen years old," she says. "To think that after Hitler, Germany does this to its citizens. Is there something wrong with the Germans?"

Tamm was one of millions of former East Germans who applied to see their own once-secret Stasi files after the communist regime fell. When she learned the truth, she made copies and sent them to her former friend's family and employers. "Now she has lost her job and is ostracized by her family," Tamm says. "We have to know the truth. What is life without truth?"

Her words come from a well deep within, a lifetime of experiences alien to most of us in the West. I've lived, studied, and worked in Germany, in Munich when the wall still stood, but I'm from the American South and now live in Mississippi, thousands of miles away, the polar opposite of sprawling Berlin with its broad boulevards, towering monuments, and giant, domed cathedrals.

Yet those words resonate with me, with my experience as a journalist in the province of Mississippi, where people also wrestle with "truth" and wonder just how much truth society can bear. It's an important question, particularly for a journalist.

The novelist William Styron saw the connection. In his book *Sophie's Choice*, he describes how the U.S. South shares with central and eastern Europe (he spoke of Poland but his words could apply to all of the region) "a sinister zone of likeness," the same long history of poverty, ethnic injustice, and political demagoguery, "the same instant cruelty and compassion, bigotry and understanding, enmity and fellowship, exploitation and sacrifice, searing hatred and hopeless love."

Mississippi has people who, like Tamm and Lembke, bear the scars of their past; they dare not let the memories of their past overwhelm them but nevertheless feel a responsibility, a duty, to remember. Mississippi is one of the haunted places scattered around the world, places where a race of people were hunted and abused, where many died, where the hunters still live among their victims, and where others—who lived through those times but were neither the hunters nor the hunted—wonder whether they did all that they could have done.

The people of these places—and you can also find them in Latin America, Asia, Africa—will point with pride to the progress they've made. Yet the past clings to them, with its calls for justice and its demands to be remembered.

As a journalist, I'm drawn to such places, and as a human being I find myself a part of them even as I observe them. I look across the latter half of the twentieth century—to Mississippi and the South, where the civil rights movement of the 1960s freed a people and inspired the world, and to central and eastern Europe, where another cataclysmic and also largely nonviolent movement did the same in 1989. I see the importance of words such as truth, freedom, and responsibility, however varyingly each may be defined, and I see how utterly vital in such times is the journalist, whose lifeblood is somehow intertwined with those words.

TRUTH AND JOURNALISM

Erle Johnston and I had a curious relationship. Both journalists fascinated by Southern politics, we were amicable enough in 1985 to travel together to the 5,800-acre plantation of former U.S. Senator James O. Eastland in Sunflower County, in the Mississippi Delta, where I conducted the last interview with the ailing, eighty-year-old senator before he died. Johnston and political crony Jack Stuart took turns leaning over Eastland's bed to relay his whispered answers to my questions. After the senator's death in 1986, I wrote a postmortem for the state's largest newspaper, the *Clarion-Ledger*, that lambasted him for the years he used his considerable power in Congress to stymie civil rights legislation and lead the South's futile legal fight against racial integration.

Johnston stopped speaking to me after that piece. It wasn't until five years later and upon my return to Mississippi from my work as a reporter in Washington, D.C., that he contacted me. He asked me to help edit the latest of his several books on Mississippi politics. I agreed. By this time, I was teaching journalism at the University of Mississippi, and Johnston was well along the way on a journey of personal redemption for his own considerable role in what historian James Silver once called the "closed society" that had been Mississippi's segregated past.

A veteran reporter, editor, and publisher of the *Scott County Times* in Forest, Mississippi, Johnston changed hats many times over his long career, serving once as mayor of Forest and frequently as political publicist for staunchly segregationist politicians such as Eastland and Mississippi Governor Ross Barnett. Most famously, or notoriously, he served from 1960 to 1963 as public relations director and then from 1963 to 1968 as director of the Mississippi Sovereignty Commission, a state-funded spy and propaganda agency committed to preserving racial segregation. The commission existed from 1956 to 1977.

In this capacity, Johnston oversaw a secret statewide network that targeted, investigated, intimidated, and threatened anyone who challenged the power structure in Mississippi. It tampered with murder cases against Klansmen; loosed police bullies on civil rights workers and sympathizers; planted misinformation in state newspapers while crushing critical coverage; compromised hundreds of blacks and whites by recruiting them as informers; used its power to ruin lives forever.

In the years before his death in 1995, Johnston worked hard to affix a more positive image of himself in Mississippi history. An affable, mild-mannered man, he offered a tribute in his 1990 book, *Mississippi's Defiant Years: 1953–1973*, to black civil rights leaders Aaron Henry and Charles Evers, and he praised the new racial cooperation in the state.

However, Johnston also insisted that his work with the Sovereignty Commission served to mollify more extremist elements that might have otherwise ruled, and he claimed that the commission's work "mostly was psychological rather than physical." In something less than a *mea culpa*, he concluded, "There is hardly a public official today who doesn't regret the injustices of the sixties. But apologies, regrets, or commiserations won't heal all the wounds or bring back the dead."

BETRAYING SOCIETY AND JOURNALISM

Johnston was fortunate that he didn't have to deal with eastern Europeans such as Ekaterina V. Ognianova, a media scholar sharply critical of the efforts of former "spy/journalists" in her native Bulgaria and elsewhere across the old Soviet bloc to gain redemption in the post-communist world.

"The spy/journalists cannot be forgiven because they violated moral principles that had been vital in Eastern Europe even during the communist regimes," Ognianova wrote in a piece for the *Journal of Mass Media Ethics* in 1993. "A democratic society should rely on journalists with no history of deceiving audiences."

Journalists in communist-era central and eastern Europe frequently doubled as spies for the government. Indeed, as the authors of the classic *Four Theories of the Press* explained more than four decades ago, the primary purpose of the media in communist societies was to preserve the socialist system and the dictatorship of the Party. When communism fell in the Soviet bloc countries, the legions of journalists/propagandists who had served the old system faced public condemnation—often at the hands of their new and independent colleagues in the press.

On April 30, 1992, for example, two daily newspapers in the still-united Czechoslovakia—the *Telegraf* and *Metropolitan*—published the names of 382 communist-era journalists who allegedly had doubled as spies for the government's secret police agency, known as the Statni Bezpečnost, or StB. Those listed were told to clean out their desks and leave immediately. The list included Jindrich Hoda, the deputy editor-in-chief of the *Telegraf*. The people on the list even were declared to be national security threats by the new government.

The release of the list of compromised journalists in Czechoslovakia was an early case in the highly controversial opening of once-secret files all across central and eastern Europe, the files of the now-defunct communist security agencies that had spied on millions of citizens between 1945 and 1990 and compiled countless volumes of information on everything from political activities to sexual habits. After the fall of communism, country after country in the region adopted laws similar to the Czech Republic's "lustrace" act or Poland's "vetting" act in releasing the files. What followed were public denouncements and the expulsion from public life of thousands of former agents and collaborators—ten thousand alone in the Czech Republic—and havoc in the personal lives of citizens who learned of the betrayals of spouses, children, neighbors, and ministers.

False accusations also resulted. People often were listed as "informants" for the most innocent of contacts with spies and agents. For example, even Lech Walesa, the former president and head of the Solidarity labor union that toppled the Communist regime in Poland, was listed as a collaborator in the files of that country's secret police. In August 2000, Poland's "vetting court" cleared him of accusations of collaboration, along with Polish President Aleksander Kwasniewski, who had reluctantly signed the so-called vetting law and soon afterward found himself facing accusations.

Spying was a major preoccupation of the governments of the Soviet bloc countries. The Stasi security force of East Germany collected 6.5 million files, enough to fill 120 miles of shelves. Using the work of an estimated 160,000 informers, the Stasi compiled reports on one in every three of East Germany's sixteen million citizens. Hungary's counterpart compiled some hundred thousand documents on its citizens, utilizing information provided by 140,000 informants.

People have had mixed views about dredging up the sins of the past, including the new journalists of the region who, unlike their predecessors, made the public aware of the files and pressed the debate on whether they should be released.

Piotr Gadzinowski, a socialist member of the Polish Sejm, or parliament, who also serves as vice editor-in-chief at the leftist satirical journal *Nie* in Warsaw, scoffs that political opportunists now use the past as a tool to provoke "historical and ideological war." Poland's communist past, he says, "is a kind of theater now for the right wing's politics." Lukasz Glowaski, a twenty-eight-year-old journalist for a Catholic newspaper and radio station in Lodz, disagrees. He remembers too well how Secret Service officers bullied him as a teenager when he innocently took a photograph of a police building, and how the government simply took his grandfather's book-printing business and confiscated the money. "A lot of people took (the Polish people's) money and built big houses," Glowaski says. "There were people killed. We don't know what happened to them. ... Now we can see the truth."

THE PAST IS NEVER DEAD

The Rev. Ed King stretches his lanky frame to relax with the glass of Piastowski brandy I've brought him, a souvenir from a recent trip to Poland. It's a warm October night, and we're on my back porch in Oxford, Mississippi, talking about Mahatma Gandhi, radical Catholic journalist Dorothy Day, and civil rights–era legends Bob Zellner, Medgar Evers, Stokely Carmichael, and Bob Moses. All of our conversation relates, of course, to the civil rights movement. Ed King is a captive of those days. All he has to do is look in the mirror to see the facial disfigurement that he'll carry to his grave. It came from a 1963 car accident that he blames on white supremacists out to kill him.

At the time, he was the white chaplain of predominantly black Tougaloo College in Jackson—a center of civil rights activity—and he was a key leader of the movement that was challenging Mississippi society to its core. A Methodist minister steeped in the tradition of Reinhold Neibuhr and Dietrich Bonhoeffer, and who himself has been compared to the German pastor and Nazi concentration camp survivor Martin Niemoeller, King was beaten, jailed, scarred. Even his parents were forced to leave the state.

Fear was the only constant in those days, he says. Mississippi was a "police state," and thus you couldn't trust the police, the judges, or even your neighbor. "You had to see yourself as part of something greater, something beyond yourself, to make the sacrifices that might be required of you."

I study the intensity in his face. He's like an old revolutionary fated to relive the defining moments of his life again and again. Faulkner, another Mississippian who lived those days, said it well: "The past is never dead. It's not even past."

In his mid-sixties now, King should be enjoying a kind of senior status as bona fide civil rights hero. But he isn't. Quite the contrary. He is today an outcast among movement veterans. Like the racists he once battled, some of his former comrades question his mental stability and even accuse him of being a likely spy and collaborator with the very police state that once filled his days with fear. The reason? He fought harder than anyone against the release of the 132,000 pages of secret, sealed documents compiled by Mississippi's segregationist spy agency, the Sovereignty Commission.

Standing his ground against the state's major news organizations and his former colleagues in the movement, King argued that simply releasing the files to the public—names and all—would revictimize those whom the state had once wanted to smear as communists, adulterers, or homosexuals, and those whom the commission had unfairly and wrongly listed as informants or collaborators. The commission collected information on an estimated eighty-seven thousand individuals and hundreds of organizations.

But King lost his battle. Most of the files were released by 1998 under a court order in a victory for voyeurism rather than truth, he insists. And here he reminds me of Bonhoeffer, the pastor, theologian, and conspirator who was executed by the Nazis in 1945. In his book, *Ethics*, Bonhoeffer insists that humanity, not truth, is what must be served first, and he ridicules the "grotesque…self-righteousness" of an Immanuel Kant who would subject humanity to a higher duty to truth even if it meant exposing a loved one who had taken refuge from evil pursuers.

Still, like Tamm and Ognianova, King knows the value of truth. He recalls too vividly how "you couldn't get the message out" in the 1960s because "the editors in Jackson controlled public opinion [and] the Sovereignty Commission was a kind of a magnolia gestapo…an agency to keep track of dangerous thought." Most journalists at that time, like their counterparts in central and eastern Europe, served the power structure.

Indeed, the state's two largest and only statewide newspapers, the *Clarion-Ledger* and *Jackson Daily News*, were owned by the Hederman family, one of the most powerful in the state and staunch supporters of the segregationist philosophy that dominated the closed society. Both newspapers propagated this philosophy relentlessly in their editorials and racist columns, in what they covered and didn't cover. Stories of the burnings of black churches were killed at the request of Sovereignty Commission agents, whereas commission propaganda was sometimes published word for word.

Journalists who tried to expose the closed society risked the wrath of the state and the vanguard of its segregationist policies, the Sovereignty Commission. Led by journalist Erle Johnston during some of the most crucial years of its existence, the commission either targeted or compromised journalists. Among those targeted was Hazel Brannon Smith, editor of the *Lexington Advertiser* in Holmes County, Mississippi. A Pulitzer Prize winner in 1964 for her courageous editorials supporting black civil rights, Smith was secretly followed and photographed by commission agents as she helped civil rights workers. The photographs were then given to state legislators, who denounced her as a traitor on the floor of the state senate. The commission also helped subsidize a competing newspaper in the drive to run her out of business.

Eventually, an economic boycott organized by the racist Citizens' Council in Holmes County broke Smith financially. The commission, which Smith attacked in a 1961 editorial as "our own home-grown variety of fascism, Mississippi-born and nurtured," provided a $5 thousand monthly stipend to the Citizens Council. Smith died in poverty and suffering from Alzheimer's disease in a Tennessee nursing home in 1994.

At the same time that the commission was joining with the Citizens Council to destroy Hazel Brannon Smith, it was working to compromise leading black journalists such as Percy Greene, editor of the state's most prominent black newspaper, the weekly *Jackson Advocate*. Documents show that Greene was on the commission payroll at least from 1957 to 1967, traveling across the country to speak on behalf of racial segregation, criticizing civil rights leaders, and publishing commission-inspired stories and editorials that tried to link Martin Luther King Jr. with the Communist Party. Greene died in 1977, the year that the commission officially ceased to exist.

Thus, the irony of the media's role today is not lost on Ed King. More than any other force in the state, the *Clarion-Ledger* fought for the opening of the Sovereignty Commission files, which had been ordered sealed by the Mississippi legislature until the year 2027. In fact, the leaking of many of the files to

Clarion-Ledger investigative reporter Jerry Mitchell led to the 1994 conviction of white supremacist Byron De La Beckwith for the murder of civil rights leader Medgar Evers in 1963. Mitchell also used information from the files to investigate the 1966 killing of NAACP leader Vernon Dahmer. Klan leader Sam Bowers was subsequently convicted of ordering the killing.

Like the trials of accused Nazi collaborators and war criminals Maurice Papon, Paul Touvier, and Erich Priebke in France and Italy in the 1980s and 1990s, the Beckwith and Bowers cases in Mississippi were widely viewed not only as a society's effort to bring about long-overdue justice but also to expiate its sins of the past.

King believes the trials were also a way to let the society-at-large off the hook. "To single out these monsters like Beckwith and Bowers, it was very easy to say, 'We didn't have anything to do with that.' This didn't rise up with anybody in the white community saying 'Let's deal with the past.' It was the *Clarion-Ledger*. ... I didn't hear any great cry (for justice) until the *Clarion-Ledger* started it. ... I don't buy that theory that we are exorcising our ghosts. I do not think the people are repenting. They are not identifying. They are not saying that it was the silence of the good whites who let all these things take place, that it was the failure of the moderates who let this police state be set up."

I recall the words of crusading Russian journalist Yevgenia Albats in an interview with a Knight-Ridder reporter in 1995: "All of us, all Soviets, we are responsible for what happened in our country. ... We made deals, we tried to compromise with government, with KGB, with authorities. We tried to survive. ... A deal with evil." Then I think of Ognianova, who castigated those journalists and politicians in Bulgaria who tried to minimize their own betrayals by saying "We are all guilty; therefore nobody is guilty."

REDEMPTION

Karl Marx once wrote, "The tradition of all the dead generations weighs like a nightmare on the brain of the living."

This is not just true in Mississippi or in Europe. It's also true in places such as South Africa, where a "truth and reconciliation commission" has inflamed old passions even as it has attempted to deal with the legacy of brutality left from the days of apartheid. In Argentina, Guatemala, and elsewhere across Central and South America, citizens have called for a public accounting of the sins of the past. In the Vatican, Pope John Paul II has publicly wrestled with the church's role vis-à-vis the Nazis during World War II and even during the Spanish Inquisition centuries ago. More recently, the Vatican has encountered controversy in its attempts to canonize Cardinal Alojzije Stepinac, a Croatian accused by Serbs of being a Nazi war criminal.

Some countries—such as Spain and Greece—dealt with the sins of past dictatorships by destroying the files of the security forces and spy agencies that kept those dictatorships in power. Indeed, some scholars believe Latin America's long history with dictatorships and political repression has been made possible in part because of society's failure there to face and deal with the past, a failure of memory that allows the past to repeat itself. Some point to a similar failure in Russia, where former KGB spy and now Russian President Vladimir Putin has reinstated many of his old KGB comrades in key positions and worked hard to reestablish an important role for security forces in his country.

"Many countries are not dealing with the past, because the past is still with them," journalist Tina Rosenberg writes in her book about the old Soviet bloc, *The Haunted Land.*

No country has been more forced to face its dark past than Germany, at least what used to be West Germany. Since the end of World War II, West Germany has paid more than eighty-five billion marks to Nazi victims and tried more than eighty-five thousand cases involving Nazi war crimes. Post-war surveys showed that more than 90 percent of Germans felt that the Nuremberg trials of Nazi leaders were fair. When Daniel Jonah Goldhagen's book, *Hitler's Willing Executioners*, appeared in 1996, pointing an accusing finger at all Germans for the Holocaust, the author was sharply criticized for shoddy scholarship almost everywhere but in Germany, where he was welcomed with open arms.

Yet the stigma that hovers over Germany may take another century to disappear.

Croatian writer Miroslav Wolf believes that justice for wrongs committed in the past must be served. However, he also believes that forgiveness and even a redemptive forgetting may be the only ways for both the sinner and the sinned-against to move beyond the past and into a new future. "The memory of sin must be kept alive for a while, as long as it is needed for the repentance and transformation to occur," he wrote in a piece for *Books & Culture* magazine in 1996. However, he said, "ultimately, forgetting the suffering is better than remembering it, because wholeness is better than brokenness."

Rosenberg counters that "a society-wide examination of how the dictatorship maintained its power" is essential if democracy is to have a chance.

To remember? To forgive and forget? To tell all the truth, or just part of it? To blame only the criminals, or also society as a whole? The divisions resulting from such questions are part of the ongoing legacy of evil, of inhumanity to man.

They're not just questions for philosophers, theologians, and politicians to discuss and debate. Journalists, perhaps more than anyone, must deal with them. It's no accident that journalists have played a central role in the debates over the release of secret spy files from Jackson, Mississippi, to Prague. Journalists can unlock doors and they can keep them locked. In Mississippi, journalists such as Erle Johnston, Percy Greene, and the Hederman family betrayed their society and they betrayed journalism. The same holds true for the journalist-spies in Europe whom Ekaterina Ognianova refuses to forgive.

Of course, despite the spies, we have had heroes, too: journalists such as Adam Michnik and Jerzy Turowicz in Poland; and Hazel Brannon Smith, Hodding Carter, and Ira Harkey in Mississippi. These are people who stood up to power at great risk to themselves but whose allegiance to humanity and to their own sense of calling and mission as journalists was too great to allow betrayal. These are the preservers of democracy—something impossible without journalism, media scholar James Carey has said. They are the ones who practiced democracy even when it wasn't allowed and who made democracy possible for the rest of us today. Their courage is a constant reminder that another past exists, a noble past that we all want and need to remember as we enter the future.

Chapter five

From Collusion to Independence

The Press, the Ruling Party, and Democratization in Mexico

by Michael Snodgrass
Assistant Professor of History
Indiana University

The year 2000 marked the end of an era in both Mexican politics and Mexican journalism. The timing was no coincidence. In July, the nation's citizens elected an opposition candidate to the presidency. The outcome ended seventy years of one-party rule. Three months after the ruling party's fall from power, a less significant but equally symbolic event transpired in the offices of *Excélsior*, a Mexico City daily long considered a ruling party stalwart. At the close of an assembly laden with shouting, fisticuffs, and mutual accusations, members of the employee cooperative ousted the long-time director, Regino Díaz Redondo, whose corrupt and authoritarian management had carried *Excélsior* to the edge of bankruptcy. Díaz Redondo's directorship began with a 1976 "coup"—instigated by the government—that overthrew an editorial board that had transformed *Excélsior* into Latin America's most prestigious newspaper. Under his twenty-four-year reign, the paper quickly forsook its critical, independent, and progressive line and returned to one that largely echoed the official ideology of the ruling Institutional Revolutionary Party (PRI). *Excélsior* returned to the status quo of what the government's opponents called "*la prensa vendida*," the sold-out press. Like so many of the capital's two dozen dailies, *Excélsior*'s financial survival resulted from decades of collusion between the government and the press. Consistent with its style of political rule, the PRI maintained a compliant press less through intimidation than patronage. The print media accepted a range of incentives—from government advertising to subsidized newsprint—and delivered the party line to readers. Economic dependency fostered self-censorship. *Excélsior* stood out only for the spectacular degree of government largesse it received.

This essay explores the historical roots of that system, its endurance into the late twentieth century, and the developments that led to its decline. It focuses on the print media and what is known in Mexico as the national press, the Mexico City dailies with nationwide distribution. Mexican newspapers have limited readership. Relatively few can afford their cost. Most Mexicans get their news from television, which was dominated by a single network until the 1990s. Although circulation figures are notoriously unreliable, only a handful of major dailies and newsweeklies exceed one hundred thousand copies.[1] But the national press enjoys a highly influential readership of intellectuals, business leaders, politicians, and the politically active urban middle classes. The development of a genuinely independent and critical press in Mexico, a process that blossomed in the 1970s, simultaneously mirrored, responded to, and promoted the nation's gradual transition to democracy. The emergence of critical investigative reporting prompted a violent backlash in the 1980s, a decade when independent journalism became a hazardous occupation. But as Mexico entered the 1990s, cutbacks in government spending and popular discontent with the ruling party forced publishers to compete for readers by offering an independent journalism free of government tutelage.

FROM REVOLUTION TO COLLUSION

Journalists experienced cycles of press freedom and political persecution for generations before the 1910 revolution transformed Mexican society and politics. The first printing press in the Western Hemisphere arrived to colonial Mexico City in the 1530s. But Spanish censors muzzled publishers during three centuries of imperial rule. Not until the mid-1700s did a daily newspaper surface in the colonial capital. In the early nineteenth century, an alternative form of journalism—subversive broadsides produced at home and abroad—circulated clandestinely in Spain's largest and wealthiest colony. This underground press spread republican ideals among the small but influential community of literate Mexicans who promoted national independence. Freedom of expression arrived with the 1823 founding of the Mexican republic. This politically charged atmosphere produced a highly polemical style of journalism. Newspapers became a key forum in which political factions waged an ideological struggle to define policy and shape national identity.[2]

Political instability, highlighted by civil wars and foreign interventions, guaranteed short life spans for most publications and the intermittent persecution of newspapermen. However, journalists enjoyed nearly complete freedom of expression by the 1860s. Indeed, a combative press helped cultivate public hostility toward a succession of Mexican presidents, a function not lost upon Mexico's first long-term dictator, General Porfirio Díaz (1884–1910). As Díaz consolidated his authoritarian regime, his government fashioned a *pan y palo* ("carrot and stick") policy toward the press, one that rewarded compliant publishers with bribes and punished defiant journalists with libel suits and jail. While progovernment papers published regularly, the independent press remained confined to the provinces. Meanwhile, a growing contingent of anti-Díaz activists published critical papers from the security of exile rather than face intermittent prison terms. Indeed, on the eve of the 1910 revolution, the issue of press freedom helped unify moderate and radical opposition forces. As happened at the time of Mexican independence, the democratic opening of revolution set the presses running again.

Contentious, polemical, and often available at popular prices, the revolutionary-era newspapers were published by various groups that represented a range of interests along the political spectrum: from wealthy families and upstart politicos to conservative Catholics and anarchist trade unions. Few survived these times of civil war, political vengeance, and economic hardship. Many came and went with each electoral season. Although the story of early twentieth-century journalism awaits its historian, it appears that the gradual onset of political stability in the 1920s and 1930s paralleled a process of consolidation in the Mexican newspaper industry. Provincial papers tied to local political factions disappeared as Mexico's multiparty system evolved into one dominated by the National Revolutionary Party, the ruling party later known as the PRI. The period gave birth to major national and regional dailies able to reach and influence a growing urban, middle-class readership. Owned by the well-to-do or well connected, papers such as *El Universal* (1917) and *Excélsior* (1917) in Mexico City and *El Porvenir* (1919) and *El Norte* (1938) in Monterrey proclaimed their independence from the corridors of political power and cast a critical eye on the revolutionary government.

The 1930s marked a rare period when the nation's more influential newspapers were more conservative than the government. As the ship of state veered to the left, the "independent" press helped rally conservative opposition to the Cárdenas government and its "red" supporters: trade unionists, agrarian reformers, and economic nationalists. Come the 1940s, these commercial newspapers' conservative line would converge neatly with official government policy. By then, the PRI had become synonymous with the state. It adopted Mexico's national colors as its own. It established a political machine that reached from the middle-class districts of the capital to isolated rural villages. And it employed a mix of patronage and fraud to win local and national elections until the close of the twentieth century. In the words of Peruvian novelist Mario Vargas Llosa, the Mexican Revolution had produced "the perfect dictatorship."

The period from the 1940s through the 1960s came to be known as the Mexican Miracle a time when sustained economic growth and political stability distinguished Mexico from its Latin American neighbors. In the revolution's aftermath, the government's progressive pro-union policies and land distribution program earned it the loyalty of workers, peasants, and intellectuals.

The state thereafter refined the arts of *pan y palo*, the carrot-and-stick program of incentives, negotiation, and repression that oiled the ruling party's political machine. After the Second World War, ruling party bosses refined the art of corruption while the government's pro-business policies promoted economic development to the benefit of Mexico's middle classes. During these early post-revolutionary years, the government honed a "culture of collusion" with the Mexican press. Indeed, some scholars perceive the media as the institution most responsible for keeping the PRI in power for seven decades.[3]

The culture of collusion dates to the 1930s. As did governments elsewhere in that tumultuous decade, Mexico's new ruling elite "understood the power of organized propaganda."[4] Both the ruling party and the government-allied Confederation of Mexican Workers attempted to shape public opinion by publishing their own dailies. The government also launched Mexico's first radio station with a nationwide network and established a state-run film institute to promote the official ideology. Of greater long-term significance, the state came to exert considerable influence on the commercial press through a web of financial incentives that fostered a remarkably durable system of self-censorship. In 1937, the Cárdenas government established the Department of Press and Publicity. The agency not only managed public relations with the media but also enlisted the press's loyalty through the placement of advertising by a host of government ministries and institutes. Authorities at the municipal and state level soon followed suit. Government allies such as organized labor also provided significant advertising revenues. Moreover, as the years passed, a diverse range of key economic sectors fell under state ownership: oil, telecommunications, broadcast media, airlines, steel, banks, tourism, and so forth. Like their privately owned counterparts elsewhere, they all depended upon advertising to market their goods and services. From a publisher's perspective, the most important state enterprise was PIPSA, the government agency that monopolized the production, importation, and distribution of newsprint. Publishers lobbied the government to create PIPSA during the mid-1930s, when inflation and a weak peso drove up the costs of imported newsprint. Thereafter, the state controlled its costs through protective tariffs and could either subsidize the basic input or fail to deliver it. For that reason, some observers later perceived PIPSA "as a means by which the government could exercise a certain control over the press when its actions seemed harmful to the nation's interests."[5]

Government advertising and subsidized newsprint allowed publishers to profit despite low readership. Commercial dailies also survived through the publication of *gacetillas*, press releases disguised as regular news stories. Thus articles that ran in many countries as paid advertising appeared to Mexican readers as hard news about the public official, political candidate, government agency, or labor union that placed the story and paid for its publication. The *gacetilla* became indispensable to a paper's survival. One North American journalist estimated that, by the 1980s, the major dailies garnered 60 to 80 percent of their revenues from the government. Therefore, as late as the 1990s, blatant *gacetillas* on how "The People Support the Government" or how the state had adopted an "Iron Hand Against Corruption" ran regularly.[6] The benefits and consequences of this system of collusion trickled down from publishers to reporters. Newspaper owners became willing collaborators of the ruling party, more interested in maintaining revenue flows than criticizing a government that could indirectly bankrupt their operations. Reporters, for their part, customarily received a commission on each *gacetilla* brought in from the agencies, enterprises, or individuals covered on their beats.

In addition to the *gacetillas*, the entire newsroom benefited from an ingrained system of payoffs designed to influence reporting. Reporters assigned to specific beats tamed their coverage in exchange for regular payments and piece-rate stipends delivered personally or to their mailboxes on a weekly basis. Those who traveled with the entourages of presidents or foreign ministers could expect additional perks, including meals, travel costs, and spending money. Government ministries and state-owned enterprises therefore included press expenses as part of their declared operating budgets. Columnists fared even better. In a society in which they are held in high regard as influential public intellectuals, columnists can shape public opinion through silence, praise, or defamation. Editors fared best of all because they took the calls from public authorities who "suggested" the stories to be highlighted, downplayed, or simply ignored. The publishers thrived under the payoff system as well. It permitted them to pay reporters notoriously low salaries. Publishers and editors also secured their journalists' loyalties by assigning them to potentially lucrative beats such as the president's office or PEMEX, the state oil company. In fact, the culture of collusion permitted a number of well-connected journalists and columnists to become quite wealthy by national standards.[7] Seen in a broader perspective, this relationship between the state and the press reflected a culture of official corruption that touched nearly every aspect of public life, from the presidential office to the local police precinct.

Economic compulsion became the root cause of the self-censorship practiced by the Mexican press. In contrast to other authoritarian regimes in Latin America, the Mexican government never censored the press directly. But as with other recalcitrant sectors of society, newspapermen who persisted in their pursuit of independent journalism often faced threats, intimidation, and physical violence. In hindsight, the 1930s proved to be a decade of tolerance. Rather than impose limits on press freedoms, the Cárdenas administration promoted its own dailies. In those days, a more progressive ruling party leadership perceived the conservative influence of the press as an obstacle to the government's radical social policies. However, as Mexico entered the postwar era, the ruling party came to share the probusiness, anticommunist agenda propagated by the major dailies. That ideological convergence abetted the culture of collusion. Meanwhile, President Cárdenas's successors proved less tolerant of a critical press. Commercial newspapers and weeklies that defied the government faced insurmountable obstacles, including vandalism by ruling party goons, the physical intimidation of publishers and reporters, and, on rare occasions, the assassinated newspaperman. Government-allied unions could also be mobilized to shut down presses or stop the distribution of troublesome papers. Publishers and journalists thus learned early on to work within the limits of the system. The president himself remained immune from criticism until his six-year term ended, while the strikes, rural unrest, or student protests that contradicted the Mexican Miracle remained taboo subjects unless reported from the government perspective. Otherwise, documenting social discontent was considered a sympathetic endorsement. Events in the 1960s would shatter this status quo and launch Mexico's gradual transition to political democracy and independent journalism.

FROM COLLUSION TO INDEPENDENCE

The year 1968 became synonymous with youth rebellion and political violence. As the decade had progressed, the gulf between revolutionary rhetoric and social reality had widened. Government statisticians charted economic growth. Glistening new skyscrapers, public works projects, and modern industrial parks dotted the Mexico City landscape. And the government prepared to showcase the Mexican Miracle by hosting the 1968 Summer Olympic Games. Meanwhile, blue-collar wages stagnated, poverty spread in the countryside, and rural migrants seeking better lives in the cities found themselves in sprawling suburban shantytowns. After more than three decades of uninterrupted rule, the PRI came under scrutiny from an increasingly sophisticated electorate, one grown tired of ruling party bossism, paternalism, and corruption. In this context, the government opted to repress dissidence rather than offer a political opening.

As strikes and campus protest escalated, the government ordered the police and military to quell disturbances. The repression radicalized Mexico City's vast population of middle-class students. One month before the Olympic games, some 300,000 protestors staged the largest antigovernment demonstration in Mexican history. The government hardened its line. Ten thousand troops seized the National University campus from striking students. Mexican jails filled with hundreds of political prisoners charged with sedition under a vague law of social disorder. The climax came on October 2, 1968, when military forces ambushed a relatively small and peaceful protest at Mexico City's Plaza of Three Cultures. The violence resulted in three hundred to four hundred deaths, forty-three of which the government officially acknowledged.[8]

What became known as the Massacre at Tlatelolco effectively silenced the opposition but eroded the long-term legitimacy of Mexico's political system. For the generation of 1968, the massacre came to symbolize the moral and political bankruptcy of the Mexican Revolution.

The Mexican press mostly adhered to its customary practices of self-censorship. Echoing the official story, the media blamed the massacre on rebellious students and communist conspirators, dismissing the violence as a military response to sniper fire. *Excélsior* proved the exception to the rule.[9] Only months before Tlatelolco, Mexico's then-leading newspaper had come under the editorship of Julio Scherer García. Known as an incorruptible journalist, Scherer quickly dropped such practices as selling the daily's headline. Many a reporter continued accepting bribes. Government advertising remained a vital source of revenues. But Scherer hired on some of Mexico's most renowned and critical intellectuals as columnists. Under his direction, *Excélsior* gained renown as the world's finest Spanish-language newspaper—the *Le Monde* of Latin America—for its investigative journalism and critical analysis of government policy. Its coverage of the massacre and its aftermath marked *Excélsior*'s first step toward independence and distinguished it from its competitors. Under Scherer, the daily would capitalize on the "democratic opening" promised by President Luis Echeverría (1970–1976), the formerly hard-line Interior Minister who many considered responsible for the 1968 massacre.

As it had done in the past, Mexico's ruling party responded to the political crisis with a reform agenda meant to appease its opponents. This time, the pendulum swung left. Echeverría distributed land to peasants, freed political prisoners, and opened Mexico to political exiles from South America. He enveloped his policy in socialist and anti-imperialist rhetoric. He attempted to prove his sincerity and restore PRI legitimacy by encouraging press criticism of the government. Scherer and other independent-minded journalists began investigating and reporting news once considered taboo: union insurgencies, land seizures, guerrilla movements, and political violence against social activists. The president expected the press to employ the "opening" to attack the previous government. But in the greatest break from an unwritten rule of Mexican journalism, that of presidential immunity, *Excélsior* leveled its investigative reporting against the Echeverría administration itself. The paper exposed high-level corruption. Reporters tracked a soaring budget deficit and foreign debt. Editorials chastised the president for failing to transform government expenditures into concrete social improvements. Corporate Mexico came under scrutiny as well, earning Scherer the wrath of Mexican businessmen. Meanwhile, Echeverría's leftist posturing earned him the indignation of conservatives, especially the big industrialists in Monterrey. That city's influential daily, *El Norte*, criticized Echeverría from the right. Its editors blamed the government for a rash of strikes and the failure to properly investigate the assassination of a local industrial patriarch by leftist guerrillas. Thus in a brief time, newspapers as distinct as *Excélsior, El Norte,* and a host of new critical weeklies came to perform the role of the loyal opposition within a political system wherein the ruling party and the president held undisputed power.

The Echeverría government retrenched on its policy of "self-criticism." It instead used intimidation, economic coercion, and political intrigue to temper the independent press. In 1974, Mexico City police raided a small, leftist weekly renowned for its reports on guerrilla activities. They vandalized its presses, kidnapped and beat the staff, and threatened the imprisoned editor with death if publication resumed. Monterrey's *El Norte* lost access to subsidized newsprint. The daily was forced to produce a more austere paper and turn away advertisers. But the financial independence enjoyed by its wealthy owners permitted it to recover by importing more costly newsprint from the United States.[10] *Excélsior's* international prestige forced the government to employ more subtle means to silence its reporting. The pressure began with a 1972 advertising boycott orchestrated by Echeverría's private allies, including Mexico's leading department stores, banks, and breweries. *Excélsior* survived the commercial boycott as well as a gradual withdrawal of government advertising. Scherer's downfall ultimately came from within the employee-owned cooperative. Throughout the Echeverría years, *Excélsior's* old guard had clamored to oust the upstart editor. In 1976, the conservative rebels demanded an extraordinary assembly at which armed outsiders made clear their intention to force Scherer's resignation. The coup succeeded after calls for police assistance went unanswered and Scherer walked out. *Excélsior* returned to the staid tradition of political conservatism and government collusion. Its readership declined over the next quarter century. The daily nonetheless prospered as government largesse, in the form of direct subsidies, low-interest loans, and forgiven debts, permitted *Excélsior* to survive and its new directors to grow wealthy.[11] Meanwhile, some two hundred loyal reporters and editors had resigned in solidarity with Julio Scherer. They became Mexico's vanguard of critical investigative reporting.

THE DEMOCRATIZATION OF POLITICS AND THE PRESS

The *Excélsior* coup marked a watershed in Mexican journalism. The reporters and editors who departed the paper in 1976 upheld their commitment to press independence and investigative journalism. Scherer was silenced only briefly. Later that year, he published the first issue of *Proceso,* a muckraking newsweekly that became (and remains) the most respected source of investigative reporting in Mexico. Other *Excélsior* alumni founded the leftist Mexico City dailies *Unomasuno* (1977) and *La Jornada* (1984). They staffed their dailies with young college graduates and an influential number of South American journalists who had sought exile in Mexico from military dictatorships in their homelands. *Proceso,* in particular, distinguished itself for regular exposés on high-level nepotism, corruption in the government and labor movement, and the rise of political repression in the countryside. Thus, although *Excélsior*'s tenure as the world's most distinguished Spanish-language newspaper ended, its offspring ensured the survival of a national press that remained openly critical of the government.[12] From northern Mexico, Monterrey's *El Norte* sustained an editorial line consistent with the city's conservative reputation. As the dominant daily in Mexico's wealthiest city, *El Norte* became the first daily to declare its full economic independence from the government. By developing a profitable base of corporate advertisers and middle-class subscribers, the paper's publishers afforded state-of-the-art newsroom technology and professionalized the staff by offering Mexico's highest salaries to Mexican graduates of U.S. journalism programs. By the 1980s, *Proceso* and *El Norte* had forbidden reporters from accepting bribes, cut government advertising, and stopped publishing *gacetillas*. Their financial independence made them early exceptions to the press's ongoing reliance on government largesse.

But after 1976, the Mexican press grew more critical and ideologically diverse. Although self-censorship remained the rule at many Mexican dailies, a degree of editorial diversity worked to the ruling party's advantage. It bolstered the government's rhetorical claims to defend press freedoms and promote a democratic opening. Government subsidies prevented a handful of influential papers from dominating public opinion by permitting some two to three dozen dailies to survive in Mexico City alone. Some media scholars assert that the system created a facade of journalistic pluralism. Others suggest that a freer press provided an escape valve for the leftist intellectuals who dominated Mexico's cultural and academic life.[13] Moreover, by the 1980s, some twenty million Mexicans received their daily news from the aggressively progovernment television monopoly Televisa, whose owner declared himself "a loyal soldier of the president." However, the press's ideological diversity also reflected the ruling party itself, factions of which represented competing class interests, business groups, regions, and political tendencies. Indeed, the PRI's survival after the crisis of 1968 owed much to its capacity to integrate leftist intellectuals and social activists into the government apparatus. Competing political families used the press to push their credentials, debate policy, or assassinate the character of their rivals. The internal rivalries erupted in 1988, an election year, when dissidents bolted the party to oppose PRI nominee Carlos Salinas.

The PRI had by then won every presidential and gubernatorial race in its sixty-year history. But, in the 1980s, a severe economic crisis and blatant electoral fraud swelled grassroots support for the political opposition: the conservative National Action Party (PAN) and a leftist coalition supporting the dissident candidacy of Cuauhtémoc Cárdenas, son of a president beloved by workers and peasants. Consistent with tradition, the major media outlets rallied behind the Salinas candidacy. One newspaper executive later admitted that his senior editor brought in one million pesos—then about $300,000—

to boost the Salinas candidacy in the months before the election.[14] For the first time in memory, however, opposition candidates received extensive and balanced coverage from a more independent press. Mexicans thus read that Cárdenas led the early returns before the electoral computer system crashed. One week later, final tallies gave Salinas a narrow victory in an election that most Mexicans considered stolen. A brief economic recovery rejuvenated the PRI's patronage machine. But its political hegemony waned. A program of electoral reforms meant to restore legitimacy coincided with a series of shocks that included an Indian rebellion in the South, another devastating economic crisis, political assassinations, and revelations of ruling party links to drug trafficking. All received extensive press coverage and analysis. Indeed, the political drama of the 1990s bolstered the circulation of such beacons of critical reporting as *Proceso*, *La Jornada*, and *Reforma*, the Mexico City daily launched in 1993 by the owners of Monterrey's *El Norte*. Meanwhile, the democratization of the press paralleled Mexico's own transition to genuine political democracy. As the 1990s progressed, the ruling party lost control of Congress, key states, and the major cities, including the capital. The process culminated in December 2000, when the PAN's Vicente Fox became the first opposition figure to be inaugurated president since the revolution.

The ruling party's loss would culminate in the gradual demise of the government-subsidized press. Its degree of dependence had become clear in the early 1980s. Reeling from the onset of economic crisis, the De la Madrid government launched a program of austerity measures that included cutbacks in government advertising. The president's own aides predicted a resulting bankruptcy of half of Mexico City's dailies. As ad revenues fell, the publishers staged such an outcry the government admitted that the system of collusion would endure indefinitely. Even the leftist opposition daily *La Jornada* continued to earn some 70 percent of its ad revenues from the government.[15] Moreover, although several dailies competed for columnists with relatively high salaries, journalists remained the lowest-paid professionals in Mexico, earning an average salary of $300 monthly in the early 1990s.[16] Although meager compared to the subsidies received by publishers, the bribes and perks offered to journalists supplemented their threadbare incomes. Journalists could benefit from the culture of collusion, and those at some dailies therefore allied with their employers as obstacles to change.

However, by the mid-1990s, a neo-liberal program meant to deregulate the economy and cut Mexico's debt had undermined the culture of collusion. Free trade policies cut tariffs and permitted publishers to import newsprint at affordable rates. The sale of hundreds of state enterprises to the private sector dramatically eliminated a primary source of government advertising. And privatization established an array of new companies—banks, hotels, airlines, utilities, and so forth—forced to compete for consumers. Thus new sources of advertising revenues emerged just as the devastating economic crisis of 1995 forced the federal government to enact further budget cuts and end its tradition of bankrolling the print media. Meanwhile, at the state and municipal level, opposition parties stormed into office and immediately purged journalists from government payrolls. The demise of collusion increased commercial competition. *Reforma*, the sister paper of Monterrey's *El Norte*, saw its circulation surpass 100,000 shortly after entering the Mexico City market. That forced old-guard dailies such as the *El Universal* to adopt a more independent line. It gained readership immediately. *Excélsior*, on the other hand, clung to the ruling party line, lost credibility, and saw its circulation tumble from more than 100,000 to less than 30,000 by the late 1990s. Publishers thus came to learn that editorial independence was not only possible but also profitable.[17]

The shift reflected broader changes in Mexican society. One was a transformation in what Joel Simon calls "the very ethos of Mexican journalism." Reporters who once established themselves by allying with a political boss learned to build their careers on solid investigative reporting. Simon attributes the change to the arrival of a younger, better-educated and higher-paid corps of journalists and editors. Moreover, a public reeling from a series of political and economic crises increasingly directed its anger against both the government and a compliant, sold-out media. Civil society demanded more transparent coverage of the scandals and crises that accompanied the end of the Mexican Miracle. The big city press responded first. The leftist *La Jornada*'s in-depth reporting on the 1994 Zapatista rebellion in southern Chiapas state doubled its circulation. The Mexico City dailies were learning that "readers would respond to aggressive coverage."[18] Public demand for transparency also prompted publishers and journalists to launch dozens of independent dailies and newsweeklies in Mexico's rural and borderland states during the 1990s. In southern Mexico, reporters documented the emergence of armed opposition groups. In northern and Pacific Coast states, courageous journalists focused on an explosion of drug trafficking and its corruptive effects on local politics and society. They did so at great risk, for these were regions overseen by entrenched ruling party bosses who used strong-arm tactics rather than financial incentives to silence the press and maintain their increasingly tenuous grip on power.

The democratization of politics and the press prompted a violent backlash from political authorities unaccustomed to the scrutinizing eye of reporters. Upon its 1981 founding, the Committee to Protect Journalists (CPJ) called Latin America "the most dangerous place in the world to be a journalist." Right-wing dictatorships ruled much of the region and death squads targeted journalists in their campaigns against "communist subversion." Mexico was exceptional for its dearth of political violence. Indeed, it remained a safe haven for many an exiled journalist. Then, as Latin America embarked on a transition to democracy, freedom of expression returned and the press became a key "mechanism of accountability" in a region where Congress and the courts remained relatively weak.[19] However, in Mexico, the process of democratization led to increased levels of political violence. In the 1980s and 1990s, violence against journalists escalated in rhythm with the repression of opposition political activists. Hundreds of predominantly left-wing activists were murdered from the late 1980s through the mid-1990s. By then, the toll of journalists killed in Mexico had mounted with each presidential term: six during 1970–1976, twelve during 1976–1982, thirty-three during 1982–1988. The violence peaked after 1988. One report documented the deaths of twenty-one more journalists during the first three years of the Salinas administration alone. Among all Latin American countries, only the journalists of Colombia faced greater occupational hazards than Mexican reporters.[20]

Political violence became most pronounced in Mexico's hinterlands. Ninety percent of murdered journalists worked in relative obscurity for small provincial papers. They lost their lives after documenting fraudulent local elections or reporting ties between political authorities and drug traffickers. Their deaths went largely unnoticed in the insular world of the Mexico City press. But even a reporter's fame did not guarantee immunity. In 1984, assailants gunned down the country's most celebrated columnist, Manuel Buendía, on a Mexico City street. The *Excélsior* writer, whose column was syndicated to more than sixty dailies, earned high regard in both ruling party and opposition circles for exposés on high-level corruption, CIA activities in Latin America, and the clandestine world of Mexico's ultra-right. Buendía died a poor man, a testimony to his famed resistance to media corruption. Yet he was seen, one colleague noted, as a reporter who "would criticize the government, but he would never criticize the system. He was part of the system, and he was useful to it." The president attended his wake. But the government failed to realize its highly publicized promises to uncover Buendía's assailants. Thus, by the late 1980s, one human rights group reported that "the death of this exemplary figure still casts its shadow on Mexico's journalists."[21] Moreover, the press faced other forms of intimidation as well: police raids on offices, vandalized machinery, bombings, kidnapping, assaults, death threats, and so forth. More insidious hazards emerged in the 1990s. Publishers faced arrest on arbitrary tax fraud charges, while well-connected subjects of press scrutiny fought back with dozens of defamation litigation suits.[22] But the ongoing violence and legal intimidation failed to silence an increasingly defiant and independent press.

In its 1999 report, the Committee to Protect Journalists found the Mexican press "covering local politics with greater confidence and independence." The drug trade "was still an extremely dangerous assignment." But the number of reporters killed in the line of duty—five—had declined notably since the mid-1990s. Moreover, the violence attracted the scrutiny of international human rights monitors, which forced the federal government to take notice and act. A more thorough investigation of press-related violence promised to increase with the creation of a journalistic protection unit within the government's National Human Rights Commission. Perhaps most important, Mexican journalists began organizing themselves in defense of their interests. For decades, ideological feuding and personal rivalries divided the insular Mexico City press corps. Reporters in the capital developed few professional ties to their provincial counterparts. Indeed, the repression of journalists generated little coverage in Mexico City. But in 1997, five reporters there suffered reprisals, including one murder, for their coverage of police corruption. In that context, the CPJ convened the first significant gathering of top Mexican journalists to discuss mechanisms of defense. Within two years, Mexico counted three national organizations aimed at defending press freedoms. As a result, violence against journalists has become front-page news throughout Mexico. Press coverage helped fuel a public outcry and the government responded by ordering federal prosecutors armed with greater independence and resources to investigate local cases. Meanwhile, annual press forums are convened to promote journalistic ethics and lobby the government to legislate a freedom of information act.[23] Today, Mexico's more independent, professionalized, and organized journalists have become watchdogs, freed from the culture of collusion and poised to oversee the nation's ongoing democratization.

NOTES

1. In a country where workers earn the equivalent of six to nine dollars *daily*, newspapers sell at prices comparable to those in the United States. As of the mid-1990s, media scholars reported a combined circulation of 700,000–1,000,000 for Mexico City's two dozen dailies. Were one to exclude sensationalist tabloids and sports dailies, the figures fall to roughly 280,000–550,000 in one of the world's largest metropolises. Estimated circulation figures do not account for high multiple readership rates. Nor do they acknowledge the ubiquitous newsstands, whose prominent displays of front-page news attract countless readers. See Raymundo Riva Palacio, "A Culture of Collusion," in William A. Orme, Jr., ed., *A Culture of Collusion: An Inside Look at the Mexican Press* (Miami: North-South Center Press, 1997), 23, 31–32; Andres Oppenheimer, *Bordering on Chaos* (Boston: Little, Brown, 1996), 135.
2. Moisés Ochoa Campos sketches the early history of Mexican journalism in *Reseña Histórica del Periodismo Mexicano* (Mexico City: Editorial Porrua, 1968).
3. Murray Fromson, "Mexico's Struggle for a Free Press," in Richard Cole, ed., *Communication in Latin America: Journalism, Mass Media, and Society* (Wilmington: SR, 1996), 115–137. The term "culture of collusion" is borrowed from the veteran journalist Raymundo Riva Palacios.
4. William Beezley and Colin MacLachlan, *El Gran Pueblo: A History of Greater Mexico*, Vol. II (Englewood Cliffs, NJ: Prentice Hall, 1994), 319–20.
5. Carlos Moncada, *Del México Violento: Periodistas Asesinados* (Mexico: Edamex, 1991), 10.
6. Alan Riding, *Distant Neighbors* (New York: Vintage, 1989), 124; Joel Simon, "A Freer Press Scares the Government," *Columbia Journalism Review*, Jan./Feb. 1993.
7. Fromson, "Mexico's Struggle for a Free Press," 117–118; Riding, *Distant Neighbors*, 125–126.
8. Elena Poniatowska, *Massacre in Mexico* (New York: Penguin Books, 1975).

9. The *Excélsior* story is recounted by Carlos Monsiváis, "El fin de un cacicazgo en ruinas," *Proceso*, Oct. 29, 2000; "El golpe a Excélsior," *Proceso*, Nov. 5, 2000; "The Coup at Excélsior," *Columbia Journalism Review*, Sep./Oct. 1976; Patrick Oester, *The Mexicans* (New York: Harper and Row, 1989), 184–190; Riding, *Distant Neighbors*, 433–34; Petra Maria Secanella, *El periodismo político en Mexico* (Barcelona: Editorial Mitre, 1983), 25–33. Julio Scherer Garcia chronicles his years at *Excélsior* in *Los Presidentes* (Mexico: Grijalbo, 1986).

10. Christopher Palmeri, "Señor Clean," *Forbes*, April 24, 1995, 132–134.

11. Carlos Acosta Córdova, et. al., "Díaz Redondo: el gobierno lo elevó, lo sustuvo y lo dejó caer," *Proceso*, Oct. 29, 2000; Oppenheimer, *Bordering on Chaos*, 136–38.

12. "Excélsior's Offspring," Ann Davis, *Columbia Journalism Review*, March/April 1992; Riding, *Distant Neighbors*, 106–107.

13. Richard Seid, "A Heavy Hand on Mexican Papers," *Christian Science Monitor*, Oct. 10, 1996; Oppenheimer, *Bordering on Chaos*, 136.

14. Fromson, "Mexico's Struggle for a Free Press," 118.

15. Fromson, "Mexico's Struggle for a Free Press," 130; Oppenheimer, *Bordering on Chaos*, 138.

16. Linda Egan, "Feminine Perspectives on Journalism: Conversations With Eight Mexican Women," *Studies in Latin American Popular Culture*, No. 12, 1993, 182.

17. Orme, Jr., *A Culture of Collusion*, 5–8; Palmeri, "Señor Clean"; Córdova, "Díaz Redondo"; Seid, "A Heavy Hand."

18. Joel Simon, "Breaking Away: Mexico's Press Challenges the Status Quo," Committee to Protect Journalists: Special Reports, 1997 (http://www.cpj.org); Simon, "A Freer Press."

19. Barbara Belejack, "Latin American Journalists Under the Gun," *NACLA Report on the Americas*, No. 32:1, July/August 1998, 6–11.

20. Article 19 (The International Centre on Censorship), *In the Shadow of Buendia: The Mass Media and Censorship in Mexico* (New York: Article 19, 1989), 6–17, 83–89; David LaFrance, "Politics, Violence, and the Press in Mexico," *Studies in Latin American Popular Culture*, No. 12, 1993, 215–220.

21. Riding, *Distant Neighbors*, 107, 125;, Article 19, *In the Shadow of Buendia*, 1–8. The government later charged the head of the Federal Police in Mexico City as the intellectual author of Buendía's assassination. See LaFrance, "Politics, Violence, and the Press in Mexico." The most detailed documentation of violence against journalists is presented in the annual reports of the Committee to Protect Journalists (http://www.cpj.org) and Reporters Sans Frontiers (http://www.rsf.fr).

22. Seid, "A Heavy Hand on Mexican Papers"; Orme, Jr., *A Culture of Collusion*, 1–3; Article 19, *In the Shadow of Buendia*, 6–17; Dianne Solis, "Mexican Press Still on the Take," *Nieman Reports*, No. 51:3, Fall 1997; Mark Pinsky, "Living Dangerously," *Quill*, No. 85:4, May 1997.

23. Simon, "Breaking Away."

Chapter six

The Outspoken Journalist Is an Expression, a Symbol of Colombia

by Stephen F. Jackson, Editor
The *Latin American Post*
Bogota, Colombia, and
Associate Professor, Stillman College
Tuscaloosa, Alabama

This account turns back the clock to December 15, 1989, one of the most pivotal moments during the notorious drug wars with the Medellin Cartel. Yet, in Jackson's depiction of the danger-wrought lives and work of Colombian journalists, this story is very much about today.

69

In Bogota, Colombia, on Friday, December 15, 1989...

Bogotanos are dancing in the streets of their beleaguered capital city. They began in the afternoon. They will continue through the night until the early hours of the morning. Colombians have a reason to celebrate. The deadliest, most ruthless player in this country's drug war has been shot and killed by the national police.

Jose Gonzalo Rodriguez Gacha's ignominious end is the greatest victory yet in the drug war declared by the Colombian government after the brutal murder of a leading presidential candidate in August. The celebration is not confined to the streets. Perhaps the largest victory party is taking place behind closed doors and under heavily armed guard—in the newsroom of one of Bogota's major newspapers, *El Espectador*.

Of course, journalists and news media all over Colombia are breathing a huge sigh of relief with the news of the killing of Gacha, the drug mafia's self-proclaimed "Enforcer" and most notorious perpetrator of violence and revenge. During the past decade, Gacha orchestrated the threats, killings, and bombings of journalists and anyone else who stood in the way of the illegal drug trade. No news organization stood more in the way than *El Espectador*.

This Friday began like any other at the newspaper in Bogota, the Andean city of "eternal Spring." Editors and reporters, by now oblivious to the cordon of armed soldiers around the newspaper building, hustle against deadline to produce not only Saturday's edition but also the special sections for Sunday. Suddenly, at 2:47 P.M., the newsroom routine is broken by the staccato voice of a newscaster from a radio on a reporter's desk. The newscaster reports: Gacha and his henchmen are surrounded at their northern coastal hideout. A wild shootout is under way with officers from the Department of Security Administration, the powerful and armed federal security and intelligence agency, or national police, known as DAS and led by General Miguel Maza Marquez.

The other shoe did not take long to drop. At 3:03 P.M., another radio bulletin comes on: Gacha, his seventeen-year old son, and five accomplices are killed at La Estrella on Colombia's balmy Caribbean coast. Gacha, the pudgy, forty-four-year-old former pig farmer and later billionaire cocaine kingpin who shared leadership of the Medellin cartel with still-at-large Pablo Escobar, is riddled with bullets by a DAS machine gunner firing from an American helicopter. Gacha dies clutching his own machine gun, running to nowhere across a vacant field. Nine months earlier he had been on the cover of *Fortune* magazine, featured as one of the world's richest and most powerful men. Soon his bloodstained body would be buried in an obscure, common grave for paupers somewhere near Cartagena.

Many Colombians had come to see their government as a *pinata*, a paper tiger, against this raging bull. The Gacha-Escobar empire was responsible for thousands of killings. Victims included judges, magistrates, police, an attorney general, a justice minister, a newspaper publisher-editor, and Luis Carlos Galan, the front-running presidential candidate who was machine-gunned on August 18, 1989. In late November, bombings—planned by Gacha with the general public as part of the target—assumed ritual status in the capital city and throughout the country. All 107 passengers aboard a Colombian airliner were killed when a cartel-placed bomb exploded in midair on November 27. Sixty-three people died and more than one thousand were injured in the dynamiting of DAS headquarters December 6.

But Gacha's death could mean a decisive turn in the war declared by Colombian president Virgilio Barco: a great victory for him and for the DAS, an agency that in Colombia combines the functions the CIA and FBI serve in the United States. Gacha's demise is a victory, too, for the journalists who have been prominent among Gacha's targets since the early 1980s—none more so than those at *El Espectador*.

With a daily circulation of 200,000, *El Espectador* is the second largest daily newspaper in Colombia. Like its larger rival, *El Tiempo* (with a 325,000 circulation), *El Espectador* is family-owned, published in Bogota, and read religiously throughout this country of forty million. Among its most avid readers are the decision makers and opinion leaders in Bogota—and, of course, the drug warlords in Medellin.

The ruthless Gacha had ordered the killing of *El Espectador*'s owner, its lawyer, one of its columnists, its Medellin correspondent, and its circulation manager. In addition, Gacha orchestrated the bombing of the newspaper with 330 pounds of dynamite in September, severely damaging the building, its computers, and its presses. The list of such deeds perpetrated by Gacha and Pablo Escobar stretches back into the early 1980s, not only against *El Espectador* and journalists but against all institutions and individuals in Colombia who stood against the cartel's power.

Owned and operated by the Cano family, many of whom work at the daily founded in 1886, *El Espectador* has become an institutional symbol, a lightning rod for exposing and crusading against the cocaine cartels and their minions.

The newspaper's patriarch and publisher is soft-spoken Luis Gabriel Cano, whose brother Guillermo was an editor and columnist at the newspaper when Escobar had him assassinated in 1986. Luis Gabriel Cano continues to operate the newspaper in the face of economic hardship due in large part to the war with the drug cartel. *El Espectador* is not part of a corporate conglomerate that can draw on outside resources to help meet expenses and payroll. The cash flow is largely the result of the newspaper's advertising and circulation revenue, although *El Espectador* is receiving economic as well as moral support from newspaper organizations all over the world. This support includes a $2.5 million fundraising effort begun in November by the American Newspaper Publishers Association and the InterAmerican Press Association. More than thirty American, Australian, British, Canadian, and Japanese newspapers have pledged or made donations.

"The help we have received from our overseas friends allows us to carry on and to move forward," Cano says.

Still, with all the killings, threats, and costly damages from the September bombing, Cano's family could easily throw in the towel and no one would question them.

But Gabriel Cano is a man on a mission. The intimidation must be stopped, he says, to preserve not only freedom of the press but also Colombia's democratic way of life. "We must find a way of fighting this tremendous scourge," he says. "The death of Gacha is the beginning of the end of this drug war." After a moment's pause, he adds, "I think."

The drug cartel ordered the murder of Cano's brother. However, the struggle is more than personal. Gacha and Escobar are responsible "for the deaths of thousands of people in Colombia," he reminds.

More than fifty Colombian journalists have been killed by the drug lords in the 1980s. As for the journalists who survive, many have been forced to leave the country because of death threats to them or to their families. Those who remain in Colombia move from one place to another, followed by heavily armed bodyguards.

"Editorial offices of the newspapers look like headquarters of the police or army in time of war," Cano says. "Personally, journalists receive death threats, their families also are threatened and, ultimately, also advertisers who use the press are intimidated by threats and by bombings if they continue buying advertising in the newspapers."

As former *Washington Post* reporter and famed Watergate investigator Carl Bernstein told an *El Tiempo* interviewer two days after Gacha's death, "Colombian journalists work under the most dangerous conditions in the world, more dangerous than being a war correspondent."

As the drug lords' principal gadfly, *El Espectador* has taken the brunt of their attacks against the press. However, even after the September bombing, no one quit the newspaper. Still, its staffers know they take their lives in their hands every day that they go to work.

The writer at *El Espectador* who most symbolizes the struggle of the press against the warlords is thirty-one-year-old Maria Jimena Duzan. A mercurial woman who fancies skin-tight blue jeans, black leather high-heeled boots, and a leather jacket cinched at her waist, Duzan has used her column, "My Zero Hour," to fight Gacha relentlessly ever since he and his tactics emerged on the scene.

Journalism is a way of life—the only way—for Duzan. "I have to understand what is happening to my country," she says. "And the only way I can do that is by being here. What is happening to my country is a part of me. I write about guerrilla violence, criminal violence, narcotraffic violence because this is my country and these things are happening here.

"We have something similar to the U.S. Constitution's First Amendment— a guarantee of freedom of the press—but the government cannot protect us, so the journalist has to protect her own life, accepting that responsibility or fate, as the case may be. I and the other journalists...in Colombia, we do not feel isolated. We feel we are backed by the people. I certainly feel that way. That is why I stay here and continue to crusade and not move to another country. The outspoken journalist is an expression, a symbol...of Colombia."

This commitment requires sacrifice, however. Duzan's sacrifices include the bombing of her home, which she barely escaped, and the assassination of her sister, a documentary filmmaker murdered at work.

"I know of no other war where journalists are the intended targets. There is a reason for this. Our governmental and political institutions have not been functioning effectively for ten years now and the narcotraffickers have been exploiting these weaknesses, these failures. The narcotraffickers threaten the stability and democracy of our country. The journalists in Colombia were the first to recognize and to speak out publicly about this illegal and corrupting usurpation of power by the cartels. We told about their power, their money, and how they were insidiously destroying our society. We told who they were. We told about their ownership of soccer teams and business fronts. We refused to condone their actions. We refused to accept them.

"To be a journalist in Colombia now is to belong to a special group. A journalist—the one who writes about the narcotrafficking—is an image, a symbol to this society. We have prestige. Whether people agree or disagree with what we write, the public in general respects us because we unmask hypocrisy and fraud. Even the narcotraffickers respect us. They know they cannot bribe us, so they try to destroy us. They desperately want acceptance from society but they are afraid of what we can tell about them, what we can show about them—that they are criminals who threaten the sovereignty of our democracy."

In a country where nineteen of her fellow journalists have been killed thus far in 1989—making Colombia the most dangerous country in the world for journalists—Duzan has indeed never been alone in her fight against the cocaine billionaires and their network of support. But the courage and commitment that her byline immediately communicates have made her a rare and prominent symbol, a beacon in the darkness, not only in Colombia but now worldwide as a result of profiles in *The New York Times* and by the BBC (British Broadcasting Company), which came to Bogota in December to produce a documentary titled *A Week in the Life of El Espectador*.

"To us in Colombia Duzan is like a matador, a bullfighter," says an official at the *Circulo de Periodistas* (the Circle of Journalists), Bogota's professional association of journalists. "She is not afraid to take on the cocaine dealers. She is not intimidated by their threats and attempts on her life. She stays close to the action in the drug war. And, this time, with the killing of Gacha, the wild bull of the cocaine cartel, she can revel in a victory far greater than any in the Plaza de Toros here in Bogota."

Even with Gacha dead, however, Duzan still does not leave her bomb-proofed apartment without armed bodyguards. Likewise at *El Espectador*, armed soldiers continue to perch on the corners of the roof with automatic weapons. More soldiers, all heavily armed, patrol outside the newspaper building. As does anyone else entering the premises, Duzan must submit her car and briefcase to a thorough search at a checkpoint in the parking lot. The security has become a routine way of life at *El Espectador*.

Ironically, Duzan almost missed the biggest news story in years. She had been out of the country and only returned to Bogota on December 13. "I had to leave the country very quickly at the end of November for two weeks due to what we considered a very serious death threat," she says. "I do not like working under these conditions anymore than I like having bodyguards. Having bodyguards makes my work as a journalist very difficult. It is difficult for me to circulate and make the contacts I need for my news stories and columns. But bodyguard protection is also a very obvious necessity ever since 1985 when drug-traffickers blew up my house. Now, I must put antibomb screens on my home. I can never have a set or established schedule or say on the telephone where I am going. I receive threatening phone calls and I receive threatening notes. But I will not stop writing."

Duzan, an intense, precise, hard-driven woman whose fast-paced style is fueled by cigarettes and coffee as well as a fire for truth, has known only one journalistic home over her fifteen-year career: *El Espectador*. The Cano family interrupted her education at Oxford when her father died and left a vacancy on the newspaper. Duzan reluctantly decided to give journalism a try when *El Espectador* asked her to fill her father's position. Now her column is read nationwide, and Duzan has become what is called in Colombia a professional violentologist, someone whose specialty is terror and violence. Hers is the top assignment, the most prestigious—and also the most dangerous—post in the country's news media. She doesn't waste a word. "My Zero Hour" is relentless in its focus on violence and on *El terrorismo*, the term Colombians have given the drug war.

But prestige doesn't quell the constant gnawing of fear that is the lot of all journalists in Colombia. "When I hear or see a motorcycle, I think my time has come," she says, referring to a particularly Colombian form of terror.

Bogota's notorious traffic mayhem provides a perfect milieu for the cocaine mob's $1,000-per-job hitmen and hitwomen, known locally as *sicarios*. Their specialty is murder by motorcycle, here called *asesino de la moto*. Motorcycle hits are truly the stuff nightmares are made of for journalists in Bogota. Trained in special schools operated by the drug lords, the *sicarios* weave in and out of the traffic, usually in pairs and armed with machine guns, and usually making their strikes with impunity.

"This is no place for the journalist to be…in the gunsight of the narcotraffickers," Duzan says. "This is the job of the justice department, the security forces, and the government. But these institutions have obviously not been able to control the narcotraffickers. Our institutions have been intimidated by the *plata o plomo* (silver or lead)—by the bribe or the bullets, by the blood or the bully—of the drug cartels. We are the victims of the failures of a lot of mistakes made in the past. The narcotraffickers were created here in Colombia. The U.S. is not the bad guy.

"Monsters like Gacha were created here in Colombia," she says, "not in Panama, not in Peru, not in the U.S. And, as journalists, we are paying for the failures of the other institutions in our society which have helped create and nourish people like Gacha. The journalists in my country have been the only obstacle between the cocaine criminals and public acceptance. This is why they kill us and bomb radio stations, TV stations, and newspapers. Because they cannot control us with their *plata* (silver). Because we have the boldness and the integrity to speak out about their lawlessness, their hypocrisy. They desperately want to be accepted. But we do not accept them."

The objectivity traditionally aspired to in U.S. journalism is a myth for the Colombian journalist, Duzan says. It's an unrealistic concept in such a society, she says. "In Latin America you cannot be neutral. You cannot be neutral under a dictatorship. You have to take a position—either for or against the dictator. We do not have the tradition of being objective. Our journalists are either for or against. But with the narcotraffickers, we have become the target. Right now our lives are in danger—our rights are threatened because we are not neutral. Because you are a target as a journalist you cannot do some of the things you would like to do. Because you have responsibilities to your colleagues and others on the newspaper. So, what happens is a sort of self-censorship."

Duzan says journalists from the United States and other countries who are amazed at conditions in Colombia must realize the scope of the battle at hand. "We are in a different atmosphere than in the U.S. We are used to the danger, to the violence, the bombs, the bullets, the blood. You in the U.S. who see this merely as a war on drugs miss the point. We are not just fighting narcotraffickers. We are struggling to preserve our democracy, our freedom of the press, our institutions which are being threatened.

"If we do not speak out, then the rulers of Colombia will be the narcotraffickers. We are on the front line of the drug war and, in many respects, we are the last line of defense. We have to fight this war because it is the only way to survive. Otherwise, we would lose our jobs, lose everything, and lose the country. That's why we are here. Being in Bogota, in Colombia, is the only way I can understand, the only way I can write about what's happening."

Maybe things will change now, she says.

"Now, with the killing of Gacha, I hope journalists will feel some relief because before we did not see much of a future for us."

Yet the continuing uncertainty about that future was obvious in the pages of *El Espectador*'s rival, *El Tiempo*, in the days immediately after Gacha's death.

"The myth of invulnerability of the drug barons is broken," *El Tiempo* editorialized optimistically the day after the shooting.

"The war is not over and journalists are still very much a part of it as targets," countered Enrique Santos Calderon, an editor, columnist, and member of the family that owns the paper. The large number of threatening telephone calls that the newspaper began receiving soon after Gacha's death is evidence, he said.

And, he said, the message of those threats is always the same: "Don't celebrate too much. You don't know what's going to happen."

The journalists in Colombia hoped that life would improve after the death of car-tel leader Rodriguez Gacha that December. However, Colombia today remains a country wracked with widespread violence. Colombia remains one of the most dangerous countries in the world for journalists. Cocaine lord Pablo Escobar was killed—with U.S. assistance—in December 1993, but the cartel has been replaced by smaller drug organizations. U.S. involvement in the war against them is grow-ing. Leftist guerrillas control 40 percent of the country. They and their paramili-tary enemies, as well as elements in the government itself, have been accused of working with drug growers and narcotraffickers to suit their own purposes, con-tinuing a cycle of violence that took the lives of forty-three reporters during the 1990s, second only to Algeria, a frightening number yet a mere fraction of the thirty-five thousand Colombians who suffer violent deaths annually. Many thou-sands of these are political killings. In the midst of a virtual civil war, journalists in Colombia are still charged with the sense of mission described in this essay. Shortly after the time depicted here, columnist Maria Jimena Duzan wrote a com-pelling book about her experiences on what she calls the "Death Beat." More than a decade later, Judith Bedoya Lima, a reporter at El Espectador, *was kidnapped, beaten, and raped on May 25, 2000. Paramilitary and police displeased with her investigative reporting are the usual suspects. All sides in this interminable Colom-bian conflict—a holocaust of biblical proportions—are partially financed through the drug trade. "Colombian journalists are concerned," says Fernando Leyva Duran, publisher of the* Latin American Post, *"that the U.S. $1.3 billion mili-tary aid package could increase their own danger and make the war worse." This story provides a window into journalism in 1989 and, sadly, today in Colombia where journalists continue to be threatened, killed, and forced into exile by right-wing or left-wing factions, drug traffickers, common criminals, and personal vendettas.*

PART THREE

In Europe

This section of *The Mission* takes you to central and eastern Europe, to countries that underwent tremendous change during the last decade of the twentieth century—change not only chronicled but also aided by journalists.

In Chapter 7, Georg Ruhrmann, chair of media science at the University of Jena in what was once East Germany, probes the media coverage of immigrants and other minorities in the reunited Germany, how that coverage has influenced public attitudes, and the ethical questions it has raised about the role of the media.

In Chapter 8 we travel to Hungary, a nation still making the transition from communism to democracy. Media scholar Ildikó Kaposi and investigative reporter Eva Vajda describe the ethical and other challenges facing journalists as they and their society as a whole adapt to the new Hungary.

In Chapter 9, Pavol Mudry, editor-in-chief and co-founder of SITA, Slovakia's first independent news agency after the fall of communism, tells how he and his fellow journalists quickly got into trouble with the would-be strongman Vladimir Meciar, who tried every means to shut SITA down. Meciar eventually fell from power, but, as Mudry tells us, SITA still continues its struggle with the authoritarian attitudes that remain the legacy of forty years of communism.

Chapter 10 takes us south to the Balkans, where Slovenian journalist Bernard Nezmah is waging a similar struggle. A fiery journalist with a sometimes biting wit, Nezmah tells of his battles with politicians and judges who are still coming to terms with having a free press in their midst.

Chapter seven

The Stranger

Minorities and Their Treatment in the German Media

by Georg Ruhrmann
Chair of Media Science
Friedrich-Schiller University (University of Jena)

My objective is to give a brief overview of the research being done on the way   79
foreigners are depicted in the German media. It is interesting to note that up
until the mid-1980s, analyses of this kind were not carried out in Germany at
all, in contrast to such countries as the United Kingdom or the United States.
Discovery of the need for media analyses lays and in general continues to lie
in social and political problems of the day. Systematic content analysis of the
image of minorities in the media consistently and clearly shows a negative syn-
drome. The more current the media coverage is, the more likely one is to find
particularly conflict-charged messages about "foreigners" or "asylum seekers."

More systematic content analysis of television coverage on the subject of
foreigners consistently shows how their social situation is dramatized. What is
shown on television represents the norm for what can typically be expected
across the full spectrum of the media in Germany. Existing prejudice is often
accentuated and in some cases reinforced. The content analysis has given rise
to questions about media practices and the function of the print and electronic
media with regard to integration. Can the media report in a manner that
would help to reduce prejudice? Would it make sense to withhold or to emphasize certain types of information? In this chapter, I deal with the following
issues:

- The development of content analysis research
- Key characteristics of media reporting on foreigners
- Proposals for journalists derived from these characteristics
- Prospects for future media research

DEVELOPMENT OF CONTENT ANALYSIS RESEARCH

In the United States, the public image of minorities has been a subject of research activity since the 1930s and more intensively since the 1950s.[1] From the outset, this research addressed questions regarding the function of the media.[2] Systematic analysis of the image of foreigners in the German media began around thirty years ago. A frequently quoted study on "guest workers" in the state of North Rhine-Westphalia maintains that press reports on the situation of the immigrants living there were full of generalizations and that this situation tended to strengthen negative attitudes that already existed in people.[3] A study carried out fourteen years later at the request of the Federal Government Commissioner for Foreign Resident Affairs—involving more than twenty-two hundred articles taken from eighteen media sources[4] as well as another analysis of seven hundred articles and letters published in six newspapers[5]—shows that reporting on foreigners accentuates social realities in accordance with specific criteria, first and foremost the fact that news tends to be negative per se. Nearly a fourth of the articles about foreigners studied dealt with the subject of the (rising) crime rate. Analysis of public debate of the "foreigner problem" shows that actions and behavior of the immigrants themselves tend to be indicated as the causes of the problem. Both studies show that media reporting distinguishes between "desirable" and "less desirable" groups of persons. The media make this distinction by, for instance, emphasizing the role played or activities carried out by the respective groups of persons. Journalists also emphasize the cultural distance between the respective nationality and their own or that of their readers. They distinguish between foreigners who are in Germany temporarily as guests—for example, artists or athletes on official visits—and foreign immigrants or asylum seekers who live and work in Germany on a long-term basis. Whereas journalists generally depict visiting artists and athletes in a positive light, journalists tend to give foreign workers and asylum seekers negative coverage. Greeks, Italians, and Spaniards, who are closer to "us" in terms of culture, religion, and traditions, tend to be depicted more positively than immigrants from other countries.

Ruhrmann/Kollmer have been able to show that nationalities who appear to be more "foreign," that is, whose cultural differences are greater (Turks in particular), are clearly over-represented in media reporting compared to the proportion of the population they account for.[6] Clear stigmatization exists in the reporting on the subject of asylum seekers. The German word "Asylant" ("asylum seeker") in connection with concepts such as "Überfremdung" ("excessive immigration") and "durchrasste Gesellschaft" ("racially mixed society"), or metaphors such as "Flut" ("flood"), "Lawine" ("avalanche") or "Schwemme" ("glut") are easily associated with similar-sounding words with negative connotations such as "Bummelant" ("loafer"), "Querulant" ("troublemaker") and

"Simulant" ("malingerer"). These metaphors in connection with the terms "foreigner" or "asylum seeker" are perceived as signs of a potential threat to German society and the German identity.

An analysis of 835 articles taken from two newspapers with national and regional circulations confirmed that journalists show a preference for negative, sensational, and conflict-charged subjects.[7] Asylum seekers often become an interesting "story" as individuals only when they can be depicted as criminals or as the victims of discrimination in the context of an exceptional situation.

The first content analysis of television reporting was presented in 1995. The leading question studied by Brosius/Esser was: "How is it possible that after major xenophobic attacks (e.g. Hoyerswerda, Rostock, Solingen) there has been a plethora of copycat attacks?"[8] The analyses show an increase in reports focused on acts of xenophobic violence with strong symbolic character. Among other things, the analyses confirm the hypothesis that television coverage between August 1990 and July 1993 led to the further spread of acts of xenophobic violence.

CHARACTERISTICS OF REPORTING ON IMMIGRANTS

Summing up the results of these and other studies, I find the following characteristics of reporting on immigrants.

Foreign Workers Are Associated with Crime

When reporters mention "foreign" workers, they often do so in connection with crimes.[9] Similar results have been found in content analyses of print and electronic media reporting in other European countries.

"Undesirable" Groups Are Over-Represented

Groups perceived as undesirable are over-represented in the media when one compares socio-demographic data with data regarding media depictions of immigrants obtained on the basis of content analysis. Undesirable nationalities include persons from Turkey as well as from other non-European countries, particularly in Asia and Africa.[10]

Popular Opinion Is Over-Represented

Popular opinion about groups perceived as undesirable is also over-represented in the media. Empirical studies show that persons interviewed greatly overestimated the numbers of "foreigners" who were perceived as being a particular threat to them.[11]

Semantics Reinforce Popular Perceptions

The definition of the foreigner problem has undergone semantic fluctuation. In the early 1980s, people spoke of a "Turkish problem"; in the late 1990s, the focus was on an "asylum-seeker problem"; since the mid-1990s, there has been a "refugee problem" and this terminology continues to be used today.[12] Systematic content analysis of television reporting shows how tabloid magazines and other tabloid formats report on cultures that appear to be particularly "foreign" in an exotic framework.[13] This emphasis reinforces feelings of foreignness; the domestic population perceives the immigrants as threatening and ominous.

Immigrants Serve as "News" without Context

Current events become news when they are surprising, novel, interesting, and important. Reporting on immigrants is also based on current events. This context places immigrants in the limelight of public perceptions and public opinion. Less topical background information that could explain current statements or place them in a broader economic, political, cultural, or religious context is neglected.[14] For instance, explaining the circumstances of wars in which people are expelled or otherwise forced to flee from their homes could be essential in understanding certain immigration processes.

News Has a Negative Focus

Conflict-related, crisis-related, and negative events are made the primary focus of public interest.[15] This focus favors media depictions of immigrants as a problem or elements of a crisis.

Negative Events Are Dramatized

Television, particularly the "live" reports, as it were, from the scene of xenophobically motivated incidents, dramatizes negative events as well as escalating trends with corresponding copycat effects.

Language Creates an Atmosphere of Threat

Communications theory and linguistic studies have shown that the media have presented the consequences of global migration processes and the emergence of multicultural trends with connotations of impending threat.[16] Social change is not depicted as something people can make decisions for themselves and control with policies but rather as something disastrous and fateful.[17] This journalistically created but unreflected transition between risk founded on human decisions and disaster as harmful danger can promote negative attitudes toward immigrants and immigration processes.[18]

Right-Wing Extremism Might Influence Public Opinion

The promotion of such attitudes applies similarly with regard to right-wing extremist tendencies.[19] In most cases, the audiovisual media show only spectacular attacks and violent incidents.[20] Only a few national newspapers deal with background information and causes. According to information provided by experts from the German Ministry of the Interior, increased use of the Internet by right-wing extremists has been noted since the mid-1990s. Extremists try to avoid prosecution by establishing their Web sites in countries where placing contents of this kind on the Internet is not illegal. However, imposing legal and technical constraints on content providers and criminal prosecution of violations does not offer effective protection against extremist propaganda.[21] It needs to be asked what influence these groups and networks have on public opinion.

In summary, all studies show that the media tend to disseminate a negative image of the immigrants living here. This image exerts an influence on the spread of xenophobia among the domestic population. It also promotes disintegrative tendencies among the foreign population, although significant cultural, economic, and socio-psychological reasons also exist for this disintegration.[22] Exploring those factors, however, would take me beyond the bounds of this essay.

PROPOSALS FOR JOURNALISTS

Based on the knowledge and experience accumulated thus far, communication researchers have formulated a number of proposals for journalists.[23]

• Journalists should consider to what extent they can avoid multiple stigmatization of "foreigners" as non-Europeans, as undesirables, or as victims. The proposal comes from the United States in its assessing of the information value of naming nationality and skin color. This sensitivity to the use of language should be implemented as a rule in the day-to-day business of journalism and should not be confused with political correctness.[24]

• The media can present immigrants more clearly, both audibly and visibly, as autonomous social and political beings.[25] Reports on successful understanding and cooperation between foreigners and the domestic population at the local and regional levels have an integrative effect. They serve as a concrete example of successful coexistence between locals and immigrants.

• Journalists can make the economic achievements of immigrants a subject of reporting. The boom in Turkish business startups in Germany is a current economic success story. Economic reporting should include coverage of problems experienced by foreign workers in the German job market. It would also seem necessary to undertake efforts to analyze the complex economic factors behind global migration processes journalistically and to present them to the public in understandable form. This reporting should not reduce immigrants to the level of purely economic factors and justify their existence with the profit they bring to the German economy. Doing so would give rise to the attitude that immigrants are guests who are merely tolerated as long as they are of economic profit to their host country.

• The media competence of the immigrants living here needs to be improved and promoted. This includes the ability to use new hardware and software or to log onto networks. Immigrants need skills that will enable them to obtain information on media developments independently and to draw their own conclusions from this with regard to any actions to be taken. A further element of media competence would be their ability to make use of certain contents and services. This means the systematic and critically reflected use of contents and services offered.[26]

• A changed personnel policy at radio and television stations and in print media newsrooms could ensure that qualified immigrants would have sufficient opportunity to work as announcers or reporters. Thus far, very little is known about the experience of foreigners employed in newsrooms.[27] Immigrants should be given a say on more subjects than just those specific to foreigners. Reduction to immigrant status constitutes a form of discrimination comparable to the discrimination that would be perpetrated against women if they were to be consulted only on matters relating specifically to women.

• Possibilities for positive identification should be promoted. Dark-skinned stars appearing in the context of attractive media presentations reduce prejudice more effectively than any moral appeals or recommendations made in the context of political education. Far-reaching efforts are needed here with regard to media policy and responsibility to see entertainment as a form of communication with a public function.[28]

• Public radio and television stations should expand programming for immigrants and the domestic population, and private television stations should introduce this type of programming as a competitive draw.[29] However, there is a need to analyze the degree to which public acceptance of public radio and television programming for immigrants has declined and what consequences those stations that are strongly involved in this area would draw from this (WDR, SFB, SWR, RB, and ZDF).

• The field of investigative journalism could be strengthened. An example would be the subject of right-wing extremism. Lengthy articles published in the tabloid press and in reports broadcast by Northern German Television revealed that right-wing candidates for the state assembly did not match up to the political, legal, and linguistic standards expected of persons aspiring to hold political office.

All these recommendations require intensive discussion with persons involved in practical media work. We need to be aware that journalistic policy interventions of this kind can also have unintended side-effects.[30] This, too, is a question I am not able to deal with in the context of this essay.

PROSPECTIVE AREAS OF MEDIA RESEARCH

The print and electronic media report on current affairs. Television also provides entertainment and relaxation, a factor that academic media researchers often overlook. Actual media reporting is based on the currentness, negativity, and conflictiveness of events. The attractiveness and credibility of programming for a paying audience is becoming an increasingly important factor. Defined academically, communication is a process that can lead to the acceptance of controversial developments (immigration) and decisions (immigration policies); it involves the study of social change as defined and evaluated by experts. Communicators (politicians and media representatives) communicate about such developments and decisions. Their statements are published by journalists in the course of their routine activity of selecting information for public consumption. Recipients can take in this information or ignore it, understand or misunderstand it, or simply forget it. In this frame of reference, acceptance of immigration and its consequences is a target variable with a very complex set of conditions based on interactive and independent variables in a process model. Further studies on effects exerted by the media would need to analyze the areas described in the following sections.

Organizations

Organizations should analyze decisions and communications, particularly when dealing with immigration policy or multicultural issues. Organizations need to assess the conditions that would or would not make undertaking strategic public information initiatives possible.[31] Analyses of this kind offer initial insights into early stages of forming (pre)judgments in the process of journalistic work.

Journalists

A further analytic task involves examining the reasons that issues such as "foreigners," "immigration," or "political multiculturalism" become issues at all. The nature of information and entertainment programming needs to be defined. It could be revealed here how certain events and issues are made current or dramatized.[32] There would be a need to analyze the conditions under which media newsrooms dealing with "foreigner" issues work and the kind of work they produce.

Media Analysis

Long-term content analyses of verbal and visual depictions of foreign cultures in the media should be carried out.[33] The subjects of migration and immigration should receive stronger consideration in the content analysis of television reports, first and foremost with regard to images and texts depicting violence.[34] This consideration applies in particular to serials and feature films. This kind of programming is of particular relevance for the longer-term integrative effects of the media in modern societies. With a view to the target groups, such as online media, there is a need to analyze what kind of programming is attractive, and why and to what extent this is so.[35]

Recipients

There is a need to register the cognitive and emotional characteristics of public knowledge (media stereotypes) in connection with audience responses to programming.[36] These characteristics also provide information on the extent to which media content and messages are linked to prior knowledge regarding multiculturalism. We need to learn more about the interactive effects of media attention and understanding.[37] The lifestyles and consumer behavior of readers, viewers, and users need to be registered in social environments reconstructed on the basis of psychographic information.[38] Only the results of analyses of this kind will make it possible to formulate target-group–specific communication policy strategies with prejudice-reducing effects.[39]

Social Change

Various dimensions of economic and social change need to be described along with their interaction with the media system.[40]

Public Expectations with Regard to Effects

Public expectations need to be evaluated with regard to use of the new media.[41] Our assumption is that growth will occur in global "audiences," society will divide further into the informed and the uninformed, with a breakup into smaller sized audiences taking place. The integrative effects of public radio and television stations for one audience will need to be redefined in more modern terms.[42]

In view of the described trends, the definition of "media"[43] and with it the concept of "media influence" need to expand.[44] I am not speaking of a linear or causal relationship between media stimulus and response. The constructive effects of a wide range of different recipients are constantly expanding as a result of an enlarged choice of media products.

Seen from a communications science perspective, it would seem appropriate to be moving towards an integrative approach. Analysis of reciprocal effects at the indicated levels will guarantee new and valid results. Studies of isolated factors are no longer sufficient. From a media practice standpoint, it will be necessary to bring together scientists and media practitioners, politicians and citizens, and decision makers and those whom their decisions affect for the purpose of establishing an intercultural dialogue. Initiatives of this kind will require broader cooperation between the business, government, and academic communities in a networked environment. Without the politically agreed objective of substantially improving the situation of immigrants in Germany, the efforts aimed at improving media reporting will not have the desired effect. No one knows this better than Americans, based on the long tradition of immigration and integration in the United States.

NOTES

1. Milton C. Albrecht, "Does Literature reflect common values?" *American Journal of Sociology* 21 (1956), 722–729.
2. Klaus Merten and Georg Ruhrmann, "Die Entwicklung der inhaltsanalytischen Methode," *Kölner Zeitschrift für Soziologie und Sozialpsychologie* 34, 4 (1982), 696–716.
3. Jesus M. Delgado, "Die 'Gastarbeiter' in der Presse," *Eine inhaltsanalytische Studie* (Opladen: Westdeutscher Verlag, 1972).
4. Klaus Merten and Georg Ruhrmann, "Das Bild der Ausländer in der deutschen Presse," *Ergebnisse einer systematischen Inhaltsanalyse* (Frankfurt: Dagyeli, 1986).
5. Georg Ruhrmann and Jochem Kollmer, "Ausländerberichterstattung in der Kommune," *Inhaltsanalyse Bielefelder Tageszeitungen unter besonderer Berücksichtigung ausländerfeindlicher Alltagstheorien* (Opladen: Westdeutscher Verlag, 1987).
6. Georg Ruhrmann and Jochem Kollmer (1987), 5.
7. Walter Hömberg and Sabine Schlemmer, "Fremde als Objekt. Asylberichterstattung in deutschen Tageszeitungen," *Media Perspektiven* 1 (1995), 11–20.
8. Hans-Bernd Brosius and Frank Esser, "Eskalation durch Berichterstattung?" *Massenmedien und fremdenfeindliche Gewalt* (Opladen: Westdeutscher Verlag, 1995).
9. Margret Jäger, Gabriele Cleve, Ina Ruth, and Siegfried Jäger, "Von deutschen Einzeltätern und ausländischen Banden. Medien und Straftaten," *Mit Vorschlägen zur Vermeidung diskriminierender Berichterstattung* (Duisburg: DISS, 1998).
10. Georg Ruhrmann, "Risikokommunikation zwischen Experten und Laien," *Universitas* 51, 603 (1996), 955–964.
11. Ulrich Neuwöhner and Georg Ruhrmann, "Das Interesse der Radiohörer an Ausländerthemen. Ergebnisse einer repräsentativen Studie in Baden-Württemberg," Meier-Braun, Karl-Heinz/Kilgus, Martin (Hg.): *Migration 2000 - Perspektiven für das 21. Jahrhundert. 5. Radioforum Ausländer bei uns* (Baden-Baden: Nomos, 1998), 109–132.

12. Thomas Knieper, "Der 'Ausländer' im Spiegel der politischen Karrikatur Deutschlands," Quandt, Siegfried/Gast, Wolfgang (Hg.): *Deutschland im Dialog der Kulturen. Medien, Images, Verständigung* (Konstanz: UVK Medien, 1998), 101–114.

13. Jaqueline Boyce, "'Exotenbonus' als persönliches Unwort," *Sage & Schreibe* 3–4 (1999), 18.

14. Georg Ruhrmann, "Ist Aktualität noch aktuell? Journalistische Selektivität und ihre Folgen" Löffelholz, Martin (Hg.): *Krieg als Medienereignis. Grundlagen und Perspektiven der Krisenkommunikation.* (Opladen: Westdeutscher Verlag, 1993), 81–96.

15. Matthias Kohring, Alexander Görke and Georg Ruhrmann, "Konflikte, Kriege, Katastrophen," Meckel, Miriam/Kriener, Markus (Hg.): *Internationale Kommunikation. Eine Einführung* (Opladen: Westdeutscher Verlag, 1996), 283–298.

16. Matthias Jung, Martin Wengeler and Karin Böke (Hg.), "Die Sprache des Migrationsdiskurses," *Das Reden über "Ausländer" in Medien, Politik und Alltag* (Opladen: Westdeutscher Verlag, 1997).

17. Franz Nuscheler, "Migration und Konflikpotentiale im Jahr 2000," Meier-Braun, Karl-Heinz/Kilgus, Martin (Hg.): *Migration 2000 — Perspektiven für das 21. Jahrhundert. 5. Radioforum Ausländer bei uns* (Baden-Baden: Nomos, 1998), 29–38.

18. Georg Ruhrmann, Johannes Kollbeck, and Wolfgang Möltgen, "'Fremdverstehen', Medien, Fremdenfeindlichkeit und die Möglichkeit von Toleranzkampagnen," *Publizistik* 41, 1 (1996), 32–50.

19. Wolfgang Kowalsky and Wolfgang Schroeder (Hg.), "Rechtsextremismus," *Einführung und Forschungsbilanz* (Opladen: Westdeutscher Verlag, 1994).

20. Klaus Merten, "Gewalt durch Gewalt im Fernsehen?" (Opladen: Westdeutscher Verlag, 1999).

21. Klaus Beck and Gerhard Vowe, "Zwischen Anarchie und Zensur — Zur Regulierung internationaler computervermittelter Kommunikation," Quandt, Siegfried/Gast, Wolfgang (Hg.) (1998): *Deutschland im Dialog der Kulturen. Medien, Images, Verständigung* (Konstanz: UVK Medien, 1996), 349–366.

22. Franz Nuscheler (1998), 17.

23. Siegfried Weischenberg, "Journalistik. Medienkommunikation: Theorie und Praxis 2," *Medientechnik, Medienfunktionen, Medienakteure* (Opladen: Westdeutscher Verlag, 1995).

24. Hermann Vinke, Friedrich Voss, Wolfgang Pohl, Gualtiero Zambonini, Ulrich Wagner-Grey and Gunter Schneider, "Vom Funkhaus Europa, SFB 4 Mulitkulti über DAB und Internet zu neuen ARD-Ausländerprogrammen — Perspektiven für neue Programmangebote für Migranten und Einheimische," Meier-Braun; Karl-Heinz/Kilgus, Martin (Hg.): *Migration 2000 — Perspektiven für das 21. Jahrhundert. 5. Radioforum Ausländer bei uns.* (Baden-Baden: Nomos, 1998), 133–147.

25. Georg Ruhrmann, "Medyanin Yabvancilara Iliskin Haberli Veris Sekli — Alamanya´daki Türk Kadinlari Imajminin Olusumuna Etkileri," Goethe Institut (Hg.): *Alman Medyasinda Türk Kadinlari.* (Ankara: Goethe Institut, 1999), 14–28.

26. Georg Ruhrmann and Jörg-Uwe Nieland, "Interaktives Fernsehen. Entwicklung, Dimensionen, Fragen, Thesen" (Opladen: WestdeutscherVerlag, 1997).

27. Jaqueline Boyce (1999), 13.

28. Louis Bosshart and Wolfgang Hoffmann-Riem (Hg.) *Medienlust und Mediennutz. Unterhaltung als öffentliche Kommunikation* (Konstanz: UVK Medien, 1994).

29. Hermann Vinke and Friedrich Voss, Wolfgang Pohl, Gualtiero Zambonini, Grey Wagner, and Gunter Ulrich/Schneider (1998), 24.

30. Siegfried Weischenberg (1995), 20.

31. Georg Ruhrmann and Holger Sievert, "Bewußtseinswandel durch Kampagnen gegen Ausländerfeindlichkeit? Zur Effektivität von Anzeigen und TV-Spots," *pr magazin* 25, 12 (1994), 35–42.

32. Bernd Scheffer (Hg.), *Medien und Fremdenfeindlichkeit. Alltägliche Paradoxien, Dilemmata, Absurditäten und Zynismen* (Opladen: Leske + Budrich, 1997).

33. Georg Ruhrmann, "Mediendarstellung von Fremden. Images, Resonanzen und Probleme,"

Quandt, Siegfried/Gast, Wolfgang (Hg.): *Deutschland im Dialog der Kulturen. Medien—Images—Verständigung* (Konstanz: UVK Medien, 1998), 35–50.

34. Klaus Merten (1999), 20.

35. Pattrick Rössler, "Wirkungsmodelle: die digitale Herausforderung. Überlegungen zu einer Inventur bestehender Erklärungsansätzen der Medienwirkungsforschung," Rössler (Hg.): *Online Kommunikation. Beiträge zur Nutzung und Wirkung* (Opladen: Westdeutscher Verlag, 1998), 17–46.

36. Helmut Giegler and Georg Ruhrmann, "Remembering the News. A LISREL Model," *European Journal of Communication* 5, 4 (1990), 463–488.

37. Georg Ruhrmann and Jens Woelke, "Rezeption von Fernsehnachrichten im Wandel. Desiderate und Perspektiven der Forschung," Kamps, Klaus/Meckel, Miriam (Hg.): *Fernsehnachrichten. Prozesse, Strukturen, Funktionen* (Opladen: Westdeutscher Verlag, 1998), 103–110.

38. Ulrich Neuwöhner and Georg Ruhrmann (1998), 11.

39. Georg Ruhrmann, "Interkulturelle Kommunikation," Jarren, Ottfried/ Sarcinelli, Ulrich/Saxer, Ulrich (Hg.): *Politische Kommunikation in der demokratischen Gesellschaft* (Opladen: Westdeutscher Verlag, 1998), 663–664.

40. Thomas Bruns, Frank Marcinkowski, Jörg-Uwe Nieland, Georg Ruhrmann, and Thomas Schierl, "Das analytische Modell," Schatz, Heribert (Hg.): *Fernsehen als Objekt und Moment des sozialen Wandels. Faktoren und Folgen der aktuellen Veränderung des Fernsehens* (Opladen: Westdeutscher Verlag, 1996), 19–56.

41. Walter Klingler, Peter Zoche, Monika Harnischfeger, and Castulus Kolo, "Mediennutzung der Zukunft. Ergebnisse einer Expertenbefragung zur Medienentwicklung bis zum Jahr 2005/2015," *Media Perspektiven* 10/98 (1998), 490–497.

42. Georg Ruhrmann, "Digitales Fernsehen und Individualisierung. Perspektiven für die Mediennutzungsforschung," Latzer, Michael/Maier-Rabler, Ursula/Siegert, Gabriele/ Steinmaurer, Thomas (Hg.): *Die Zukunft der Kommunikation. Phänomene und Trends in der Informationsgesellschaft* (Insbruck Wien: Studienverlag, 1999), 329–346.

43. Roland Burkhart, "Was ist eigentlich ein 'Medium'?" Latzer, Michael/Maier-Rabler, Ursula/Siegert, Gabriele/Steinmaurer, Thomas (Hg.): *Die Zukunft der Kommunikation. Phänomene und Trends in der Informa-tionsgesellschaft* (Insbruck Wien: Studienverlag, 1994), 61 72.

44. Pattrick Rössler (1998), 35.

Chapter eight

Between State Control and the Bottom Line

Journalism and Journalism Ethics in Hungary

by Ildikó Kaposi, Central European University
and
Eva Vajda, *Népszabadság Online,* Budapest, Hungary

Freedom of expression and freedom of the press have been inextricable from   91
the concept of democracy in Hungary. Following the demise of socialist Hungary, where all media were state owned and controlled by the party-state, it seemed that the natural way to achieve this much-awaited freedom was through the privatization of media outlets. Hungary has a population of ten million, making this central European post-communist country a relatively small market for capitalist-style developments in the media. However, recent years tell a story of rapid expansion in the country's communication and media industries.

The press went first, sold partly to Western media giants and partly to local players busy building their own media empires. The outlines of a new structure for the television market started emerging in 1997, when two terrestrial television frequencies were auctioned to international bidders. The complete deregulation of broadcasting and the demolishing of the dual system of public service and commercial broadcasting in favor of an all-commercial television and radio system are not on the agenda in Hungary. The country's television scene is based on the dual-system characteristic of western Europe: commercial channels deliver commercial broadcasting and tax-funded state channels cater to the public service programming. Hungary's case clearly exemplifies that democracy is also a learning process. The country needs to come to terms with very different paradigms of development if it is to evolve into a western European-style democratic market economy in addition to rediscovering and preserving a national heritage.

Following the general enthusiasm that greeted privatization as the means of ensuring freedom of the press, it soon dawned on journalists that private ownership may have brought independence from political influences, but nothing exists to protect the media should the new owners abuse their power (including blocking articles, a former privilege of the communist regime), or should advertisers put the media under pressure by threatening to withdraw advertising in case journalists intend to publish sensitive materials about them. Yet, apart from the insistence that public service broadcasting should continue, journalists maintain a strong resistance to the idea of state intervention in the media market. Ideas such as a press subsidies system elicit reactions from journalists akin to that of conservative Westerners along the lines of Rupert Murdoch, who claim that the only way to guarantee the freedom of the press is through the free market.

This is not the only case in which Hungarian journalism is faced with the same dilemmas as its Western counterparts. The sidelining of the public in public communication is also an issue that is likely to cause more problems in the future, although the extent to which journalists reveling in their newfound watchdog role are aware of this threat remains unclear. Journalists in Hungary tend to rely on official sources for nearly all their stories. More often than not, exclusive publication of stories depends on how close a working relationship a particular media outlet maintains with political actors in the position to supply the story. This implies that such stories will inevitably reflect the angle from which the source views the events, and the news agenda remains rather firmly in the hands of politicians. This, in turn, works against real competition among media for news (that is, new information).

We are not suggesting that excessive scoop-journalism or check-book journalism would be desirable. Still, turning on commercial pressure for the media would probably force journalists to take into consideration what the public wants from them and become innovative in delivering it, rather than allow them to rely on old, well-established routines of reporting. Characteristically, it is the tabloid news bulletins of the commercial television stations that regularly produce exclusive breaking-news items, even if these consist of inevitably soft, human interest, sensational news.

It could be said that journalists in Hungary are struggling with the benefits and drawbacks of the market structure introduced to the media after 1989. Maintaining the professional status quo of the past decade means that Hungary's media have avoided the downward tabloidization trend, but they also have yet to develop the skills necessary to survive in a competitive environment, most notably being more inclined to give the public what it wants, not just what the journalist understands to be necessary.

THE JOURNALIST IN HUNGARY

The role of the media and journalists was different in eastern Europe and Hungary than in developed Western democracies. This was mainly due to historical reasons. In the communist era, journalists had extremely limited access to information in the first place, and even the information acquired had to pass several strict filters before appearing in the news. Journalists formally had the task of informing the public, but in practice their role was restricted to repeating official communiqués and points of view. For example, when party leader János Kádár gave a speech at a party conference, his speech had to be reprinted word for word, just as MTV, the acronym for Hungary's state-owned television channel, had to broadcast the full speech. Journalists were not allowed to comment on or interpret the news they covered, let alone editorialize. Many of those journalists with insight into the internal affairs of one-party politics were forced to find alternative means of performing their professional duty of informing the public, of telling them what was really going on. They developed a technique of writing in an ambiguous way, which enabled people to read between the lines.

This mode of communication was so pervasive that even a year or two before the collapse of communism it was still widely used. On one occasion in the late 1980s, the government raised the price of bread. The state-owned television channel's evening news bulletin covered the story but the channel was not allowed to include the public's reaction to the price hike. However, the editors had a story from Tanzania about riots among starving Tanzanians that they broadcast right after the Hungarian bread story. This was an indirect-yet-sophisticated way of commenting on the news of the price increase affecting many people's lives.

As a consequence of such malformed structures of public communication, journalism was not able to evolve into a profession with standards such as using diverse sources, double checking, and providing background and context, not to mention investigating. The lack of these standards meant that journalists seriously underperformed not only as watchdogs but also as providers of information to society. The latter role proved to be more difficult to tackle in the long run.

After 1989 journalists became free to reveal cases when authorities abused their power, but, in our opinion, they still fail to properly inform the public. In a transitional society such as Hungary, people need to understand and come to terms with concepts, structures and institutions they never heard of or experienced before. This process would require journalists to provide even more background, context, and analysis than in developed democracies where people are born into an environment of well-established democratic structures and institutions. In many cases, Hungarian media fail to give comprehensive coverage of issues because journalists themselves do not understand all the aspects involved, which is partly because most of them never had formal training in journalism skills.

Apart from the courses run by the Hungarian National Association of Journalists (MÚOSZ), no opportunities existed for learning journalism in an academic environment either during or before the communist years. The lack of college-level journalism education inevitably led to the everyday newsroom experiences of senior journalists serving to introduce young people to the profession. These experiences were defined and shaped by the thoroughly undemocratic political environment outlined previously, which was also the environment that conditioned the trainers in the courses at MÚOSZ. The need for professional journalism training was demonstrated in the number of journalism programs started by universities as well as by several media outlets and private enterprises after 1989, although this boom did not bring with it the necessary diversity of professional background and experiences among lecturers and trainers.

Ten years of democracy have not been enough to transform Hungary's unfortunate journalistic heritage. The country is currently in a state of transition en route to complete social transformation, and ethical standards and the concept of the journalists' role in society are also in disarray, although formally the institutional framework of democratic media has been set up. General ethical guidelines have been laid down in a code of ethics by MÚOSZ, but in practice the impact of this attempt at transparent regulation is ineffective.

In practice, most journalists are employed not as staff writers but as freelancers who are paid by the column. Although nothing seems wrong with this on the surface, freelancers in fact are so underpaid that their fees usually do not even cover the expenses of putting together a column. This system makes journalists' interests lie in producing as many columns as possible in the shortest period of time instead of focusing on the quality of the pieces they write. Furthermore, to avoid strict taxation, journalists form bogus companies that look real on paper but in reality are the means of cheating on taxes. This also holds true for the staff writers who have low salaries, making them look for different venues of earning more. Put in a simplistic way, the simplest kinds of such bogus companies require one or two persons and minimal capital. The persons employed by such companies need to pay their own taxes, pension, and social security contributions, which could amount to half of the gross salary of "regular" employees. Journalists often form such companies with their spouses or family members, locating the company headquarters at their home address. This setup enables them to deduct nonwork-related expenses (for example, home telephone bills) from their taxable income. Such subtle ways of blurring the line between the private and public activities of journalists would undermine the moral legitimacy of the profession anywhere in the world, and they put an especially powerful weapon into the hands of state-controlled tax authorities should they decide to turn on the heat under an overinquisitive journalist. For what moral basis exists for watchdog activities if journalists can be caught at cheating on their taxes at random tax supervisions?

This financial setup drives many journalists (who nonetheless on the average still make considerably more than, for example, public officials or high school teachers), both staff writers and freelancers, to grab at opportunities for earning extra money. Media outlets are usually aware of these practices but choose to turn a blind eye to them. Their attitude is something like this: "That is the way it goes in Hungary. Everyone is trying to make ends meet."

Following are specific ethical dilemmas faced by journalists in Hungary. Each reflects the challenges these journalists face in making the transition from communism to a market society.

Staff Journalists Freelancing for Other Employers

An editor at one of the national newspapers regularly publishes analyses (on the same area she routinely covers) in a weekly paper that is not owned by the same company. Her newspaper owners tolerate this because they do not consider the weekly a competitor. The same practice is widespread at the national public radio, where employees also work for the national public television and newspapers. In a rather extreme case, a female journalist employed full time by a financial weekly decided to use a male alias to publish different articles for alternative publications. She used the sources she developed on her beat at the weekly, not always telling them that on this occasion the article would be published in a different media outlet.

Putting Expertise to Corporate Uses

An editor specializing in banking issues at one of the leading financial weeklies regularly edited the newsletter of a commercial bank, even though he was also covering that bank in his articles. Hiring journalists to write annual reports for commercial banks is also common practice because they charge less than an independent expert would do. In an extreme case, a leading editor of the stock exchange section at a financial daily accepted a position on the board of supervisors at a listed company.

PR Activities

A journalist covering banking issues for one of the national newspapers set up a public relations consulting firm whose clients include the same banks he covers. Newspapers also regularly run special sections on specific (chemical, banking, energy, and so forth) industries sponsored by the major actors of the industry. Although these sections are good for generating extra revenue for the paper, the articles appearing in the special sections are written by the same journalists who normally cover the area. Thus they conduct promotional interviews with the people they normally use as sources for news articles.

Accepting Gifts

In Hungary, companies offering gifts to journalists at press conferences and at Christmas time is an established practice. It is up to journalists to judge what they can accept. Only one publication on the national newspaper market limits the value of acceptable gifts. Its limit is 5,000 HUF (the Hungarian currency, equivalent to $20 to $25). By the way, this is the most affluent weekly in Hungary. However, a journalist working for this publication says that he does not believe that setting limits is an adequate way of managing the problem, because presents distributed at press conferences do not have price tags attached to them, nor is it possible to ask how much the item costs. Apart from this weekly, media outlets leave it to the judgment of their journalists to decide how to handle offers of presents. The results of this hands-off policy are mixed. For example, when a multinational company opened a subsidiary in Hungary in recent years, it distributed hi-fi systems as Christmas presents to the journalists who had covered them. It was up to each of the journalists to accept or reject the gift.

The most common incentive for favorable coverage is to organize trips abroad for journalists. For example, a major insurance company flies journalists covering them to exotic locations every year so that journalists can recover from the hardships of reporting. In 1999, a travel agency specializing in Greek destinations offered two-week vacations to journalists in exchange for articles about their holiday experiences that mentioned the company's name. A less direct way to influence journalists (and decision makers) is exemplified by the way an American firm flew several journalists to its U.S. headquarters while their application for the privatization of Hungarian power plants was being processed by authorities. Officially, the aim of the trip was to give journalists a better idea what the company was doing in preparation for the time when they would operate in Hungary. However, the early fruits of the gesture could be read all over the press. (Eventually, the company lost out to the other bidders.)

Cronyism

Top journalists are integral parts of a country's elite corps. The same is true for Hungary, where many top journalists grew up and went to school with decision makers. Although this circumstance puts them in a good position when it comes to getting information from old friends and acquaintances, an inherent danger of cronyism exists in such relationships. This is especially true considering that the different types of public roles are just being defined after decades when Western-style separation of roles were not applicable. In the case of journalists, this means that they are unable to distinguish between private chats with friends and public interviews with the same people, because for them both are parts of an ongoing dialogue. The resulting articles or interviews may often feature information journalists pick up at informal events, and because their professional instincts are dormant in a relaxed atmosphere, they end up passing on the information without checking on it. Cronyism may also intrude into public interview situations in which the interviewee feels free to change the content afterwards, citing his or her relationship with the journalist as the basis of trust between them. In extreme cases, the interviews can be conducted in a collaborative effort, with the interviewee writing his or her answers and sometimes even the questions. Similarly, prominent public officials are known to give interviews to electronic media outlets under the condition that they are informed of the questions in advance. Cronyism can also be detected in the practice of journalists inviting fellow journalists to their programs to act as experts.

Journalists for Sale

Despite a lack of evidence for it, a general belief exists among members of the elite that every journalist has his or her price. News coverage can be influenced by handing money to the journalist to report favorably on the person or company who pays. Incidents of this kind are often no more than unconfirmed rumors, but the very fact that such rumors circulate is an indication of major problems with the social standing and credibility of the profession.

THE CHALLENGE FOR THE NEW GENERATION OF JOURNALISTS

We must add that all the practices described in the previous section are carried out by journalists who consider themselves independent professionals.

Although the media in Hungary are privately owned, standards or the know-how of Western journalism have not been imported to the newsrooms of even those outlets that are owned by Western media companies. One reason for this situation could be the language and cultural barriers separating Western newsrooms from their Hungarian counterparts, although the transplantation of Western work ethics did happen with multinational companies.

Private media outlets are also commercial enterprises in Hungary, but running them purely like a business is sometimes still impossible. When a profitable publication continues making money, the owners often do not feel the incentive to force major changes in the established structures of the newsroom.

When new, foreign owners take over, they are usually unable to read Hungarian and therefore have to rely on the judgment of their Hungarian editors, who are typically products of former times.

In other cases, the owner may be content simply with the prestige offered by owning a quality newspaper, and thus is willing to use his or her other, profitable Hungarian media interests to cover any financial losses from the prestigious publication.

New challenges emerged recently in Hungarian media with the launching of two terrestrially transmitted commercial television channels. Here the ethical traps usually affecting the autonomy of Hungarian journalists were successfully eliminated through new hiring policies that strictly regulated terms and conditions of employment. However, under commercial pressure, these stations inevitably went down the road to tabloidization. One of the casualties of the growing trend toward tabloidization has been the fundamental rights of citizens featured in the news. For example, even if the victim of a crime is underage, his or her face and name are still often revealed on television. Prime-time sex and violence are also staple fare now on commercial television. In reaction to this phenomenon, an advisory sign system has been proposed to alert viewers as to the recommended age limits for programs.

Despite all the negative tendencies and phenomena discussed here, the prospects for a democratic Hungarian public sphere are not hopelessly bleak. Not yet robust, Hungary's fledgling democratic institutions are proving stable enough to enable some classic democratic procedures to unfold. In the first half of 1999, for example, two incidents occurred involving public officials who were forced to resign as a result of investigative articles published in national newspapers that uncovered their abuses of power. In these cases, all democratic institutions functioned the way they are supposed to: parliamentary committees were set up to investigate the affairs, the companies involved started internal investigations, and the stories were picked up and covered extensively by all media outlets, which in turn added their own research with new information and angles.

Still, a decade after the democratic turn in Hungary, public institutions rarely perform this well. The judicial, legislative, and other state supervisory bodies are burdened with too many ongoing cases at one time. The fact that the media perform neither better nor worse than all the other public institutions, however, does not exempt them from trying to fulfill their crucial democratic role. The media in Hungary are instrumental in ensuring that democracy works. They must strive to do better in informing, educating, and entertaining the public and in serving as the watchdogs for society.

It is high time that Hungarian journalists learned to face their situation and the actual professional environment they operate in. The same rules and expectations of transparency they are now applying to elected public officials should apply to them, the nonelected watchdogs monitoring these officials and others in positions of power. Journalists should realize that they have considerable individual responsibility in shaping the standards and maintaining the credibility of their profession. The structural-institutional background of the Hungarian media is sufficiently developed now to aid them in this process.

At the moment, however, the clarification of ethical issues in journalistic practices is not on the agenda. Publicly inquiring into the ethical misconduct of the journalistic community is something of a taboo. The rationale underlying this blind eye to the ethical issues of the profession is a variation of the old argument that "everybody does it." The good news is that not everybody does it. The generation of young and dedicated journalists who look to Western ethical norms for guidance poses a challenge to the established ways of the profession. In the long run, this challenge is bound to have a redeeming impact on journalism in Hungary.

Chapter nine

SITA

Slovakia's First Independent News Service and Its Battles with the Huey Long of the Danube

by Pavol Mudry
Editor, General Manager, and Co-founder
SITA

Vladimír Meciar conceded his election defeat and announced his impending de-
parture as Slovakia's prime minister/would-be strongman in September 1998, lit-
erally with a song on his lips—albeit a bitter song. "God be with you," he unex-
pectedly crooned during his concession speech on national television, employing a
tear-stained, a cappella rendition of a Slovak folk tune. "I did not hurt any of
you." Of course, the ex-communist, ex-boxer, post-communist nationalist and pop-
ulist demagogue was lying. During his six-year rule, the then-fifty-six-year-old Me-
ciar had done everything he could to muzzle what for him was the most aggravat-
ing aspect of the fall of communism: the press. And no organization in the media
was more aggravating to him than the Slovak News Agency, or SITA, the nation's
first independent, privately owned news agency. In this essay, the co-founder and
general manager of that Bratislava-based agency tells the story of SITA's rise and
Meciar's fall. Meciar, sometimes called the Huey Long of the Danube, barred SITA
and other "oppositional" media from government press conferences, announce-
ments, and interviews. Just as he scapegoated Hungarians and other ethnic mi-
norities for Slovakia's social and economic problems, Meciar loved to target the in-
dependent media, threatening them with such actions as 400 percent tax increases.
It got worse than threats. Meciar and his cronies were suspected of engineering a
host of crimes, ranging from kidnapping, beatings, and murder to the theft and
property destruction you'll read about in this essay. Meanwhile, he showered favors
on his kept media, such as the newspaper Slovenska Republika, *and even created*
his own media organization, called "Journalists for a True Picture of Slovakia." A
coalition of opposing political parties finally ended his rule in 1998, but his legacy

lives on. In October 2000, the state-subsidized and formerly pro-Meciar TASR news agency filed a 92 million-SKK (Slovak currency, roughly equivalent to $26 million) lawsuit against SITA, alleging that the agency illegally obtained information from TASR databases. The amount of the lawsuit is three times the annual budget of the news agency. "It has already become a nightmare for us," SITA co-founder and general manager Pavol Mudry said of the lawsuit. "We would never try such unfair actions. It is an attempt to liquidate SITA. But we fight, and (we) have good support from the media here."

In order to tell you about the establishment of our news agency in Slovakia—the nation's first independent agency—I must first describe the political situation and the reasons that such an effort had to be undertaken.

After the breakup of the Czech-Slovak Federation in 1993, the official press agency CsTK split into two parts, but the main operations remained in Prague as they had been before. In Slovakia at that time, the regional office of CsTK had to be developed into a full-fledged national news agency. Based on a law passed just before the breakup in mid-1992, the Press Agency of The Slovak Republic, or TASR Slovakia, was established. The agency was, and still is, financed directly from the state budget, and the appointment of the director general is a cabinet-level decision.

In March 1994, Prime Minister Vladimir Meciar and his party, HZDS (an acronym that stands for "Movement for a Democratic Slovakia"), lost their majority in Parliament. With the additional loss of a parliamentary vote of confidence, Meciar was forced to turn over rule to an interim government led by a former confidant, Democratic Union leader Jozef Moravcik. During this political upheaval, TASR gave Meciar its support, a decision that signaled the end of any independent, free and unbiased reporting at that agency. Still, the support didn't prevent Meciar's temporary fall from power—he returned after another round of elections seven months later—and the subsequent recall of TASR general manager Dusan Kleiman.

The broad coalition of anti-Meciar parties that won in the March 1994 elections established a new management for TASR with the goal of getting the agency out from under the government's influence. The idea was to transform a state agency into a corporation whose owners would consist of media and industrial associations with a minority stake remaining in the hands of the state. The Moravcik government, however, eventually balked at this idea and reasoned that with oncoming elections, the agency should indeed provide support to the government. Moravcik and his supporters came to regret this decision when the elections that September brought Meciar back to power and former general manager Kleiman back to his post at the head of TASR. Upon his return, Kleiman fired those who had sought the transformation of the agency!

TASR again became a staunch supporter of Meciar and HZDS, so much so that it even published fabricated documents from the official state secret service, SIS. Curiously, the other media in Slovakia, despite private ownership and efforts to be independent, still were willing to obtain news from the obviously biased TASR.

Meciar's ruling coalition—including HZDS, the strongly nationalist Slovak National Party, or SNS, and the extremely left-wing Association of Slovak Workers—maintained a communist-era attitude toward the media after its September 1994 victory. This attitude is best summarized in the saying, "Who is not with us is against us." Meciar and his cronies viewed independent media more or less as the opposition media of their political enemies. They maintained a direct influence on TASR and on state-subsidized and perennially underfinanced public radio and television. This situation continued even through the year 2000 despite a rapidly changing political landscape.

Still, the years between 1994 and 1998 were an aggravating time for Meciar in the emerging democracy that was his homeland. Only one of the eleven national daily newspapers—the HZDS-controlled *Slovenska Republika*—supported his governing coalition. The privately owned media consisting of newspapers, radio, and television were generally critical, a fact that led to reprisals. The coalition ordered state-owned enterprises and private firms to withhold advertising from the critical press. Legislation to hike taxes on media organizations with any degree of foreign ownership was introduced in October 1997. In protest, all ten of the non-Meciar–controlled dailies ran blank front pages on the same day! The protest worked: the Parliament killed the proposed tax hike. The debate also resulted in an intense and growing demand for independent sources of news.

THE SEEDS OF SITA ARE PLANTED

In early 1995, a group of managers and staffers who had been fired from TASR—including myself—began to discuss the feasibility of establishing a privately owned news agency that would be free of the influence of whatever clique is ruling in Bratislava. We knew the difficulties that lay ahead, first and foremost in finding investors to help provide the basic resources. A majority of the business leaders in Slovakia at that time supported Prime Minister Meciar and his newly elected government. They showed little interest in supporting a source of information that could not be controlled by government.

We received offers from various foundations, especially foreign, to run the agency as a nonprofit organization. We decided, however, not to accept those offers because we felt that maintaining the profit motive was the best assurance of quality in our product. This is, after all, a regular business: news agencies produce information as goods to be sold. The better the product, the better it can be sold. Finally, in late 1996, I made contact with investment bankers, financial advisory companies, and others who agreed to raise funds to establish the news agency SITA. Their attitude was that their companies needed reliable information on business and financial affairs. Such information is available from the major news agencies such as Reuters, Bloomberg, and Dow Jones, but over the long term these services are very expensive. Plus, they do not provide their clients here with sufficient information about Slovakia's economy. The idea was to cover Slovakia as completely as possible and to then, in turn, exchange this information with the international agencies and other resources.

SITA Ltd. was established on January 15, 1997, with a basic capital of 4 million SKK (at that time equivalent to approximately $120,000). We immediately began to search for adequate space and for a computerized editorial system. Locating office space wasn't a problem. But finding the special software system needed for the writing and editing of news in a modern news agency as well as for the distribution of the news product was more difficult. The most-used systems are produced in the United States or Switzerland, are extremely expensive, and have to be adapted to Central European conditions.

SITA contacted POSAM, a Slovakian software company that created programs based on the Lotus Notes system. Within one month, POSAM presented to us an editorial system that it created after consulting both with potential users of SITA's news product and with us to determine our software needs. This system continued to develop and evolve over the next two years to enable us to export our news stories to other agencies.

Still, establishing and launching SITA operations posed many problems. I took over responsibility for general management, editorial operations, and special contacts while Martin Vahancik assumed responsibility for financial operations. I believed my role at that time especially to be to explain the urgent need for an unbiased agency that stands in sharp contrast to the state-owned TASR. I needed to convey this need to our future clients as we sought to establish our special niche in the market. Another major responsibility of mine was, of course, to conduct the search for a good and responsible staff of reporters and editors.

Ours was not an easy task, particularly in view of the political situation in Slovakia. But we saw that the information market held a definite niche for us, with its great demand for unbiased information, for real-time, online business, and economic news about Slovakia. No organization in Slovakia had ever provided business information online before SITA except Reuters. However, Reuters focused primarily on banking and macroeconomic issues, rarely providing news about individual firms and corporations, people in business, or other microeconomic issues.

In 1997, the Central European Office of Reuters evaluated the possibility of establishing a special business news service in Slovakia. After we came up with our plan, we spoke to the Reuters management in Vienna, Austria, the office that is responsible for coverage in Slovakia and the region. We agreed on a trial period for SITA, during which Reuters would assess the quality of the business news that SITA could provide for its use. During the next two months, Reuters received SITA news stories free of charge, checking it for quality and evaluating the costs of ultimately paying for the service as compared to establishing its own Slovakian-based service with headquarters in Bratislava. The trial was a success, and SITA won its first important contract and reference.

Staffing the newsroom at SITA brought its own special challenges. No tradition of business news existed in communist Czechoslovakia. We decided to seek out new graduates or even current students of the University for the Economy in Bratislava and give them the chance to create a working place for themselves for the future. This probably was the best decision we made. We established three desks—general news, business news, and news in English— and we hired three relatively experienced agency and newspaper journalists to lead the operations. After three months of training the staff and sending out news "blind" (which means to nobody but Reuters), we felt ready to go on the wire and announced that wire operations would begin by June 15, 1997. At the time, we had a staff of approximately twenty. Meanwhile, before our first story ever made it to the wire, we found ourselves under heavy attack from Meciar, the HZDS, *Slovenska Republika*, and TASR, all of whom attempted to raise questions about SITA investors and stir controversy about the threat of United States or other foreign influences.

We announced our start at an International Technologies Fair two weeks before real operations were to begin. But one week before start up we received a bad surprise. On Saturday, June 7, 1997, I was called by the police to come to the SITA office. A break-in had occurred. I did not know what to expect but quickly found out. The complete computer system—all the equipment including servers with the saved editorial codes and information—had been stolen! This apparently had occurred during a busy Saturday afternoon at our location in the heart of Bratislava. The loss came as a real shock. We spent the whole night with the police drawing up a list of the stolen equipment. The police never really investigated the robbery, however, and three months later they reported to us that they still had not found the thief.

We immediately began to contact our technology suppliers. To our surprise, they offered to provide us with substitute equipment and to postpone payment deadlines. We agreed to their terms and on Wednesday morning, June 11, we started operations again.

The robbery brought us a great deal of publicity and subsequent media support from every corner, except, of course, TASR and *Slovenska Republika*, which even accused us of stealing our own computers in order to create suspicion of the ruling coalition!

Meanwhile, we found ourselves facing another battle. In a letter sent to state administration offices, the ministry for culture labeled SITA an "oppositional" organization financed by mysterious sources and warned officials not to give the agency any information. This happened at a time when SITA had yet to get its first story published. With every roadblock put in our way, however, came offers of help from others. Among those was the United States Embassy in Bratislava, which pledged its support of media plurality in Slovakia and offered to seek a grant to fund new equipment. We stressed to them and all our supporters that we welcomed assistance but could never accept any that was politically aimed.

With all these events swirling about us, we started our real operations as a wire service on June 17, 1997, offering our stories to all media free of charge during a two-month trial period. The Meciar government fought us from day one. It could not prevent us from attending press conferences, from reporting on parliamentary sessions or committees meetings, or from attending press briefings after the meetings of the cabinet. But what the politicians of the ruling coalition could do was refuse any comment or answer any questions posed by a SITA reporter, and this is what they did. We solved this problem in a way that was unique for Slovakia. SITA's management decided that publishing their "no comment" responses can be a good story in and of itself, a good indication to the public and to voters of the attitude of the politicians who claim to represent them. This lasted for about three months, at which point the so-called people's representatives recognized that their silence could affect their popularity with the public.

As we faced down the politicians on one side, we encountered an even more important problem on another: our marketing. Privatization in Slovakia at this time was characterized by much currying of favors from the government, which was still determining the rules for privatization. We therefore were having trouble finding commercial customers. The owners of financial institutions and new business enterprises were afraid to use SITA's business news service despite our growing reputation for quality. This trepidation lasted until early 1998.

With upcoming general elections, everyone knew that 1998 was going to be an important year for Slovakia—and for SITA. The majority of the political parties in Slovakia now recognized the importance of an independent news source free of the propaganda that dominated the news organizations close to the ruling coalition or to the other political parties. In fact, we had decided from the outset not to respond in our own news stories to the special attacks launched against us by media close to the ruling coalition. Those attacks, usually aimed at our alleged foreign financiers or lack of commitment to an independent Slovakia, had a political purpose, and we didn't.

In late 1997 and early 1998, a strong coalition of some 11 political parties organized with one major goal in mind: the defeat of Vladimir Meciar. Huge media campaigns were launched. The attitude of Meciar and his aides toward the media remained the same: You're either for us or against us. They were correct, in a sense. Nearly all of the non-state–backed media, along with a majority of the population, opposed Meciar and desperately wanted a change in the country. These media organizations joined opposition political leaders in pushing hard for a major voter turnout in the elections, and they got what they wanted. The result was 85 percent participation at the ballot in the September elections, including a huge turnout of young and first-time voters. These, by and large, were anti-Meciar. Throughout the campaign and elections, SITA was widely recognized as the most reliable source of information, a recognition that in turn strengthened our position in the market.

One way that we put the lie to accusations of bias from Meciar and other politicians during the pre-election campaign was through our Original Text Service, or OTS. For a fee, we publish the full-text statements delivered to us by political parties. With OTS, no political party could accuse us of refusing to publish its platform or other statements. Every party had the chance to sign a contract with SITA and get its full-text statements on our wire. The service includes a SITA statement disavowing any responsibility for the contents of the text.

In Slovakia, the OTS and accompanying SITA statement proved an important step. SITA was able to avoid the problems other media organizations faced, such as lawsuits and court actions brought by political parties as a result of stories they didn't like.

On the other hand, SITA was and is diligent in acknowledging errors and accepting responsibility for them. This attitude is atypical in Slovakia, where news organizations generally do little or nothing to correct misinterpretations of stories and rarely apologize to readers, clients, or the subjects of those stories. SITA's willingness to do so went far in ensuring its credibility.

Ironically, after the 1998 elections, leaders of the winning, anti-Meciar coalition offered to provide SITA assistance, but I declined, saying, "We do not need any help or aid from the government. Simply let us do our job."

TRAINING, ETHICS, AND THE FUTURE AT SITA

In doing our job, we at SITA believe that good training is of utmost importance and is the most effective way to keep errors to a minimum. SITA has its own system of education for its staffers. At the agency's beginning, the more experienced staffers designed a special agency style book and a separate manual for reporters and editors. These materials are continuously being updated with new information necessary in the gathering of news. As the new century dawned, SITA also remained the only media organization in Slovakia with its own editorial statute or code of conduct. This code requires that, in writing their stories, journalists maintain their independence from any political or economic influence, not only from outside the agency but from the agency owners as well.

Every newcomer at SITA must go through a trial period of three months, during which he or she works with one of the more experienced reporters or editors on the same news beat. The newcomer and the veteran both file stories, which are then compared and discussed. A newcomer generally will not see his or her first story published until one or two months have passed. Frequently, we send staffers out to take courses or participate in exchanges with different journalistic institutions in Slovakia or abroad. All reporters at the business news desk have studied and are knowledgeable in economics.

Another milestone was reached by SITA in September 1999: the news agency finally was in the black in its balance sheets. This seemed truly a miracle in view of the obstacles we had faced, particularly after only two years of operations. In developed democracies, new agencies often need seven to ten years to reach such a business goal.

As I look back, I have to say that in spite of everything maybe we owe a debt of gratitude to Mr. Meciar and his aides! They proved to be great public relations agents for us, provoking a demand for our services from other independent media and helping us to prove our mettle.

But what of the future? First, we have to continue to stabilize our market position by maintaining a high quality of service. I think that the time for state-run or state-dominated agencies such as TASR is over. In nearly all of the Central or Eastern European countries in transition, we have noticed similar small, privately owned, independent news agencies like SITA starting up. SITA has already joined in cooperative agreements with ONASA in Bosnia, BelaPAN in Belarus, and BNS in the Baltic States. We intend to broaden this cooperation to as many as 15 agencies across the region. My sense is that we will have a united Europe within 15 years, and a potential market of some 200 million readers in our region. Large agencies such as Reuters and Bloomberg will invest big amounts to penetrate such a market. Small, stand-alone agencies such as SITA will have no chance to survive unless they learn to cooperate and form some sort of association among themselves. Only this cooperation will earn them the chance to gain more respect and treatment as a partner by their larger and stronger counterparts. Such an association also will help hasten the deaths of the current competitors—the stage agencies. The future of SITA and similar agencies lies in close mutual cooperation and in a resulting exchange of products and experience. The first step in this type of exchange occurred when SITA, in tandem with its software company, provided access to its excellent editorial system to ONASA in Bosnia. That was only the start.

A STATEMENT OF PHILOSOPHY

Thanks to the 1989 "velvet revolution," we rid ourselves of state censorship and started a new era. As a consequence, we lost one generation of experienced journalists from the communist time. I am not qualified to judge whether this consequence was desirable in every case, but I respect it as a fact. Now, very talented but inexperienced youngsters have filled the gap. My experience has been that they are generally good and don't have the burden of the past that the older, still-active journalists carry.

On the other hand, the education of these younger journalists is often not satisfactory. And there is something else. Many of them have been spoiled. Everything has been allowed, and this has meant no self-control in the sense of ethics, no double or triple checking of facts and sources, for example. Too many of them follow the lead of the Slovakian Huey Long, who used to enjoy disclosing unchecked, embarrassing information on opponents by saying, "I found this on my desk." These are the journalists who like to publish without checking first.

Not to be overly pessimistic, however, I must say that a lot has been done already to change and improve the level of journalism in Slovakia. We have many good, respected journalists—young, clever, and well-educated journalists who are strong enough to stand all the pressures they face. They put much stress on quality in their work and are justly proud of what they have done. They will help determine the future of journalism in Slovakia. My generation—those of the age of 50 or older—will someday fade, but it is our obligation to create conditions as favorable as possible for the new generation. A lot of us are eager to do it. I know that I am.

Chapter ten

Holding Politicians' Feet to the Fire in Slovenia

by Bernard Nezmah, *Mladina* magazine, and
Assistant Professor, Faculty of Philosophy, Ljubljana
Ljubljana, Slovenia

In Slovenian journalism, ethics are relative. Let me tell you about three occasions when I faced ethical dilemmas as a journalist in my country both during
and after the communist era.

PRIOR RESTRAINT—SLOVENIAN STYLE

In 1987, when I was editor of the weekly magazine *Mladina*, I wanted to publish a letter to the editor in which the Slovenian-born, Georgetown University
professor Ciril Zebot asserted that the civil war that occurred in Slovenia under the Nazi occupation (1941–45) was actually started by Tito's Partisans—a
contradiction of official dogma. The local public prosecutor was so vigilant
that she ordered to be impounded all the copies of the offending pages even
before they were bound into the finished magazine. She said she was acting out
of concern that Zebot's letter would gravely disturb the public.

In those days, of course, all the media, all school texts, and indeed all books
preached the exact opposite of Zebot's version of the civil war between the Partisans and Nazi collaborationist forces. His claim definitely struck a taboo.
Such an alternative version of history was not permitted. Indeed, it was considered such a blasphemy that the courts ignored existing laws requiring that
the first three copies of a publication first be sent to the public prosecutor before the issuance of an order to seize an offending publication. In our situation, this necessary condition did not yet exist because the magazine issue con-
taining the letter had yet to be actually published. Thus, our courts allowed

the prosecutor to seize what did not yet legally exist. Not only that, the courts proscribed more than what the prosecutor demanded. The prosecutor targeted only one sentence as illegal, but the court decided that the entire letter was offensive.

Worse, this was a time when a sort of legal Catch 22 existed allowing the seizure of any text that, in the opinion of the court, might disturb the public. The decisions were entirely arbitrary because the judge simply decided each case based on his or her own feelings. No objective measure was available to distinguish between what might create mild as opposed to grave disturbances of the public. The accepted social creed of the time was that the people had to be protected from writers who might arouse and disturb or upset them.

When I decided to publish this "disturbing" letter, I knew what I was doing. It was more than clear to me that politicians, prosecutors, judges, and, indeed, the public might not be pleased with the contents. My journalistic impulse was precisely that we should offer to the public even the most upsetting views of history, regardless of whether officialdom had determined they had no right to exist. From the viewpoint of the Partisans who had fought and died in the struggle against the Nazi occupiers, it was profoundly unethical to publish a letter that glorified the collaborationist forces whom the Nazi occupiers had supplied with arms. However, my desire for absolute freedom of expression, my tendency to be skeptical about received truths, and, I admit it, my enjoyment in rebelling against the authoritarians in power were the motives that inspired me.

CHALLENGING A BALKAN BOSS

Another run-in with questions of ethics occurred when I came up with an idea for a series of articles on the retirement of the then-vice president of Yugoslavia. I'll admit I just arbitrarily decided on a date for one of that era's most powerful politicians to leave politics. I simply pulled the date out of a hat. Perhaps you might see this as a rather grave transgression of journalistic ethics, but I thought of it as my journalistic contribution toward the democratization of our society.

What excused my behavior? Well, in 1987, I was interviewing the man in question, Stane Dolanc, a quasi-god of Yugoslav politics, and during the interview, Dolanc confided that he was soon going to retire. When a year passed and there was yet no sign of his pending departure, I simply calculated that, if he did not do as he promised, the rotational presidential system of the time would make him the president of the country in May 1989. And so, in September 1988, I started the official countdown to the May date that I had established for his retirement. At the start of the series, I announced that 249 days remained.

Once a week for the next thirty-six weeks, I waxed sarcastic at his expense, using a combination of photographs and excerpts from his speeches and appearances that I found in the archives. For instance, in Yugoslavia it used to be the practice to honor people with the title of Hero of Labor. At first, this honorific was reserved for real laborers who had outpaced others in their various fields of endeavor. Later, similar titles such as Hero of Socialist Labor was by extension given to politicians. Because Dolanc, the hero of my series, was, of course, a decorated Hero of Labor, I put him beside the legendary miner Alija Sirotanovic, who in the first post-war years would single-handedly mine several wagonloads of coal in one day. I included in my report a photograph of the exceedingly corpulent Dolanc next to one of the thin-as-a-reed miner.

In another story, I juxtaposed a photo of Al Capone, who looked uncannily like Dolanc, with one of the politician. Both of them were champing on cigars in the photographs. The caption was this: "They say that the Mafia operates only in Sicily and America."

At the time, this series was one of the most popular in the country. After all, it was doing something heretofore unheard of. Our magazine was having a good time, almost childishly poking fun at the iron fist of Yugo-communism. One of the Belgrade papers openly wondered how Dolanc quietly accepted all this, the same Dolanc who in the old days would fire entire newspaper departments for the smallest perceived slight. He had been a top member of the League of Communists of Yugoslavia and became Minister of Police a year after the protests in Kosovo in 1981 that resulted in at least 11 killed, 257 seriously injured, and 1,600 imprisoned. That was the official tally released by Dolanc in a press conference after the incident. During that press conference, he accused the protesters of counter-revolution. No media had been allowed at the scene of the protest.

Knowing that my countdown risked overstepping the bounds of what was permitted, we were admittedly afraid, and that's why for several months the series went unsigned. Then I decided one day that our readers should know the author of this hagiography, and I signed my name to it.

Fortunately, the series appeared at a time when a new type of Slovenian politician was assuming power. The new politicians looked for opportunities to advertise themselves as more liberal than their dogmatic, old-fashioned, iron-fisted rivals. The new breed liked the articles. The series had another major result: its hero did indeed retire on the predicted date. In fact, just before the end of his vice-presidential mandate, the strongman even granted me another interview. Like many others, he was seeking a public catharsis that would allow him to survive the coming fall of communism. But his gesture had broader dimensions. It showed that in the new era, the authoritarian politician and his harshest critic could sit down together in a spirit of reconciliation and even look amiably at one another while remaining professional antagonists.

LITERARY SARCASM

A third case even landed me in a book about journalistic ethics as an example of impermissible writing about politicians. In 1993, in *Mladina*, I began writing a no-punches-pulled series called "Pamphlet." In 1995, I ended up before the courts because of an article that the then-mayor of Ljubljana, Dimitrij Rupel, found offensive. Rupel had previously been the country's foreign minister and is its foreign minister again today. The words that got me in trouble were "madness," "schizophrenia," and "dementia." Here is the story:

In 1994, Rupel, the former foreign minister and then still a member of Parliament, ran for the post of mayor of Ljubljana. In his campaign, he promised to devote all his energies to being mayor. And yet, after his election, he refused to give up his seat in Parliament. Thus he spent his mornings at the parliamentary sessions and was mayor only in the late afternoon. In doing this, he violated the city charter and became the first mayor in two centuries to work part time. In an interview, he said that he was quite capable of performing all of his three functions as a member of parliament, mayor, and university professor, but that if he had things his way, he would prefer to give up all three. He said, furthermore, that politicians were not normal people and that he did not consider himself unusually pathological given that he was a politician. Among other things, he also claimed that the state television was purposely excluding him from its news reports and that cameramen had instructions not to shoot pictures of him at public functions. The editor-in-chief of the TV network later called the mayor a liar and demanded proof of his claims.

I give you all this juicy local lore as background to what then happened. Because the mayor did not reply to the editor's demands, I had some sharp things to say in my weekly column about the mayor: "It appears that the mayor has succumbed to madness, given that he is speaking in the papers about his fantasies. He seems to be succumbing to schizophrenia when he at the same time says that he is capable of performing all his three functions and yet says he would rather chuck it all. That the gossip about his dementia is not without foundation can be seen in his interview, in which he says that among politicians he finds no normal people." In my admittedly sarcastic commentary, I did make certain that I stuck to the basic rule that all my inferences be based on the mayor's publicly spoken words. The very next day after my commentary, the mayor sued me in court, charging defamation of character.

Let us fast forward to the judgment. The judge in his decision did not accept the defense that the words "madness," "schizophrenia" and "dementia" were assessments of specific political actions and statements. He decided that they amounted to the simplest name-calling and that, in effect, I was attacking the honor and good name of the mayor. My column showed disdain and disrespect for Rupel, the judge said. Neither freedom of expression nor the norms of morality would excuse the use of words that tread underfoot a politician's dignity, he continued. After giving me this stinging moral lesson, the judge meted out a sentence of one month in prison—to be suspended on the condition that in the following year I do not commit a similar deed. The probation would help me in the future to know what separates constructive criticism from defamatory judgments, the judge said.

Numerous protests against this ruling came from sociologists, philosophers, and even some politicians. *Reporters sans frontières* railed against it, as did the Pen Club, Article 19, and the Index on Censorship. All insisted that the judgment would encourage self-censorship and maintained that a judge should not be allowed to decide arbitrarily where the bounds of permitted criticism lie.

I appealed the judgment, citing examples from the world press in my defense. *The Economist*, for example, once published this headline about then-Prime Minister John Major: "Mad, bad and dangerous." *Le Canard enchaîné* had written about "L'amnésie du maire de Paris" in reference to the mayor of Paris. Neither paper was accused of defamation of character. I argued that the judgment essentially forbade sarcasm as a literary device. I demanded that the court take into consideration European precedents and cited the decision in *Lingens v. Austria*, in which the court had said that politicians must expect more criticism than ordinary citizens and that the function of a press is precisely to critique the actions and behavior of politicians.

All these arguments were to no avail: the higher court denied the appeal and said again that my criticism had gone beyond the bounds of good taste. I then appealed to the Supreme Court, where I argued for my constitutional right to speak freely about my political beliefs. I protested that the lower Slovenian courts did not take into consideration the principles and practices of the European Court of Human rights. I offered the example of an Austrian journalist who had called nationalist leader Jörg Haider an idiot. The journalist was cleared of charges because the European Court argued that he had the right to write such commentary in view of Haider's own provocative statements.

The Supreme Court did finally nullify the judgment against me. More important, for the first time in Slovenian legal history, it based its judgment on precedents set by the European Court of Human Rights. It accepted the principle that criticism of politicians is precisely what journalists are meant to do. The high court said that the public's right to be informed about political leaders takes precedence over those leaders' right to their good name. Needless to say, this right applies only when the politician in question has with his or her actions given cause for such criticism. It is important to note that the Slovenian Association of Journalists kept silent throughout the process. I might add here that the president of the association was a sympathizer of the mayor's political bloc. Paradoxically, the court did more to affirm journalism as a profession worthy of respect in Slovenia than did our own association.

The above case occurred while post-communist standards of journalism were just being formulated. After the initial euphoria following 1990 came an

avalanche of lawsuits from public figures unhappy with what was being reported about them. Typically at this time, the lower court found the journalist guilty, after which the journalist appealed and won in the higher court. The
effect of the lower-court rulings, however, was nevertheless a kind of judicial
repression, for it guaranteed self-censoring. The higher courts, meanwhile, set
precedents that put a stop to the growth of lawsuits. In their rulings, they defined journalism as a socially useful profession that had the right to react even
offensively to the beyond-the-pale actions of politicians.

Initially the offended politicians sought criminal penalties, including prison
terms, against offending journalists. Later, their lawsuits began to focus on
monetary damages. The former vice premier of Slovenia, Marjan Podobnik,
for instance, sued *Mladina* for 25 million tolars ($120,000) because of alleged
false reporting and the subsequent pain it had caused him. The magazine had
reported on a conversation between Podobnik and a corporate official in
which the politician, as president of his party, agreed to help a corporate director win a parliamentary race in exchange for financial support from the corporation. A lower court found that the magazine was unable to prove that the
conversation indeed took place, even though evidence was provided showing
that the corporation did provide illegal financial assistance to the political
party. In its Solomon-like ruling, the court faulted the weekly for failing to
prove the existence of the incriminating conversation but still denied Podobnik's damage claims. What it didn't resolve is how future courts might measure
pain and suffering, a question also left unresolved in recent case rulings.

JOURNALISTS AS POLITICAL ACTIVISTS

Let us now attempt to define the atmosphere that exists in Slovenian journalism today. Under the old regime, a journalist was a socio-political worker. For
instance, whoever became an editor-in-chief automatically became a member
of the Central Committee of the Party. In his or her writing, the journalist
played the role of party activist. It was the journalist's job to translate the party
program and principles into the language of journalism. The result was a vi-
sionary style with the journalist as a sort of enlightened Moses, describing
what society ought to do to realize the goals of a communist society.

Has this perception of the journalist truly changed in the post-communist
era? The average reader still thinks of political journalism as political agitation.
In letters to the editor, calls to phone-in broadcast programs, and public opinion polls, you hear again and again the conviction that journalists are merely
activists for particular political parties, that journalism is nothing more than
political propaganda.

Now why is this the case? In Slovenia, not a single daily newspaper is openly
aligned with a political party. Thus, one might conclude that the media are indeed politically independent. The reality, however, is closer to the public per-

ception. The largest daily, *Delo*, for example, published large photographs of the president nearly every day during the recent presidential campaign. Meanwhile, the other candidates in the race were relegated to short news items on the inside pages. When the president was reelected, eyewitnesses claimed that the editor of the second largest daily, *Vecer*, proclaimed, "We won!" This same editor, by the way, was also president of the journalists' union.

Here are some reasons for the popular perception of journalists in Slovenia today:

1. Journalists constantly file as political candidates. After their political forays, many return to journalism in a constantly revolving door.

2. Even today, the president grants interviews only to the state television network, and then only to a handpicked journalist.

3. The Slovenian Association of Journalists has no will and no credibility. The association did not protest when the courts handed out suspended jail sentences to members who had published articles critical of politicians. When a public debate took place about whether journalists should be allowed to return to their old jobs after serving stints as politicians, the association president insisted that the political experience made such journalists ideal commentators and analysts.

Still, the association offers certain material advantages to its members. They receive a 10 percent discount when they buy automobiles from certain select companies, and hefty discounts when they buy clothes from certain clothing manufacturers. Whether they can subsequently write objectively about these gift-bearing companies isn't certain.

PRESS CONFERENCES, POLLS, AND CENSORS

Press conferences in Slovenia are staged events in which the journalists faithfully reproduce what they're told, ask few tough questions, and essentially provide support to the images and messages the events are designed to convey. For instance, a major firm will summon journalists to boast about recent successes. The journalists do not question whether the firm's success has been affected by cutbacks and layoffs rather than by any new dynamic initiatives. The same rule holds for press briefings given by politicians and also by sports figures or organizations. If someone wants his or her name in the media, that person simply calls a press conference. Journalists will passively march to the staged event. Thankfully, this is not an absolute. Some journalists are professional enough to go to these conferences asking real questions. They are the exceptions.

What we have in Slovenia is the paradox of the passive reporter on the one hand and the activist reporter on the other. During a six-month period in 2000, when a coalition of right-of-center parties briefly ruled, the left-leaning mainstream media daily reported the number of senior civil servants and directors of government agencies being replaced. As the count continued, their vocabulary changed dramatically with neutral words such as "replace" and "change" falling to the wayside as emotionally charged words such as "dismiss" and "purge" took their place—words that in the minds of Slovenian readers evoke Fascist and Stalinist times.

The partisanship in the mainstream Slovenian media can also be seen in the opinion polls that they publish regularly. According to these polls, the politicians of the left are without question the most popular and beloved in the country. However, the polls and election results often seem to suffer from a lack of connection. In the parliamentary elections of October 2000, for example, media polls typically showed center-left politicians far ahead of their center-right opponents. Then, on election day, the results often came out exactly the opposite. Perhaps the science of polling needs further evolution in Slovenia.

If the biggest daily media are slanted to the left, why doesn't the political right establish its own favorable media? Two such attempts, the dailies *Slovenec* (1991 to 1996) and *Jutranjik* (1998), failed. The reason is simple: the attitude of the right toward its media tends to be a carbon copy of the old communist-style authoritarianism with its accompanying ignorance of how journalism operates in a market-based society. This is evident in the media's recruitment of journalists. The first criterion of acceptability is ideological correctness rather than professional competence. Add in constant interference with editorial policy and you have a formula for failure.

Censorship and self-censorship are still specters hovering over the Slovenian media today. In the old one-party system, politicians were interviewed by one of their own, a member of the Party. The Slovenian public was regularly offered the cozy spectacle of a journalist interviewing a politician in the politician's living room, while wearing slippers generously provided by the politician himself! Things grew feistier by the end of 1980s, but even then only authorized and sometimes altered versions of the interviews were released.

I once interviewed the director of a hospital who later became Minister of Health. Presented with the text of the interview, the man nonchalantly changed all his responses in order to present them in a more concise and effectively argued manner. On another occasion, during the period of Slovenia's first attempts to assert its independence, my interviewee said that he favored Slovenia having its own currency. Later, as he checked his answers before giving his authorization to print them, he became afraid of his own daring and changed his position to the exact opposite.

In the mid-1990s, I held a conversation with Dutch colleagues and learned that their interview subjects could change only incorrectly stated facts and nothing else. That has been my position ever since, and it's a system that seems to work.

THE ANTI-CHURCH REFLEX

I want to add a note here about a special characteristic of many Slovenian journalists nowadays: their anti-church, anti-Catholic bias. A leftover from the days of communism, it remains a given even with our post-communist journalists. Comrade Lenin liked to call religion the opiate of the people, and certainly the pre-October Revolution masses seemed to humbly accept all manner of injustice as the will of God instead of rebelling and launching a class struggle.

Today, the perception is still widespread—certainly it is in the press—that everything connected to the Church except a quiet, personal, and interior faith is *a priori* harmful to society. Despite a Slovenian law of denationalization that seeks to return properties nationalized by the Communist authorities to their original owners, the press rarely fails to champion any effort to deny a church request for a return of its own property or holdings. And if a brass band from the local police department should show up at a church picnic, what a scandal that is in the papers! With few exceptions, the press typically speaks with the same voice on such issues that it employed in communist times.

THE STRUGGLE TO PRACTICE REAL JOURNALISM

In the last years under communism, the basic principle that guided me was my desire for freedom of expression. I wanted to possess the courage to destroy taboos. To do so, I had to pay careful attention to my style, and I had to find genres that would allow my sharp criticism to survive the scrutiny of the courts.

This was a rare time in which a journalist actually could feel what every journalist wants to feel: that he or she is creating history. Today is a time for redefining the basic principles of journalism as an independent profession.

Here is what I strive for now. I want to have a readable style. I want my readers to enjoy reading what I have to say even when they don't agree with me. And I want to look at events from a perspective that is different from that of the powerful, whether in politics, economics, finance, or sports. Even though my writing these days tends to be closer to the views of the opposition, I am not going to become its spokesman. My stance is that of the critical intellectual. But to communicate with my readers, I try to avoid clichés as I seek to give *le plaisir du texte*.

PART FOUR

In the Middle East and Africa

Few regions of the world have put journalists to greater tests than the Middle East and Africa, where the forces of religion, culture, and history have made the concept of a free and independent press often tenuous at best. These are also regions where great changes have taken place, changes that demonstrate just how central the role of the media is in all societies.

In Chapter 11, Nabil Dajani, a leading scholar on the Lebanese and Arab media, describes how the role of the all-important medium of television in Lebanon—where a 15-year civil war between 1975 and 1990 took its toll on the media as well as the nation as a whole—has been undermined by the self-serving interests of government and the private sector, robbing the public of the opportunity for a real discussion of issues crucial to Lebanese society.

In Chapter 12, Regina Jere-Malanda, a Zambian and journalist now based in London, describes how intense partisanship threatens the promise of the free press in the emerging democracies of Southern Africa.

In Chapter 13, Minabere Ibelema, a Nigerian who teaches communication studies at the University of Alabama-Birmingham, describes ethical practices in Nigerian journalism and the failures and successes of journalists in contributing to the marketplace of ideas in that nation.

Chapter eleven

Lebanese Television

Caught Between Government and the Private Sector

by Nabil Dajani
Professor of Communication
Chair of Department of Social and Behavioral Sciences
American University of Beirut, Lebanon

This essay is an expanded, updated and completely revised version of a part of a   123
chapter on Lebanese television in the author's 1992 book Disoriented Media in a
Fragmented Society, *which was published by the AUB Press in Beirut.*

This chapter surveys the development of television in Lebanon historically,
from its inception until the introduction of satellite broadcasting. The influence of the political and professional changes that took place in this tiny
Mediterranean republic is inspected within the background of the Lebanese
civil war and the confessional system of the country. The struggle between government officials and media practitioners over television operation is not directed at public service. Government officials and political bosses are concerned with the control of television news and programs that might threaten
the status quo. Television officials' concern lies more with financial profit. Public interest is given only lip service.

Lebanese television broadcasting lacks professionalism, social responsibility,
and civic commitment. The government, on the other hand, needs to provide
the climate of freedom that is conducive for the broadcasting medium.

THE CHANGING SCENE OF LEBANESE TELEVISION

The past decade has witnessed radical changes in the structure and role of television in Lebanon, yet little has been written on the subject. Consequently,
much of the available literature on the topic is outdated.[1] Most of the rest is

either too general or lacks precision.[2] This essay attempts to fill this gap by providing firsthand information based on the author's experience of more than forty years as a media practitioner, researcher of the role of the media in the Lebanese society, as well as a friend and adviser to various media practitioners and officials. The material in this chapter, therefore, is based on the analysis of the available written material in both Arabic and English as well as on information collected through personal contacts with media and government sources.

LEBANESE MEDIA AS A PRODUCT OF ITS SOCIETY

Media scholars often address the relationship between government and television in the context of either a Western societal structure, where this medium usually operates within the private sector, or a Third World structure, where the medium customarily operates within the public sector, typically as a government arm. Lebanese media institutions, however, do not fit either the Third World model or the Western model of media operation, for the existing societal forces in every state determine the structure, content, and operation of media institutions. The mass media, therefore, are unique to their society. They cannot have identity or effects outside the concrete instances within which the different forces operate.

Lebanon is a curious country with many contradictions, a country of extreme pluralism and of deep divisions. It is a society fragmented along sectarian lines, which is going through a controversial identity shift: Its institutions are torn between a state of transformation, which is exhibited in its relatively modern laws and perspective, and that of persistence, which is demonstrated by the performance of its political and religious bosses, who put obstacles before the introduction of change or application of laws that may lessen the sectarian nature of the system of government.

Although newspaper readership is not widely spread in Lebanon or in the Arab world in general, radio and television are available in almost every household in Beirut. For this reason, the focus of this chapter is on the television medium rather than the media as a whole. Television reception is not limited to the Lebanese local channels; the cable connection is widely spread in Beirut and the major Lebanese cities. This spread is enhanced by the inexpensive cost of cable subscription in Lebanon. For a little over twelve U.S. dollars a month, a Lebanese household can receive some seventy channels, including most of the Arab satellite stations, CNN, the BBC, al-Jazira, and numerous movie and other specialized channels. In some heavily populated areas, this subscription could be as little as five U.S. dollars a month. Unlicensed satellite television distribution companies have mushroomed in the past few years and have penetrated almost two-thirds of Lebanon's households.[3]

The Lebanese media situation is an example of the contradictory state of transformation and persistence that Lebanon is going through. The existing media laws specify that television institutions be not directly managed or run by the government or private individuals or politicians. The practice, however, is different but is congruent with the special socio-political structure of the Lebanese society.[4]

An examination of the development of television in Lebanon suggests that the measures taken by government to regulate television broadcasting since its inception in Lebanon were not intended to encourage television officials to deal with themes of significant concern to the average individual, mainly those emerging from the civil war. Themes that deal with the need for the cooperation of the different sectarian groups in the reconstruction of the country and in bringing about the unity of its people are almost absent in Lebanese television. The examination proposes that the different government legislations introduced were aimed not at promoting original productions, nor at providing more opportunity for local talent and developing responsible and professional organizational structures. Rather, the examination points out that state legislation in the area of television broadcasting was aimed at allowing government officials and the ruling political bosses to exploit this medium for their own political goals.[5]

The assessment of the growth of television in Lebanon shows that government officials and political bosses endeavored to legalize their monopoly over television news and to control programs that might threaten their political ambitions or the status quo. Additionally, it shows that the friction between television authorities and the government during the past four decades was due to the interest of the television officials in financial gain more than their interest in securing increased freedom to produce programs that address themes relevant to the social and economic problems confronting the country. No serious investigation has been carried out by the media about claims of corruption in the government, which were often voiced by senior government officials.[6] Additionally, no serious program, to date, has been produced to deal with the sectarian conflict that plagues the country.

EARLY STAGES OF TELEVISION IN LEBANON

Unlike as in most developing countries, the initiative to establish television in Lebanon belonged not to the government but to businessmen who had little experience in the necessities of television broadcasting. They conceived of their project in essentially business terms, giving little or no attention to its social implications and responsibilities.[7] In this aspect lies Lebanese television's main weakness, for the logic of a commercial enterprise in developing countries often runs counter to that of public service and societal well being.

The first attempt to start television broadcasting in Lebanon goes back to October 1954, when two Lebanese businessmen, Wissam Izzedine and Alex

Arida, submitted an application to form a television broadcasting company. After two years of negotiations, an agreement was signed, on August 1956, granting a license to La Compagnie Libanaise de Television, SAL (CLT). The license was not for the monopoly that the applicants had requested. It was simply a license to broadcast television signals on two VHF channels, one devoted to programs in Arabic or with Arabic subtitles, the other for foreign, mainly French, programs. CLT thus became the first commercial television station in the Arab world.[8] The station inaugurated its service on May 28, 1959. It began transmission with the power of half a kilowatt.

The agreement between CLT and the Lebanese government left the door open for other companies to apply for television broadcasting licenses. The most important terms of the twenty-one–article agreement were that Lebanon would not give the company monopoly rights and that television was under official government scrutiny. The agreement further stipulated that the company was not permitted to broadcast programs that would threaten public security, morals, or religious groups, nor could it enhance the image of any political personality or party.

Under the terms of this agreement, television programs were to be restricted to education and entertainment. Although the agreement allowed the company only a restricted and inadequate freedom of political expression, it was quite generous in giving it all the time it needed for advertising. Advertising messages could cover up to 25 percent of the total broadcast time. The agreement also required that the company should undertake to broadcast, free of charge, news programs and official bulletins submitted by the Ministry of Information.[9]

In addition, television was to be subject to all laws and regulations pertinent to the rights of the press and of authors, as well as all national and international laws and regulations dealing with wireless communication and with broadcasting. Television was also required to exchange sound programs with the official Lebanese radio station. The agreement was for fifteen years, at the end of which the government had the right to buy the television installations.

In April 1959, another group of Lebanese businessmen, backed by an American corporation, ABC, approached the government with a request to set up a second television station, Compagnie de Television du Liban et du Proch-Orient (Tele Orient). An agreement identical to the one granted to CLT was concluded in July 1959. Transmission of one program began on May 6, 1962.

After a number of unprofitable years that witnessed tough competition and lack of adequate organization, especially in selling advertising time, the two companies agreed to coordinate and develop their advertising sales methods and to coordinate the scheduling and marketing of their programs. Before the beginning of the civil war in 1975, the two companies were making large profits. Revenue from television advertising was increasing. Total television income from advertising showed 19.5 percent increase over 1973 and constituted 35.3

per cent of total 1974 advertising expenditure in Lebanon. Additionally, both companies sold locally produced programs to television institutions in the Arab countries[10].

In December 1974, the Lebanese Council of Ministers renewed the license of CLT. The renewal existed for a period of nine years only. The new agreement sought to institutionalize and formulize the political control of broadcasting by the government. Under the terms of the new agreement, the Lebanese government would buy the transmission installations and lease them to CLT. It decreed that two government censors be present at the station and requested CLT to broadcast a daily one-hour, early-evening program prepared by the government. The agreement also required that CLT pay 6.5 percent of its net advertising revenue to the government. It authorized a maximum of nine minutes of advertising per hour, with a maximum of three minutes during the news programs.

The 1974 agreement made vague requests that TV programs should be "of the highest possible standards" and that CLT should "train its staff in the artistic and technical fields." It required CLT to provide national television coverage. The government, however, was not in a position to implement these provisions, first because many of these requirements were left vague, and second because of the outbreak of the civil war, which diminished the ability of the government to execute such an agreement. Thus between December 1974 and December 1977, two sets of regulations for television broadcasting existed, one applying to Tele Orient under the provisions of its 1962 license, the other applying to CLT under its 1974 agreement.

TELEVISION DURING THE CIVIL WAR

During the first two years of the civil war (1975–1976), the two companies faced their most difficult challenges. The war seriously reduced advertising, and both companies incurred heavy losses. Although both stations managed to maintain their technical equipment and keep their transmitters operational, they could not keep their production studios functioning. New programs could not be produced, and television officials were eagerly seeking programs to fill their airtime.

This situation continued until March 1976, when an unsuccessful coup d'etat resulted in the occupation of both stations by militias representing the two warring factions. Consequently, the news program in the west Beirut station was run by the "nationalist forces" (mainly Moslem) and the program in the east Beirut station by the "Lebanese forces" (mainly Christian). Coordination between the two stations in presenting a common news program was severed, but they maintained the coordination of scheduling their entertainment programs. The split of the broadcast media also marked a serious escalation in the war. Broadcasting installations became targets for the warring groups. Television installations were badly damaged as each station had installations in the areas occupied by opposing factions. Transmission was also badly affected by power failures, which now became acute. Power supply became irregular and rationed.

The heavy losses incurred by both companies as a result of the war moved them close to bankruptcy. The only prospect for them to continue in operation was to secure financial assistance from the government. They officially requested the interference of the government at the end of 1976. At that time, a new president, Elias Sarkis, was elected and the pace of hostilities diminished. People were hopeful that the new regime would bring an end to the civil war.

The first government of the new regime was faced with a dilemma. If it refused to aid both companies, Lebanon would be without television. This would add a further blow to the already battered image of the country and would be a bad beginning for the Sarkis presidency. If the government agreed to extend aid, the new regime would have to aid other institutions affected by the war. To add to the urgency for action, the license of Tele Orient was due for renewal.

To meet these developments, the Council of Ministers appointed a special committee to examine the state of affairs of television in Lebanon. The committee was charged with the task of suggesting the role television should play in what was believed to be the post-war period, and the task of making recommendations to maintain the operation of this medium.

The committee's report urged the Lebanese government to take a more active role in the development of television. It recommended replacing CLT and Tele Orient with a new company, of which the government would control 50 percent and the private sector would control the remaining half. It further recommended that the two existing companies be given the option to purchase the shares of the public sector. The Council of Ministers, which had then been given temporary legislative powers by the parliament, approved the report.

A legislative decree was issued on December 30, 1977, legalizing the birth of a new television company, the Lebanese Television Company (*Tele Liban*).[11] The company was formed "to manage, organize, and utilize the various television transmitting installations, and to undertake all commercial and television production tasks." The new company was given monopoly over television broadcasting in Lebanon until the year 2012. Its capital was distributed equally between the government and the two then-existent companies. *Tele Liban* was to be managed by a board of directors of twelve members: six representing the Lebanese government and the remaining six representing the two companies. The chairman of the board was to be appointed by the Lebanese Council of Ministers.

The formation of *Tele Liban* was, therefore, not a result of a new policy by the Sarkis regime aimed at defining the role of television in Lebanese society but simply a result of *"force majeur."* It was the only possible move that the government could take at the time in order to support television and maintain its service. The main contribution of the Sarkis regime to the television medium was to provide it with financial liquidity. This financial support made rebuilding and improving the existing transmitters possible in order to cover all the Lebanese areas as well as increase the hours of transmission.

An examination of the terms of the early agreements granting television licenses, as well as of the directives by the different Lebanese governments concerning the operation of this medium, suggests that the official Lebanese policy was mainly seeking to legalize censorship of television programs in order to keep this medium under control by limiting its political influence. Government agreements with the early television stations did not require improvement of standards or widening the appeal of the programs.[12] Similarly, the clamor made by a number of television officials seeking public support[13] to help "provide more freedom for television" was prompted more by financial interest than by public service. They did not offer a plan that would provide better alternatives.

The merger of CLT and Tele Orient could have played a more positive role in improving the conditions of broadcasting in Lebanon. The function of *Tele Liban*, according to an official at the Ministry of Information, was "to bring together the best of what the public sector has to offer—its primary concern for the needs of the country—and the strength of the private sector in dynamic management and profit making." However, both government and the private sector, which jointly managed television under the *Tele Liban* plan, continued to provide programs that were determined by their private political or economic interests more than by the public interest. Hardly was there a time when the handling of television by either the government or the private sector paid serious attention to the production of local programs, or to the selection of foreign imported programs, that were relevant to the needs of society.

Thus, one observed on Lebanese television, for example, an imported program such as "Eight is Enough," which in one of its episodes showed a U.S. teenager approaching her father for approval to "get on the pill," contrasting oddly with the values of a country where "honor crimes" are condoned by law.[14] In the same week, on another popular local program, *"Abu Milhim,"* the Lebanese viewer heard the program's hero telling a young girl who lost her virginity in a bicycle accident: "I wish you had lost your eye and not your virginity." Not a single local television program was produced to address the serious sectarian problem that plagues the Lebanese society and was one of the main causes of the civil war. And although television, and the print media in general, give their audiences an "overdose" of political discussions, we find an almost total absence of public affairs programming and lack of investigative reporting about issues that affect the livelihood of the average Lebanese, such as the shortage of water and electricity supplies.[15]

The creation of *Tel Liban* did not improve public service. The private sector involved in television felt secure and free of the fear of losing its license now that the government was its partner. Lebanese officials were content with their control of the overall management of this medium. Their attention was focused on improving the physical aspect of broadcasting that was ruined by the war. No efforts or plans were made to tie the programs of *Tele Liban* to social policies and plans. Thus, instead of both groups joining efforts to improve public service, they adopted a policy of "let the public be damned."

THE INTRODUCTION OF DE FACTO STATIONS

The deterioration of the state of affairs in Lebanon and the further weakening of the central government during the Amin Jemayel presidency in the mid-1980s encouraged some of the warring factions to establish their own pirate television stations. Most important among these were the Lebanese Broadcasting Company (LBC), which was the official organ of one of the warring militias, and *Al-Mashrek* Television, which was established by politicians opposed to the patrons of LBC. Among the important pirate stations at the time was the New Television (NTV), which was established by the Lebanese communist party and later was bought by independent businessmen.

LBC went on the air in August 1985 and in a short period captured a wide Lebanese audience and became the leading TV station in Lebanon in terms of the variety of its programs and the size of its audience. *Al-Mashrek* (the Orient) Television began its experimental broadcasting in 1989 and started airing regular programs in April 1990. By the beginning of 1991, it became a serious competitor for both LBC and *Tele Liban*. Its heavy use of Arabic programs and films attracted large audiences. New Television began its transmission in April 1991. It was mainly commercial and aired programs that had no relationship to the ideology of the communist party.

As was the case with *Tele Liban*, LBC became the subject of a struggle not only of the warring groups but also between the U.S. and French interests that sought to dominate its programs. The early U.S. influence on LBC did not please the French, who consequently were able, early in 1988, to prevail on LBC to devote a special channel for strictly French programs. This channel (C33) was, however, on the UHF band that was not widely used in Lebanon at the time.

With the creation of de facto television stations, both the Lebanese government and the private sector involved with *Tele Liban* faced a new challenge. The deterioration of the quality of the human element and technical skills at *Tele Liban* allowed the de facto stations easily to attract Lebanese viewers to their programs and consequently draw advertisers to them. They were also able to attract viewers from different factions to their foreign programs that were of a better quality and more up-to-date than those of *Tele Liban*. Additionally, they paid more attention to addressing the daily concerns of the average citizen and attracted audiences to several of their local programs, which were relatively better than those of *Tele Liban*. All television stations, however, were generally indifferent to the public needs for the coverage of subjects that relate to their livelihood (such as the problems of the shortage of electricity and water, pollution, and the high cost of living).

The success of the de facto stations led to heavy losses by *Tele Liban*. Faced with such competition, its officials had to improve their programs. They imported up-to-date foreign serials and arranged for the direct relay of many special world events. They also attempted to introduce administrative reforms within its structure. Additionally *Tele Liban* officials filed a lawsuit requesting large financial compensation from the three leading de facto stations at the time: LBC, *al-Machrek*, and NTV.

During a 1989 retreat in the Saudi town of *Taif*, Lebanese members of the parliament were able to arrive at a regionally and internationally supported agreement that marked the end of the Lebanese civil war. Among other things, the *Taif* Agreement, which was later incorporated into the Lebanese constitution, called for the reorganization of the media in Lebanon. The deliberations of members of the parliament clearly called for legalizing the existing de facto radio and television stations. Consequently, upon the signing of this agreement, many politicians and businessmen hurried to set up television stations to establish their "right" for a television license. According to an ITU expert, forty-six television stations were set up in a matter of a few months and some ten of the new stations were on the air by the end of 1991, transmitting on UHF channels as all the VHF channels were already in use.[16]

TELEVISION LEGISLATION BECOMES AN URGENT NEED

The increasing number of television stations resulted in confusion and chaos in the broadcasting medium. This increase happened at the beginning of the Elias Hrawi presidency, which had the enormous job of reestablishing government authority after the civil war. The first Hrawi government felt the urgency for introducing new legislation that put order into the broadcasting field. Thus in 1991, the minister of information recommended the reorganization of television broadcasting in Lebanon. The proposed reorganization was to grant licenses to stations whose total assets were Lebanese and require new stations to broadcast exclusively on UHF channels. To oversee broadcasting, the minister recommended setting up an Independent National Communication Agency that would grant broadcasting licenses and ensure that the different broadcasting media operated within the technical and professional regulations set by it.[17]

To avoid upset to the delicate status quo, the minister recommended that

Tele Liban be requested to lease some of its channels to the de facto stations in return for a fee. Doing so would ensure the rights of *Tele Liban* and would provide it with funds to improve its facilities and services. At the same time, this arrangement would allow the de facto stations to continue their operation.[18]

The recommendations of the minister were referred to a special ministerial committee. The committee's deliberations were the basis of a January 1992 Council of Ministers decision, which stated that "all television institutions which are presently operating de facto and in contradiction to the existing laws as well as anybody who wishes to invest in television must submit, within a period of one month, an application for commercial television broadcasting." The Council of Ministers also requested the ministerial committee to "draw out, for the consideration and approval of the Council of Ministers, the conditions for rental of, and investing in, television channels."[19]

The decision by the Council of Ministers raised a public uproar not because of what it stated but because of what was reportedly said in the deliberations of the ministers. According to press reports, the deliberations dealt with the possibility of restricting television news to *Tele Liban*.[20] Press reports suggested that both the president and the prime minister called for an end to the chaos and lack of restraint in the operation of media institutions.

Several members of the Council of Ministers and numerous politicians issued statements criticizing the deliberations. The ambassadors of England, France, the United States, and the Vatican also made statements supporting freedom of the press.[21] One paper reported that an ambassador of a prominent country declared that suppressing news on television was a demand "forced on the government" from outside but that "freedom in Lebanon is a red line which may not be crossed without negatively affecting the country."[22]

A spokesman for the prime minister promptly denied that a decision was taken to restrict television news to *Tele Liban*.[23] The ministerial committee quickly addressed itself to the task of drafting proposals for legalizing the de facto stations. It recommended that, until a new law governing broadcasting in Lebanon is issued, the de facto stations be given annual leases, not licenses, on the available UHF channels.

Two years of indecision and delays lapsed before the Council of Ministers finally approved a draft law regulating the chaotic use of the broadcasting channels in Lebanon. The new law was adopted with minor modifications by the Lebanese parliament in November 1994.[24] The influence of the very active audio-visual lobby was clear in the amendments adopted by the parliament, notably abolishing the item limiting the time devoted to advertising. No time limit for airing advertisements exists under this law. Also under the terms of this law, *Tele Liban* was to be fully owned by the government and its exclusive television broadcasting right was to be revoked in return for granting it the right to broadcast on all the VHF channels and one UHF channel. No compensation by the de facto stations was granted to *Tele Liban*.

The law requires that establishing TV stations inside Lebanese territories or its national waters be subject to prior licensing (chapter 2, article five). The duration of the license is sixteen years, renewable (chapter 5, article twenty-six). Licenses are granted by a government decree after consulting a new council established by this law, "the National Council of Audio Visual Media" (National Council). This council has the power to recommend the suspension or closure of stations. It consists of ten members appointed jointly by the government and parliament (chapter five, article seventeen).

The law classifies television stations according to the following:

First Category: TV stations that transmit visual programs, including news and political programs, covering all the Lebanese territory.

Second Category: TV stations that transmit visual programs, except news and political programs, covering all the Lebanese territory.

Third Category: TV stations that transmit coded signals that can be received only by subscribers who possess the necessary technical equipment.

Fourth Category: International TV stations that transmit via satellite and whose coverage goes beyond the Lebanese territory (chapter three, article ten).

According to the new law, granting a broadcasting license requires, among other things, obtaining approved technical transmission standards, meeting the necessary operational standards in terms of human and physical resources, and presenting evidence of ability to sustain expenses for at least the first year of licensing. The law, furthermore, compels the station to broadcast a volume of local production that is fixed by the "terms of conditions" of broadcasting in Lebanon (chapter two, article seven)

The law provides for a technical committee, "The TV and Radio Transmission Organization Committee," to draw up the "terms of conditions" for broadcasting and to study all the technical broadcasting aspects and submit recommendations to the minister of information (chapter two, article eight).

Furthermore, the law limits granting radio and television licenses to Lebanese citizens or companies. The number of licenses is also limited to one for individual companies or persons. It does not allow "for a person or entity to own directly or indirectly more than ten percent of the total company shares. The husband or wife and all direct relatives are considered to be one person or entity" (chapter four, article thirteen).

Under the terms of the audio-visual law, broadcasting stations are not allowed to operate at a financial deficit for a prolonged period. The licensed station has to submit to the Ministry of Information a statement of its accounts. The technical committee entrusted to draw the "terms of conditions" for the operation of TV stations proposed a number of meaningful technical and environmental requirements but failed to require the quality and quantity of local programs essential for a country that is flooded with canned programs. The "terms of conditions" sets the required local programs to 16.6 percent of the total aired programs. It requires only half an hour of weekly transmission of local educational programs and another weekly half an hour for rural and agricultural programs.[25]

The new law was faced with immense public debate. Again the influence of the very active audio-visual lobby was clear in the press campaigns and statements by politicians warning against "the dangers to freedom in Lebanon." Clearly, owners of the de facto stations and the political opposition were afraid of the way licenses will be granted. They were correct in their fear. In September 1996, the government granted licenses to four television stations other than *Tele Liban*. The four belonged to members of the government or their relatives, maintaining the sensitive religious sectarian balance that is of paramount importance in Lebanese politics.

The stations that received licenses were the following: *The Lebanese Broadcasting Company International* (LBCI, formerly LBC), which represents the Maronite Christians and whose shareholders included prominent members of the government; *Future Television*, representing the Sunni Moslems and owned by the then-prime minister; *Murr Television* (MTV), representing the Greek Orthodox Christians and owned by the family of the then-minister of Interior; and *The National Broadcasting Network* (NBN), representing the Shiite Moslems and owned by the family and supporters of the speaker of the House of Parliament.[26]

The government decision created a public uproar because it was based more on political and sectarian rather than professional grounds.[27] Stations that were not licensed refused to stop broadcasting. The government used both threats and promises to implement its decision. In some instances, it used force to close some stations; in others, it allowed some to appeal the decision. Only one additional television station, *al-Manar*, the organ of the Islamic Hizbollah Party, which started broadcasting in June 1991 and spoke for the resistance against the occupation of South Lebanon, received a license—in July 1996.[28] However, a Christian religious station, *Tele Lumiere*, continues to broadcast without a license but with tacit government approval.

This implicit consent by the government encouraged the Moslem religious authorities to begin experimental broadcasts for the *Holy Koran TV*, and a number of other religious stations asked for similar treatment but no official action was taken. Because religious authorities are very powerful in Lebanon, the Council of Ministers decided to provide the opportunity for the different religious communities to air their religious programs through a special channel to be made available to them by the government-owned *Tele Liban*. Until this channel is made available, the authorities keep silent about the de facto (illegal) operation of these stations. In a newspaper interview, the Lebanese

Minister of Information declared that the government expects the programs aired by the religious stations to be in agreement with the Lebanese basic positions and with the constitution of the country in a way that will strengthen common citizenship and the service of the nation.[29]

An opponent of the previous regime, Salim el Hoss, headed the Lebanese Council of Ministers when a new president, Emile Lahoud, took office. The new government reconsidered the applications rejected by the previous regime and, consequently, granted three more licenses. Interestingly, the stations receiving the new licenses were ones that had opposed the former prime minister, Rafik Hariri. These stations and their licensing dates are as follows: the *New Television* (NTV), June 1999; *The Independent Communication Channel International* (ICNI), September 1999; and *United Television* (UTV), also September 1999.

As previously stated, newspaper readership is not widely spread in Lebanon and the Arab world in general, but radio and television are available in almost every household in Lebanese urban areas.[30] Television reception includes not only Lebanese local channels but also cable, which is widely spread in the major Lebanese cities.

DEVELOPMENT OF SATELLITE BROADCASTING

The early 1990s witnessed the accelerating spread of satellite broadcasting in the Arab world. Lebanon was no exception. Satellite reception dishes became among the fastest-selling commodities in Lebanon and the Arab Gulf countries. At least 400 to 450 unlicensed satellite television distribution companies are presently supplying satellite subscription to some 250,000 households. December 1998 statistics by *Ipsos-Stat*, a media research company, suggest that 58.2 percent of all Lebanese households had cable subscription to satellite stations.[31] The cable operators usually subscribe to the different satellite systems, such as ORBIT, or they install reception dishes and then distribute the signals they get through a cable system (or they do both).

The major cry against the illegal operators comes from the local television stations that are losing a major share of their audiences to the cable system. The satellite stations are not very concerned about this phenomenon because the Lebanese market is very small and they wouldn't get all the present subscribers now watching them to actually pay the high fees for a smaller selection of stations. They are, however, considering raising their subscription fees paid by the operators.

Lebanese businessmen and television stations saw an excellent profit potential in this new development of satellite broadcasting. Two stations ventured into this field even before becoming officially licensed. They were LBCI and Future Television, who established LBCSAT and Future International SAT, respectively. Both satellite programs were ranked among the leading satellite programs in the Arab Gulf countries, which are an important source of advertising income for the programs.[32]

Founded in February 1993, Future Television started in October 1994 as a trial satellite broadcast over the footprint of Arabsat 1D. The testing period lasted two months. It was then launched on Arabsat 2A. Future International Television has five-meter and seven-meter dishes installed in its Beirut and Sidon sites. An additional thirteen-meter dish was later installed in the government earth station in *Jouret el Ballout* as a redundant uplink facility. Future International TV covers the Middle East, North Africa, and Southern Europe. It does not currently reach the American continent, Australia, or the Far East. Future International TV is not coded and is available on Arabsat 2A medium C-band, downlink frequency 3863.75 Mhz.

Realizing the commercial and professional importance of satellite broadcasting, LBCI plunged into this field in April 1996 when it established LBC-SAT, a free satellite channel. The channel has been broadcasting twenty-two hours a day since January 1997. Later in 1997, LBC launched three new encrypted channels: LBC Europe, LBC America, and LBC Australia. Today, LBC Europe is broadcasting sixteen hours a day while the two other channels broadcast around the clock. A number of recent audience studies indicate that LBCSAT has a leading position in Saudi Arabia and the Arab Gulf countries. LBCSAT programs are available on Arabsat 2A, 26 degrees east, C-band, downlink frequency 3740.75 Mhz.

Faced with the success of both Lebanese satellite stations, the government decided that the best way to respond was to have its own station, *Tele Liban*, get into satellite broadcasting. An official government decision was reached late in 1999, and *Tele Liban* began its satellite broadcast in the first week of March 2000. The TL satellite service is available simultaneously on ArabSat A3 and NileSat, covering the Arab world and part of Europe. However, it is now merely broadcasting its terrestrial programming via satellite, not special programs to satisfy Arab viewers or the Lebanese Diaspora. A fourth station, *al-Manar*, requested a license for satellite transmission. The government approved the request in April 2000 and the satellite service of *al-Manar* began a four-hour satellite on the eve of May 24, 2000, the day of the liberation of South Lebanon. After the Palestinian *"intifada"* broke out, on September 28, 2000, *al-Manar* increased its satellite broadcasting to eighteen hours per day.

The success of Lebanese satellite stations encouraged two other stations to get into this field. MTV began its satellite service in November 2000, on the eve of its ninth anniversary, and New TV, which was expected to go on the air in December 2000, announced that it will also start its satellite service. Technical and financial difficulties, however, delayed the implementation of this plan. New TV has already embarked on a six-hour experimental broadcast, but no announcement has been made as to the new date of regular operation.

Satellite broadcasting in Lebanon faced a number of obstacles at the beginning, during the regime of President Hrawi and Prime Minister Hariri. The first obstacle was to get government clearance to get a satellite connection. The second and more serious one was for the stations to secure the right to broadcast news. At the beginning, the Hariri government did not permit both stations to transmit news on their satellite channels. The argument by the government was that Lebanese news programs might negatively affect Lebanon's relations with some Arab countries inasmuch as these countries may not tolerate the freedom enjoyed by the Lebanese media.

LBCI challenged the ban and continued airing its satellite news program. The Hariri government reacted, late in December 1996, by deciding to censor "all news as well as direct and indirect political programs prepared for satellite broadcasting." A special "censorship team" was named that included a number of well-respected journalists. Again, LBCI challenged the decision and sought a ruling from the state's judiciary advisory council. The council supported LBCI; consequently, the Lebanese satellite channels won another battle.

CONCLUSION

The main problem facing broadcasting in Lebanon today is not that of government meddling, for this interference is carried out within the "rules of the game" of Lebanese politics. It is primarily one of both the government and media institutions lacking the adequate structures and professionalism that would provide the opportunity for this medium to contribute to its society's unity and cohesion as well as to address issues that are relevant to the everyday life of the average citizen. Instead, this medium gives predominate attention to commercialism at the expense of professionalism and social responsibility. Lebanese television officials, as do the majority of their Arab colleagues, view the television medium essentially as one for passing time, thus we find that about half of the programming on *Tele Liban*, for example, is of the entertainment type.[33] Additionally, their news programs focus mainly on news of politicians, with little reflective coverage of issues that concern the general public.[34] Examining the content of television programs gives one the impression that television officials believe that their viewers will accept whatever is given to them. Therefore, television officials see no need to make more effort to provide viewers with content about issues concerning their livelihood or that relate to their culture, social norms, and values.

Lebanese television broadcasting and the Lebanese media in general lack both professionalism and civic commitment. They are in urgent need of reorganization in order to cope with their expected role in the reconstruction of a country that has suffered from a long and costly civil war. Television and the Lebanese mass media have succeeded in achieving a high level of freedom of expression but have chosen to focus on presenting the disorienting views of the different political, sectarian, and ethnic groups. The media have failed to bridge the gap between these different groups and consequently have been unable to bring about national accord. Without such accord, no society can move toward real democracy and genuine development.

The Lebanese media have failed to promote an informed civil society that can rebuild a just society and an enlightened citizenry. After a long civil war that is still alive in the messages of many media institutions, Lebanese television as well as the other mass media have failed to reexamine their role in a changing society and changing living conditions. They missed the opportunity to serve as a genuine channel of communication between the citizens and the government, and among the different citizen groups within the society. They failed to serve as an objective and responsible watchdog to protect the average citizen from abuses of political institutions as well as from public and private interests.

The problem of the Lebanese media today does not lie in the lack of a proper climate conducive to freedom of expression. It lies in a wrong outlook by the media people concerning this freedom, an outlook that gives primary importance to private interests and lacks social responsibility. The real danger to the freedom of the press is that the Lebanese media spend more time avoiding information that does not agree with their gatekeepers than they spend objectively seeking information about public issues of real concern to the citizen.

It is no longer acceptable for the media to use the principle of "freedom of expression" to justify securing a special status allowing them to be above the social order. Democratic codes, including the declaration of human rights, encourage the media to be a tool for the service of the citizen and not the contrary. The citizen in Lebanon has become the target of influence by the media instead of being the focus of attention, with his or her best interests providing the main factor determining news and program selection.

Democracy requires openness to the citizens first, before the authorities, be they political or financial. It also requires the active participation of the average citizen in the public debates on matters that concern his or her welfare. The mere guarantee of the freedom of expression to the media does not *ipso facto* guarantee the ability of all groups to express their views. This ability can be realized only by guaranteeing media diversity.

To claim that "the media only reflects society" is not precise. The media select what they communicate and thus they set the agenda of what the people can think about or discuss. To achieve true democracy, the media need to be beside the citizen. The citizen in Lebanon is permitted merely to play the role of a bystander or spectator while the role of the media charger is confined to politicians as well as to finance or business groups. The basic mission of the media should be to serve the citizens, not those in power, be they politicians or business or finance groups.

The Lebanese media do not lack freedom of expression as much as they lack the proper ethical and professional structures that are needed to bring about a climate of dialog between the divergent groups in the society, and between these groups and the government. Perhaps this is mainly due to the inability of the Lebanese media to maintain their own independent financial resources; consequently, they have failed to achieve their financial viability.

Protecting the freedom of expression by the media does not necessarily safeguard the rights of the individual and promote public interest. The freedom of the media can only be guaranteed inasmuch as this freedom secures the right of the individual to receive accurate information about public issues as well as provide her or him with the opportunity to be an active and enlightened citizen.

Finally, the Lebanese media urgently need to reevaluate their role in society and to reject the domination of private interests as well as abandon their sectarian-tribal political course of operation.

NOTES

1. See, for example, Douglas Boyd, "Lebanese Broadcasting: Unofficial Electronic Media During a Prolonged Civil War," *Journal of Broadcasting and Electronic Media* (35:3, 1991); Donald Browne, "Television as an Instrument of National Stabilization," *Journalism Quarterly*, 52 (1975), 692–698; and Dajani, Nabil, *Disoriented Media in a Fragmented Society: the Lebanese Experience* (Beirut: American University Press, 1992) and *Lebanon: Studies in Broadcasting* (London: International Institute of Communication, 1979).
2. See, for example, Douglas Boyd, *Broadcasting in the Arab World* (Ames: Iowa State University Press, 1999) and William Rugh, *The Arab Press* (Syracuse: Syracuse University Press, 1979).
3. "TV networks prepare to wipe out satellite pirates," *The Daily Star* newspaper, February 25, 1999, 2.
4. For an understanding of Lebanon's sociopolitical structure, see, for example, Leonard Binder, *Politics in Lebanon* (New York: John Wiley and Sons, 1966); Carole Dagher, *Bring Down the Walls: Lebanon's Postwar Challenge* (New York: St. Martins Press, 2000); Nazih Richani, *Dilemmas of Democracy and Political Parties in Sectarian Societies*, (New York: St. Martins Press, 1998); and Kamal Salibi, *A House with Many Mansions: The History of Lebanon Reconsidered*, (London: I.B. Tauris, 1988).
5. See also Marwan Kraidy, "State Control of Television News in 1990s Lebanon," *Journalism and Mass Communication Quarterly*, 76(3) (1999) 485–498. Michael Johnson in "Political Bosses and Their Gangs: Zu'ama and Qabadayat in the Sunni Quarters of Beirut," in Ernest Gellner and John Waterbury (eds.), *Patrons and Clients in Mediterranean Societies*, (London: Duckworth, 1977), suggests that governments in Lebanon are run by a coalition of political bosses (zu'ama) who are assisted by tough guys (quabadayat). When the law is in conflict with the interest of these zu'ama, it is superseded.
6. Such accusations were voiced among others, at different occasions, by former President Elias Hrawi, Prime Minister Rafik Hariri, and Minister Walid Jumblat, all when they were in office.
7. No union or code of ethics exists for television in Lebanon, although the most recent legis-

lation moved in the direction of creating a board that may facilitate developing such a code of ethics.

8. The first noncommercial television station in the Arab world is the Iraqi government television station in Baghdad, which was established in 1957.

9. At the time, the ministry was named Ministry of Guidance and News.

10. Samir Makdisi, "An Appraisal of Lebanon's Post War Economic Development and a Look to the Future," *The Middle East Journal* (Summer 1977), 267–80.

11. Legislative decree number 770.

12. Early agreements required that the television stations accept, and even provide offices on their premises for, two government censors: one representing the Ministry of Interior (who would censor imported programs), the other representing the Ministry of Information (who would censor local programs).

13. The personnel of *Tele Liban* staged a number of unsuccessful general strikes.

14. A person who kills a female member of the family for losing her virginity outside wedlock or otherwise tarnishing "the family honor" receives a reduced sentence in Lebanon.

15. For an account of television programs in Lebanon, see Nabil Dajani, "An Analysis of the Press in Four Arab Countries," in *The Vigilant Press*, (Paris: UNESCO Reports and Papers on Mass Communication, No. 103, 1989), 75–88, and Dajani, *Disoriented Media in a Fragmented Society* (Beirut: American University Press, 1992), 114–119 and 132–140.

16. "Ministry of Transportation's study on audiovisual channels," *an-Nahar* newspaper, Tuesday, 23 January 23 1996, 5.

17. "Minister Mansour presents his plan for reorganizing the audiovisual media," *an-Nahar* newspaper, 9 August 1991, 3.

18. *an-Nahar*, ibid. 9 August 1991, 3.

19. "The story of the decree that raised a storm: How it was, how it became, and how it was issued," *as-Safir* newspaper, 15 January 1992, 3.

20. "Is the Press facing a new battle for its freedom?" *an-Nahar*, 21 January 1992, 3, and "A dangerous proposal." *as-Safir*, 11 January 1992, 3.

21. "Opposing and supporting positions towards the reorganization of the media," *as-Safir*, 11 January 1992, 2.

22. "The issue of information raises more than one question," *as-Safir*, 13 January 1992, 3.

23. The government did not keep this promise. In March 1994, it restricted broadcasting political news to *Tele Liban*. The parliament, however, voted to remove this ban a few months later.

24. *Official Gazette*, Law No 382, special supplement to issue No.45, 10 November 1994.

25. "Terms of Conditions for Licensing Television Broadcasting," Chapter 5, general rules. See also "Terms of conditions for licensing television broadcasting", *an-Nahar* newspaper, 2 February 1996, 6, and "Terms of conditions for licensing political and non-political television broadcasting," *al-Liwa* newspaper, 5 February 1996, 3.

26. *Official Gazette*, No.47, 16 September 1996, 3315–3319.

27. See "The information scandal shows, with detailed names, that the freedom of the Lebanese is in the hands of the politicians," *ad-Diyar* newspaper, 5 October 1996, 1.

28. *Al-Manar*'s Web site describes its mission as follows: "Lebanese TV channels have been overwhelmed by a trend of movies and programs that can only be described as immoral. At the time when the Lebanese—such as any people coming out of a devastating war—needed what could erase the effects of that conflict and work on building the personality of good citizenship, numerous TV channels have been broadcasting programs that would decay one's ethics and provoke his or her instincts in addition to instigating violence and identifying with western living patterns which are quite remote from our Islamic and Eastern values and culture...," http//www.almanar.com.lb

29. *As-Safir* newspaper, 6 March 2000.

30. Findings of a study in progress by the author of the media habits among two groups (polit-

ical elites and workers) in the capital of Lebanon, Beirut, show that all the elite members have television sets and 98 percent of the workers have at least one television set.

31. "TV networks prepare to wipe out satellite pirates," *The Daily Star* newspaper, 25 February 1999, 2. Findings of the study in progress by the author show that 90 percent of the Lebanese elites have cable access, compared to 44 percent of the workers.

32. According to surveys conducted by the Pan Arab Research Center (PARC) during the period December 96–January 97, and by the Middle East Research and Consultancy (MERC) during the period March–April, 1997.

33. See Dajani, *Disoriented Media in a Fragmented Society*, 132.

34. See Nabil Dajani, "Managing the crisis of public services in West Beirut," in Beyhum, Nabil, *Reconstruire Beyrouth* (Paris: Etudes Sur LeMonde Arabe No.5, 1991); 195–208, and Dajani, *The Vigilant Press*, (Paris: UNESCO Reports and Papers on Mass Communication, No. 103, 1989) 75–88.

Chapter twelve

Press Freedom and the Crisis of Ethical Journalism in Southern Africa

by Regina Jere-Malanda
Associate Editor, *New African* magazine
London, England

Since the dawn of democracy in Southern African states in the 1990s, concern for the ethical practices and conduct among journalists has been growing. The feeling is widespread that the media's watchdog role in the fledgling democracies of the region is being undermined by the unprofessional behavior of journalists.

To understand the current state of journalism in Southern Africa, going beyond polemics about press freedom is important. I want to focus on what journalists themselves are doing to harm the hard-won and still-fragile freedoms that they now enjoy, and the resulting loss of faith in the public they aim to serve.

The terms "media" and "the press" are used interchangeably in this chapter, and they refer to the print media, both private and official. I use the term "independent" with reservations in reference to the media and thus employ quotation marks. This essay does not take into account broadcast journalism, which functions on a very different terrain in Africa and has its own complicated muddle.

A Nigerian journalist once summed up media practice in emerging democracies in these terms: fiction is news; prejudice is patriotism; recklessness is courage; fabricated stories are investigative journalism; bias is balance; the headline is the story; personal opinion is objective analysis; incompetence is professionalism.

He was referring to the West African media, but he could just as easily have been describing the media of Southern Africa over the past decade. We African journalists have either sadly misinterpreted or have yet to grasp what press free-dom is and what its role in a democracy should be.

According to the Media Institute for Southern Africa (MISA), which mon-itors the region's media environment, media ethics violations in Southern Africa have never been higher. Why? Could this increase be simply a reflection of a more open society? Does it mean that we now have a vibrant and active free press and thus more transgressions against good conduct? Before the 1990s, many cases of media oppression went unreported because the victims feared retribution if they talked about it. We knew to keep our ordeals to our-selves because that way was safer.

Today, plenty of cases of media harassment still occur. However, we also en-counter many cases of journalists themselves crossing beyond the perimeters of good conduct.

My idea of good journalism as it pertains to Africa is that which provides readers with relevant information in the most responsible and ethical manner possible, as opposed to the confrontational, conflict-fueling, insulting slurs and the dull official propaganda that has inundated us in recent years.

What are the factors that determine the character of the Southern African press today? The list would have to include the legacy of history—colonialism, apartheid, dictatorships—as well as cultural traits, poverty and other economic pressures, poor salaries, and working conditions. Add to these factors the nag-ging questions about journalistic education and training as well as the grow-ing impact of global media, particularly Western media.

Professor Francis Kasoma of the University of Zambia contends that it is time our journalists practice what he calls "Afriethics." He says that African journalists work under conditions and in a cultural setting unique to them, and from these they must develop their own sense of principled behavior and ethics.

THE JOURNEY THUS FAR

With the ushering in of democracy in the 1990s, Southern Africa saw the un-precedented birth of hundreds of private or "independent" newspapers.

Southern African governments today, in theory, endorse the principles of freedom of assembly and expression and claim support for the privatization of the media. In nearly all countries in the region, the media industry indeed has been liberalized, and anyone is free to set up a new publication or radio sta-tion if the financing is available. With the exception of South Africa, however, the governments of the region still hold a tight rein on mainstream newspa-pers, radio, and television.

In Zambia, for instance, the press is polarized into two opposing camps: the official, such as the *Times of Zambia* and *Daily Mail*; and the private, such as *The Post* and *The Monitor*. While the official press serves as a mouthpiece for government, the private press provides its own opposition propaganda. Within months of democratization in 1991, a number of privately owned newspapers hit the newsstands, including the *Weekly Post* (now *The Post*), *The Daily* and *Sunday Express, The Eagle, The Herald, The Sun*, and *The Weekly Standard*. But today, apart from *The Post* and *The Monitor*, most of the new papers have folded, disappearing as quickly as they came into being. Among the survivors, partisan journalism reigns, and so does simplistic coverage of important issues. Zambian laws do not specifically guarantee press freedom, although it is inferred. The media still operate under many restrictive precolonial press laws that, for example, effectively give the President power to ban any publications and declare illegal "false reporting," insults against the President, sedition, and defamation. Journalists can also be imprisoned under the Parliamentary and Ministerial Code of Conduct Act. The situation is similar in other former British colonies in the region.

A discussion of media repression in Zambia must take into account the "independent" *The Post* newspaper and its managing editor, Fred Mmembe. *The Post* is not only Zambia's leading "independent" newspaper but also its most harassed, having faced more than 80 libel cases, with its staff members making some 200 court appearances. To its critics, *The Post* is a reckless, professionally irresponsible newspaper that is constantly fighting with authorities. To its supporters, it is a champion of clear thinking and free expression in contrast to an official press that slavishly propagates the ruling party line.

"When we consider our sense of purpose, most of us do think about the issue of responsibility," says Miriam Zimba, a senior reporter at the *Times of Zambia*. "We know the public expects us to highlight issues that directly affect them like education, health care, poverty, but the problem is the issue of 'he who pays the piper calling the tune.' The same applies to the independent media. Most of us know that journalists cannot operate effectively in an environment of poverty like ours."

Although both the official and the private press are guilty, it is usually the "independents" that bear the brunt of accusations for professional misbehavior. As one journalist at the *Times of Zambia* once put it: "If there is Pulitzer for fiction, the private press in Zambia deserve one. They know what they do best—gross distortions and misinformation."

In neighboring Malawi, the emergence of a multiparty democracy in 1994 was accompanied by the launching of nearly 30 newspapers where only two had existed before, both of them official and owned by the late dictator Kamuzu Banda. Yet the sudden abundance of journalistic activity soon raised concerns similar to those elsewhere in the region. This is the assessment of the Media Institute of Southern Africa (MISA): "There has been a deplorable attitude of most reporters and editors who refuse to stick to the ethics of the profession (and this) remains the biggest problem facing media development in Malawi. ... There is a lack of independent editorial judgment and policies, and the media struggles with extreme cases of ethical violations in the name of free press."

Unlike the Banda days when journalists were threatened with becoming food for crocodiles, the government of Bakili Muluzi has thus far refrained from imposing restraints on the press, and Muluzi claims he is a "friend of the press." He even "forgave" *The Democrat* newspaper for using an old picture of him in a prison uniform that dated back to the 1970s when he spent time behind bars on a theft conviction. The caption read: "Can you trust this man? Once a thief…!"

Botswana, which gained its independence in 1966, has enjoyed years of comparative economic and political stability as well as a relatively free press. Yet, according to MISA, "cohesion is the greatest challenge to media efficacy in the country." In the past decade, Botswana also saw a proliferation of private newspapers and magazines, but as in Malawi and elsewhere in the region, many failed financially and ceased to exist. Low managerial and financial skills are frequently cited as a cause of these failures.

In South Africa, the media history is as complex as its political history. Although the end of apartheid ushered in a unique new climate for freedom of expression, the media situation is confronted by new challenges. The issue of race continues to be a major theme in South Africa as both black and white journalists operate in a still white-dominated newspaper industry.

Soon after President Thabo Mbeki took over from Nelson Mandela, the ruling African National Congress (ANC) accused the country's mainstream private media of practicing "racist journalism" and complained about reports portraying black leaders as corrupt, antidemocratic, and dictatorial. The ANC gained support for these claims from both the general public and from other black leaders and journalists. The South African Communist Party (SACP), a close ally of the ANC, has angrily described the private (mainly white-owned) media as a "racial oligarchy serving the interest of wealthy whites."

The mainstream media has responded by saying that its critics ultimately are targeting free speech and press freedom in the new South Africa.

A report released by the South African Human Rights Commission (SAHRC) in February 2000 concluded that indeed the South African media is a "racist institution" and recommended more diversity in media ownership and better training for journalists in so-called racism-awareness sessions.

In Zimbabwe, the government of Robert Mugabe has earned a reputation of being one of the region's worst enemies of free speech, a situation aggravated in the ongoing debate over minority white ownership of vast tracts of land in the country and Zimbabwe's involvement in the war in the Democratic Republic of Congo. Mugabe and other critics have charged Zimbabwe's "independent" press with lacking patriotism and with holding on to colonial-era attitudes and ways. The arrest and torture of journalists Mark Chavunduka and

Ray Choto in 1999 proved the pressures that the media face in Zimbabwe. Chavunduka and Choto, both from the "independent" *Standard* newspaper, were arrested under the 1960 Law and Order Maintenance Act for publishing "false news" that was "likely to cause alarm, fear, or despondency" in the country. The "false news" referred to was a story by Choto in which he quoted unnamed South African intelligence sources saying that a military coup against Mugabe had been quashed and that 23 army officers had been arrested. The story of the two journalists' ordeal received widespread attention—the two became international press freedom heroes—and Zimbabwe's Supreme Court acquitted them on a constitutional technicality.

In Namibia, where celebrations marking a decade of press freedom in Africa took place on World Press Freedom Day on May 3, 2001, the media is also relatively free, but journalists working for official newspapers practice a high degree of self-censorship to protect their jobs and earn promotion. Of course, this is also true in Zambia, Botswana, Swaziland, Malawi, and Zimbabwe. The country's largest and most popular "independent" daily is the *Namibian*, which despite sporadic skirmishes with officials operates with relative freedom.

THE NEED FOR JOURNALISTIC RESPONSIBILITY

As a journalist who has worked for both African and Western international media, and taking into account our limitations as well as our values and inspirations, I am inclined to add some personal commentary on how "reporting Africa" the way we do affects ordinary citizens as well as our nations as a whole.

I have always argued for a free press in which journalists will report facts sensibly, accurately, and objectively as best as they can, even under the most difficult circumstances. I espouse the belief that freedom of expression is inseparable from truth telling and that our calling and ethical obligation are to facilitate peace, accountability, and social harmony in the society we serve. This is why I passionately agree with John Whitney, who as chairman of the *International Herald Tribune* in 1958 said that a newspaper has to be a force for good, reason, and understanding in its community. He said that newspapers must be devoted to truth and conscience, the obligation of freedom.

This is a challenge to all of us African journalists today.

Let me also cite the words of former Director-General of UNESCO, Amadou-Mahtar M'Bow, as quoted by the World Press Freedom Committee: "Freedom and irresponsibility are incompatible because history has shown that when freedom neglects values on which society's implicit consensus is built, anarchy begins to spread and conflicts loom, and from that moment, the reign of freedom starts to wane and intolerance takes over."

And here is the advice Pope John Paul II gave journalists while on a trip to

Nigeria: "Here you are at the initial stages of the development of your mass media, while the more industrialized countries have already reached a high level of development in this sector. This situation increases your responsibility while giving you a unique opportunity. Through actions, your professional honesty, and dedication to the cause of truth, you can make a decisive contribution to this continent. By orienting the mass media properly to the service of man and in favor of objective information, Africa can determine its own future development."

ZAMBIA AND *THE POST*

Fred Mmembe of the "independent" daily, *The Post*, has often spent more time in court defending himself against libel charges than in his own newsroom. In March 1999, Mmembe and his entire editorial staff were arrested and charged with espionage for a *Post* story that detailed Zambia's military deficiencies. They were later cleared of the charge by the Zambian high court. Mmembe makes it clear that he will never cringe at official intimidation in his work as a journalist and in his right to write what he calls his "wrong editorials."

"The intolerance of our leaders has torn many journalists between the pursuit of truth and their desire to be on good terms with the powerful," Mmembe, an accountant by profession, said in his speech in Namibia commemorating World Press Freedom Day. "Social climbing on the pyramids of power is the most important form of corruption in African journalism today. ... It makes us feel curiously shy about calling a lie a lie or twit a twit. Press freedom is a farce if it means merely to report pleasant things.

"...I have written more than 200 editorials...they may all have been wrong, but that does not bother me much. What bothers me is the prospect of not being able to write another wrong editorial because those in government are going to legislate away my right to write wrong editorials."

As a bitter opponent of the ruling Movement for Multi-party Democracy (MMD), Mmembe has often been accused of taking on the role of an opposition party and of being a government in waiting. His response: "So what if we are political parties? Yes we are parties...parties for all political parties, parties for all people in their diversity and complexities."

Press Association of Zambia (PAZA) president Hicks Sikazwe, formerly news editor at the government-owned *Times of Zambia*, contends that whereas every journalist was happy when democracy brought in media diversity, the resulting high level of partisanship and lack of real objective reporting is hardly what people initially anticipated. "There is clearly a divide between the state and privately owned media, with each side taking a partisan line. The state media (are) more inclined to purveying government propaganda, while on the other hand privately owned outlets are more concerned with activities in opposition parties…. Thus the atmosphere has put our objectivity in question, and it has become difficult for readers, viewers, and listeners to contend with the two extremes."

With the government threatening to impose a legislated Media Council to oversee the press, the PAZA (which draws its members mainly from journalists who work in the state media) created in early 2001 the Media and Ethics Complaints Council (MECC) to monitor press ethics in the country. Journalists from privately owned media have their own Independent Media Council (IMC), which defends freedom of the media while ensuring high professional standards and adherence to the principles of responsible and factual reporting.

Despite such efforts, self-regulation remains elusive and difficult to implement in Zambia, and this is likely true in the entire subregion. This difficulty is particularly acute in the new generation of young journalists. The mere excitement of expressing oneself freely has enticed many untrained young newcomers into journalism. Sadly, many of them wrongly associate the profession with stardom and are more concerned with instant fame than with the legal and professional rules that go with good journalism.

ARE JOURNALISTS BEYOND CRITICISM?

The press in Southern Africa often has a thin skin. Criticizing the media is popularly interpreted as an attack on press freedom. Those journalists who condemn unethical conduct are branded cowards or government sympathizers.

Malawian journalist Sunday Mkandawire has told how a call for a responsible and ethical press in his country is usually condemned as an attack on press freedom. The 1994 democratization in Malawi saw the rise of such virulent partisanship that "no newspaper will accept charges of bias, or of irresponsible, unethical behavior," he said in a MISA newsletter that year. "Journalism has gone overboard and been replaced by uncivilized political propaganda from all sides. Is this really the press freedom we are yearning for?"

Mkandawire said the press "is not an exclusive property of the media alone but for all citizens in whichever country." And he disputed the notion that unprofessional conduct is due to lack of professional training. "Some of the worst culprits in Malawi are the most experienced journalists the country has ever produced and have been in the business for years."

SOUTH AFRICA AND THE RACE CARD

When in September 2000, after months of investigating the country's media environment, the South African Human Rights Commission (SHRC) declared that "subliminal racism" permeated the country's predominantly white-owned press, the news did not come as a shock. The country's history of apartheid was too recent. But the declaration cut deep wounds in the South African media anyway. Newspaper editors responded angrily and declared that press freedom was under attack, but many South Africans agreed that the post-apartheid press has been used to fuel anxieties among whites about their future in a South Africa under black leadership.

Black South African author and journalist Njabulo Ndebele, in a hard-hitting article published in the *Index on Censorship* journal in February 2000, questioned the fairness of the South African media in its coverage of the black-led government. He said the *Mail and Guardian* newspaper in particular "persistently show(s) disdain to the new black-dominated government, by giving constant biased reporting, slander by innuendo, unsubstantiated allegations of corruption and incompetence, unprofessional annual ratings of government ministers and attacks on reputations of black public figures."

The *Mail and Guardian* and other newspapers responded that such allegations are a veiled-but-orchestrated attack on press freedom by the Mbeki government.

"The mandate of journalism in South African urgently needs revision," Ndebele contended. "Public confidence needs to be restored in a sector that has a responsibility to project more complex images to our society. We need a press that is trustworthy; that deepens public knowledge, enriches social insight, nurtures a vigorous and courageous atmosphere of public discussion and, above all, respects its public."

This type of press will not be easy to achieve. A recent example of the racially charged atmosphere in the country was an article in the Caxton Group-owned *Citizen* newspaper that claimed President Mbeki was a "womanizer." Frederik van Zyl Slabbert, chairman of the Caxton Group, later apologized. "The report (was) in extremely poor taste, politically irrelevant, and journalistically parasitical," he said. The ANC, in turn, charged the *Citizen* with returning to its former role as a propagandist for apartheid.

WESTERN MEDIA INFLUENCES AND AFRICAN SOLUTIONS

In African culture and tradition, taste, decency, and respect for elders are paramount and indispensable. African journalists are, after all, African and must take this into account as they practice their craft. The offensive language that is wantonly used in some sectors of the private press today is indeed offensive to the public. Derogatory and insulting language is viewed with contempt. Ironically, the growing use of it can be linked to the Western style of journalism that is preached as gospel throughout the continent. Many African journalists religiously believe that Western journalism is the best model for Africa.

As in other parts of the world, the rise of democratic institutions in Southern Africa over the past decade brought an influx of Western media "experts" resolutely determined to teach their style of good journalism. Kasoma has lamented that the aims and objectives of African media institutions thus have been modeled on those of the media in industrialized societies. Kasoma believes journalists in Africa should look to the continent's own rich customs in establishing the ethics of their profession. He believes it is important for journalists to practice ethical tenets that are intrinsic to their societies. Hence his term "Afriethics," deriving from the need he sees for Africanness in African journalism.

I know from my own experiences as an African correspondent for Western news agencies how the indigenous journalists are used to help reinforce the hackneyed image of a self-destructive, conflict-prone, violent and ravaged Africa that is beyond redemption. This is the "African news" that will sell, and correspondents, indigenous ones included, will cross all ethical boundaries to obtain "the story that sells," even where the story does not exist. At the end of the day, the African-born correspondent, paid in foreign currency, knows he will be financially better off than his local colleagues, and given economic circumstances, this monetary "gain" outweighs any potential negative effects from "the story that sells."

Although many positive things can be gleaned from Western journalism training and textbooks, I dispute the belief that good journalism in Africa must be modeled on the West. In the past decade, many African journalists have interpreted this Western model to mean that a completely adversarial role is necessary—to a point that negates questions of national interests and security. These journalists, in their enthusiasm for press freedom, sometimes see themselves as above the law. They ignorantly believe that the Western media operates without rules and laws and the same should apply to Africa.

As *New African* magazine editor Baffour Ankomah puts it, "The notion that the Western media is free to publish whatever they want is the biggest hogwash to be found this side of heaven. In reality countries like Britain have rings of laws around the media that keep them in check…but British journalist are able to operate (freely) because they obey the rules. We do not. In Africa the journalism training we receive tends to encourage us to disobey the rules. There lies the problem."

As an example, Ankomah cites the so-called "D-Notice Committee" in England, which was established in 1912 as a supposedly voluntary system of self-censorship whereby editors agree not to publish information on subjects relating to defense and the activities of security and intelligence agencies. National interests and security are taken seriously in the Western media and journalists respect the rules that protect them. Many African journalists don't. In Britain, the editor makes sure that his journalists are aware of the more than 40 defamation laws, Official Secrets acts, the D-notice, the Data Protection

Act, and Contempt of Court and Libel acts that potentially affect the journalists' work. This is not the case in African journalism, in which an alarming ignorance of media laws is all too evident.

In conclusion, journalists in Southern Africa have yet to clearly define what they really mean by press freedom and, despite a decade of democracy, many still don't have a real sense of professionalism. Too many use their work as journalists to engage in highly personal and over-dramatized clashes with political opponents and to settle scores with past and current enemies.

Journalism is not politics, but in Africa the two are too often crowded into the same cage. We African journalists need to redefine our sense of purpose if we are to enjoy the real fruits of true press freedom.

Our hard-won freedoms as citizens need to be accompanied by a strong sense of responsibility, and it is not too much to ask that both the official and private media strive to achieve higher standards of practice, to avoid malpractice, and to make the journalist's role a truly vital one in our emerging democracies.

Chapter thirteen

Nigerian Press Ethics and the Politics of Pluralism

by Minabere Ibelema
Assistant Professor of Communication Studies
University of Alabama-Birmingham

Any analysis of press ethics in a non-Western country such as Nigeria has to grapple with the question of whether ethics are universal or relative. I therefore note at the outset that this essay is premised on three contentions:

1. Some ethical values are universal and some vary by time and place.
2. Universal ethical values are ideals for which the potential for full attainment varies, depending on material circumstances.
3. Like all principles, ethical values sometimes conflict with one another, requiring judgment as to which should be given primacy. Such judgments vary from culture to culture and, within the same culture, from situation to situation.

To illustrate the first contention, truth as what has been called a protonorm is a universal value in journalism, as is the commitment to fairness and justice.[1] The quest for truth may be said to be inherent in every culture. No society values lies, per se, although differences may exist in how societies prefer to tell the truth. A tactful and respectful expression of the truth might be preferable to the abrasive and abusive style, for instance.[2] Yet, both approaches can reflect a commitment to the truth. Journalists anywhere who engage in overt propaganda, distortion, and outright lies have to be fully aware that they are engaging in nefarious activities even if they justify them on the basis of necessity or commitment. Despots, too, want to know the truth, though they may not want their subjects to know the same. The emperors who didn't want to be told that they had no clothes are extinct (or soon will be). Thus, failure to report the truth is, per se, an ethical breach in every society, provided that this principle does not conflict with another, as suggested in the third contention listed previously. How that truth is expressed, however, and, for that matter, how it was obtained and for what purpose, are relative ethical matters and the standards vary.[3] Similarly, objectivity is a relative concept, as is the extent to which the press maintains an adversarial or collaborative relationship with the government. It has been argued that in traditional African communications, facts and opinion are proffered in tandem,[4] a case that can also be made for traditional communications everywhere. This argument raises ethical questions that can be answered only in context. Even within the U.S. news media, the standards vary. Television news, especially of the local variety, for instance, is typically delivered in editorial and emotional wrappings. And news magazines, more so than newspapers, offer analyses that combine news and commentary. These practices violate universal ethical standards only when they infringe on the truth or other universal principles such as fairness. Some have argued, for instance, that the Nigerian news media should take an Afrocentric approach to news framing rather than reflect the Eurocentric values inculcated through Western training.[5] Given that news frames are essentially ideological, such an approach should be regarded as ethical within the community if the results approximate the truth.

It has also been argued that Western standards of journalism are at odds with African countries' commitment to development journalism, a concept in which journalism is expected to aid a nation's economic, political, and social development.[6] Here again, however, one can make a distinction between the universal and culture-specific. Were one to conceive of development journalism as that which uncritically disseminates government information and, for the most part, desists from unfavorable analysis of government performance, this argument would be true. But theorists of development journalism have consistently rejected this conception as inconsistent with its goal of disseminating all substantive information and ideas that help move the society forward.[7] This approach does not de-emphasize critical reporting or commentary but does de-emphasize the trivial and scintillating. This implicit commitment to the truth and public welfare is a universal principle though its coloration in practice will vary. Studies have shown that journalists who are constrained from engaging in honest reportage and analysis are typically aware of the shortcoming of their practices, irrespective of the society and culture.[8] A study of Nigerian journalists, for instance, shows that those at government-owned newspapers were fully aware of such ethics even though they sometimes violated them to keep their jobs.[9]

This point leads to the second major contention regarding whether the attainment of universal ethical values. Even when a journalism ethic is universal, the degree to which it is reflected in practice in any press system falls short of the ideal and necessarily reflects the particular conditions and circumstances. A study of Australian journalists, for instance, concludes that "the commitment of these journalists...is, however, highly idealized; what they do in practice does not always match the theory." [10] The same can be said of journalists anywhere on any ethical issue.

Even the capacity of the news media to report the truth depends on the facilities at their disposal to seek the truth. Journalists in developing countries, for instance, have far less capacity to obtain and verify information than those in developed countries. In Nigeria, despite a recent spurt in the growth of telephone lines, only a small percentage of the people can be reached by phone. And the major cities are congested with auto traffic, making transportation from one part of a city to another sometimes an all-day affair. The use of online technology has improved access to and transmission of information, but again its usefulness is limited by the marginal availability of these technologies to the general public and even in government offices. Inevitably, the propensity to publish unverified information in Nigerian mass media is higher than that in, say, the U.S. press. This, incidentally, is also true of the propensity of the broadcast or daily press in any country relative to its weekly press and periodicals.

Regarding the third contention, even the most noble principles sometimes come into conflict with others just as noble. For instance, the protection of life is a fundamental value in every society and other values tend to be subordinated to it. This principle by extension is applied to national security, the threat to which is greater or lesser depending on the overall security circumstance of a society. Therefore, journalists may ethically withhold even the truth when doing so serves the immediate end of protecting life or national security. To what degree such withholding may be ethical depends, of course, on the magnitude and imminence of the danger. And on this, well-meaning individuals disagree, as do people of different cultures. It should be noted in passing that governments, both democratic and despotic, exploit this reality to pressure journalists and, in some cases, to impose self-serving censorship and repression.

The analysis of the Nigerian press ethics that follows is guided by the foregoing conception of ethics. It should be evident that not much distinction is made here between journalism ethics and professional standards. As has been suggested even professional competence is an ethical issue.[11] As the title of this chapter suggests, it focuses on political pluralism as a major factor of Nigerian press practices and ethics. But other factors are also discussed, especially those related to economic and infrastructural development. These factors are now summarized, along with a general description of the Nigerian press.

THE NIGERIAN PRESS ENVIRONMENT

As a political entity, Nigeria is a British creation. Before British colonial incursion in the nineteenth century, the territory that is now Nigeria was made up of disparate ethnic and nationality groups, which constituted city states, kingdoms, emirates, empires, and loosely formed political entities, especially in the east central part of Nigeria. By the end of the century, the British had created what they called the Northern and Southern Protectorates. In 1914, both protectorates were amalgamated to establish Nigeria as a country. But the ethnic and regional groupings retained distinct political identities, which have since driven Nigerian politics and, in turn, its journalism.

Nigeria's early press was inspired by political advocacy, first as a crusader for the rights of Nigerians under colonialism, then for political independence, and then as the voice of partisan/sectional political causes after independence was within reach or attained. Thus, some of Nigeria's early political luminaries were also newspaper proprietors. The most notable were Herbert Macaulay, Nnamdi Azikiwe, and Obafemi Awolowo. Macaulay, who is credited as the father of Nigerian nationalism, was also a journalistic trailblazer who founded the *Daily News* as an organ of his National Democratic Party. Azikiwe, Nigeria's first indigenous president, established what may well be the first newspaper chain in black Africa. Awolowo, who became the premier of the then Western region of Nigeria and subsequently served in the federal cabinet, also established a newspaper chain, which propagated the cause of his Action Party.

Political divisions, from the federal government to the regional and more recently state governments, also own the news media. Until the 1990s, broadcasting was exclusively a prerogative of the federal and state governments. Private broadcasting only recently began to make an inroad, but the airwaves are still government dominated. (Some of the growing pains of the private broadcasters are noted later.) The federal government sponsors a national television network with local stations in the state capitals. Several state governments also have their own television stations, which typically broadcast from the state capitals. Radio broadcasting reflects a similar parallel structure. The Federal Radio Corporation of Nigeria (FRCN) reaches much of the country with broadcasts from regional stations, and most of the thirty-six states and the federal territory, Abuja, also operate theirs.

A major development in the Nigerian press landscape is the recent growth and dominance of independent newspapers and magazines. For the first time in Nigerian press history, the major publishing houses are not overtly affiliated with any political party, movement or government although their political sympathies are readily discernible if not transparent. These realities of Nigerian politics and media ownership are central to the emergence of Nigeria's brand of journalism and the related ethics.

Also significant is the country's economic situation. When Nigeria attained political independence from Britain in 1960, it was one of Africa's most promising countries in economic development. With a large population, enterprising people, and considerable natural resources, including crude oil, the country had high expectations from within, in Africa, and around the world. Then a catastrophic civil war broke out in 1967. Before it ended about thirty months later, approximately one million Nigerians had lost their lives.

With the end of the war in January 1970, Nigeria undertook a large-scale program of reconstruction. The program and the rise in crude oil revenues engendered an economic expansion that was unprecedented in sub-Saharan Africa. By the end of the 1970s, Nigeria was being classified as one of the elite nations among developing countries. However, the economic expansion, was short-lived. The collapse of crude oil prices in the 1980s threw the Nigerian economy into a downward vortex from which it is yet to recover. A long stretch of military government only compounded matters. The military took over power in 1966, just before the civil war, and kept it for about thirteen years. Barely four years after relinquishing the power to an elected government, the military seized power again. This time, it would govern the country until the mysterious death of the last dictator, General Sani Abacha, in 1998 cleared the way for another election in 1999.

During the second stretch of military government, Nigeria's economic situation worsened. The military government's repressive measures, including executions and imprisonment of political opponents, led to some formal sanctions and, worst of all, a bad international image. Nigeria, which used to be black Africa's flag-bearer in attracting international businesses and associations, came close to becoming an international pariah. These developments took their toll on the economy. Today, Nigeria ranks among the poorest countries by most human development indices compiled by the United Nations Human Development Programme. For instance, in 1999 it was ranked 146 out of 174 countries on the index of "information flows," which reflects the availability and use of telephone lines, television sets, fax machines, personal computers, Internet hosts and tourism.[12] The index included a 1995 telephone density of four per one thousand people, one of the lowest in the world.

The Nigerian press operates, and in recent years has expanded enormously, in this environment. These infrastructural realities are a major factor of the press's ethics, perhaps second only to Nigeria's history of pluralist and contentious politics.

POLITICS, ETHICS, AND THE TRUTH

As with the press in any country, the range of issues to discuss regarding Nigerian press ethics has no limit. As the examples in the introduction may have suggested, this chapter revolves around the ethic of telling the truth. This emphasis is chosen for two related reasons: to give this discussion a focus and because virtually every other ethical issue is directly or indirectly related to the question of truth. What is it, how should it be presented or expressed, when may it be suppressed, how should it be accessed? Accuracy, balance, objectivity, and issues of context are all about proper presentation of the truth. Resisting censorship and pressing for access to information are, in principle, means for attaining the truth. The following discussion focuses on how the Nigerian press has performed in these regards.

First, one should ask, who guards the truth in the Nigerian press? The Nigerian press is governed—and the term is used loosely here—by several professional organizations. Among them are the Nigerian Union of Journalists (NUJ), the Nigerian Guild of Editors (NGE), the Newspaper Proprietors Association of Nigeria (NPAN), the Nigerian Press Organisations (NPO)—a coalition of the NUJ, NGE, and NPAN—and the Independent Broadcasters' Association of Nigeria (IBAN), among others. These are all freely established associations that deal with issues related to the particular industry, make representations before governments, and sometimes lobby as groups. However, political differences exist within the organizations, often reflecting ethnic and regional allegiances. Some of the associations also include personnel or representatives from both government-owned and independent media, and that often makes difficult any agreement on issues and implementation of policies.

In 1978, the military government promulgated a decree establishing the Nigerian Press Council (NPC), an idea that was first recommended in 1968 by a government committee during Nigeria's civil war,[13] apparently in response to the instigating role the press played in precipitating that war. The council was inaugurated with a retired jurist as chairman and charged with improving journalism ethics in Nigeria. "Unfortunately, since its establishment, this Nigerian press council has remained non-functional, in spite of the fact that it has…an office in Lagos and some staff."[14] Several factors caused this version of the council to be stillborn. First, journalists condemned several clauses in the decree as too constraining to press freedom. Among these were the power of the council to register journalists, in effect, determining who was a journalist. Journalists also objected to the dominance of the council by non-journalists. Rather than cooperate with the council, the NPO established its own code of ethics the following year, reflecting the standards of the International Press Institute.[15] Moreover, the military handed over power to an elected government in 1979, making enforcement of the press council decree even less practical.

The NPC has been reconstituted several times since then. In 1988, about ten years after the first press council, another military government reconstituted the council by another decree. Though the NPO was consulted in formulation of the new NPC's policies, the government's role in its creation, continued objections to some of its regulatory powers, and the Nigerian press's tradition of free-wheeling journalism kept the new NPC still ineffectual.

It didn't help that crackdowns on the press during this repressive era were often preceded by public admonition of the press by the NPC. In some cases, the sequences of events might have been coincidental. In other instances, the military complained to the NPC fully expecting the council to issue a public statement against the press. Then it would use the NPC's statement to vindicate whatever actions it took. Such cynical machinations were all too common during this period of draconian rule. Though the NPC's admonitions were typically warranted, the impression that they were issued to justify subsequent military measures against journalists and press houses damaged whatever credibility the NPC had. Its directives and admonitions were therefore routinely ignored.

Tony Momoh, who served as the chair of NPC's Rights and Privileges Committee in the mid-1990s, often expressed exasperation with both the press and the government. As the former editor of the *Daily Times* and later Federal Minister of Information, he had experienced press-government relations from both sides. In his role with the NPC, he often excoriated the press for being irresponsible to an extent that would be intolerable anywhere. He also criticized the government for being heavy-handed in dealing with the press, including the proscription of responsible and respectable media houses whose only offense was stepping on the government's sensitive political toes.

A fresh attempt has been made since 1999 to reconstitute the council, but journalists continue to oppose several aspects of what appear to be regulatory requirements rather than voluntary codes. The Nigerian Guild of Editors, for instance, opposes aspects of a recently proposed code pertaining to registration and documentation of journalists. The guild demanded that "the inauguration of the (new) Press Council should be suspended until all contentious issues are resolved."[16]

The latest call for a code of ethics came from a senator, who complained that one of Nigeria's major dailies, *The Comet*, published false claims that he was scheming to bring down his successor as the Senate president. The story, which ran in the September 24, 2000 edition with the headline, "Okadigbo's group plots Anyim's ouster," prompted the Senate to vote unanimously to ask its Information Committee to develop a liaison with the NPC to establish a journalism code of ethics. The Senate may have actually intended to find an effective way to improve professionalism and ethics rather than to establish codes. For, in reality, ethical breaches have not resulted from the lack of codes of ethics but rather raise the question of how to improve adherence.[17]

In a speech delivered a few weeks before the inauguration of Nigeria's current democratic rule on May 29, 1999, Dan Agbese, the editor-in-chief of Nigeria's *Newswatch* magazine, described the Nigerian press's ethical responsibilities as follows:

The press should subject every decision to publish or not to publish to this adaptation of the famous four-way test:

- Is it fact?
- Is it fair to all parties concerned?
- Will it help to build a better society and promote good governance?
- Will it enhance the integrity of journalism?[18]

Before this, he had asserted that "the primary role of the press, above everything else should be the sustenance and the robust defense of democracy and the rule of law." As Agbese notes in the speech, the Nigerian press's performance has been checkered on all scores.

ASSERTING THE TRUTH

Babatunde Jose, the then chairman of the *Daily Times* publishing group, has been quoted as saying that "almost any editor of any important newspaper (in Nigeria), including those owned by the government, has seen the inside of a police cell or army orderly room."[19] This statement best reflects the Nigerian journalists' general tendency toward editorial independence. Such independence is, of course, necessary for an open discussion and the possibility of arriving at the truth of any matter. The tendency is enhanced by the country's pluralist politics, which impel journalists to take stands that reflect commitments to nationality or ethnic groups, regions, religions, ideologies and other factors.

Such commitment has ensured a robust press through the early years of Nigerian nationhood, when the press crusaded for the rights of natives vis-à-vis the colonialists. It galvanized the press during the nationalist crusade for independence, especially in the 1940s and 1950s. The press may have reached its peak in feistiness during the brief period of parliamentary democracy between 1960 and 1966, when virtually every news operation of note, except the *Daily Times* group, was tethered to a political party, government, or both. Laws to rein in the press were relatively ineffective, in part, because the news organizations had the backing of major political blocks, making any measures against them the equivalent of attacking a particular political constituency. Although the federal government had control of the police and armed forces, the four regional governments at the time were so powerful that any measures against them carried the threat of civil disorder.

Thus the press operated in what has been described as "cross-territorial exercise of press freedom," a situation in which the press of one region has little restraint in reporting and commenting on people and institutions of another.[20] As I discuss later, such journalistic practices have played havoc on the Nigerian polity, but the point here is that the political pluralism ensured a relatively unfettered flow of information—for better and for worse.

The Nigerian press continued the tradition of robustness through successive military governments, including especially that of General Sani Abacha from 1994 to 1998. Despite widespread arrests and imprisonment, extended proscriptions of newspapers and magazines, confiscation of issues, and attacks by security personnel and hired hands, the press continued to attack and question the policies of the military government and its very legitimacy. So thorough was the press in discrediting the military that when General Abacha died mysteriously in 1998, his successor rapidly instituted a transition to democracy and handed over to an elected government the following year.

It could be said then that, on the whole and in both historical and contemporary terms, the Nigerian press has upheld the ethic of free expression. In the process, many Nigerian journalists have paid dearly. Some were killed for their works, scores of others were imprisoned, and some went on self-imposed exile, especially during General Abacha's regime. One of the most dramatic instances of the supreme sacrifice occurred in 1986, when Dele Giwa, the editor-in-chief of *Newswatch*, one of Nigeria's leading news magazines—certainly the most respected at the time—was killed by a letter bomb. The magazine, which routinely carried investigative pieces on the military government, was conducting one at the time. The circumstance and professionalism of the attack and the government's failure to find the culprit left Nigerians with little choice but to conclude that the military government of General Ibrahim Babangida was responsible for the murder. The general denied any involvement. Yet the prevalent view is that if, indeed, he didn't know anything about the plan, his aides did.

Similarly, aides of General Babangida's successor, General Abacha, are believed to have carried out an assassination attempt against Alex Ibru, a wealthy industrialist and publisher of *The Guardian*, Nigeria's most prestigious daily. A number of General Abacha's close military aides, including his chief security officer, are under trial for the attempted assassination.[21]

Of course, not all Nigerian journalists risk the government's ire to protect open expression. To many journalists working for government-owned news media their jobs are more like those of civil servants than those of journalists. Some are so concerned with their security that they fail to exercise the privileges allowed them. In some cases, for instance, broadcast journalists seek the approval of officials in government ministries when such approval is not required. They prefer not to make independent decisions that could displease someone above.[22]

In some instances, government news media serve not just as mouthpieces for the federal and state governments but also as their attack dogs. In at least two instances, this has resulted in the odd situation in which government-owned news media accumulated so many libel awards that they are unable to pay. In a recent and most dramatic instance of this, four vehicles belonging to the daily paper, the *New Nigerian*, were impounded by court order in October

1999.[23] The paper, which was one of Nigeria's most widely circulated and the authoritative voice of the North, was acquired by the federal government in 1976. With its mission not so clear, it began a gradual demise that reached its depth during General Abacha's military regime. By 1998 its circulation had fallen to just a few hundred and its schedule was so irregular that a critic later wrote that "it became some kind of publishing Halley's Comet, sighted by a lucky few armed with the requisite equipment."[24] Its content was largely government written or inspired news, some of which were attacks against opponents of the government.

Ironically, the libel case that led to the seizure of the vehicles was filed by General Abacha's adviser. And according to the editor of the paper at the time of the seizure, the offending story was planted by General Abacha,[25] apparently to discredit his own adviser. Such was the political quirk of the military government. Though the government often preempted court rulings against it, its desire to maintain the illusion that the *New Nigerian* was operating independently apparently kept it from preempting the judgments against the paper. When the military was in power, the courts might have been reluctant to order confiscation of the property of a government-owned newspaper. But Nigeria became a democracy again in 1999, and the courts exercise their powers more freely.

The future of the *New Nigerian* is being debated as of summer 2001. The federal government is considering privatizing it, but the northern states, which used to sponsor the paper—first through the government of what was then the northern region, and then through a joint effort of the states—are again trying to take over the paper.

The *Daily Times*, another newspaper that suffered a steep decline after the federal government purchased 60 percent controlling shares in 1976, is also burdened by libel awards.[26] The obvious irony in these cases is that government ownership, which ought to ensure responsibility, actually resulted in burdensome illegalities. Part of the problem was that some of the best talent at the papers, especially at the *Daily Times*, abandoned them for the privately owned papers, and they had to be replaced with less skilled recruits. A government-commissioned report on the newspaper's near collapse also cited ethnic rivalry and staffing policies that deemphasized excellence and merit.[27]

Like government-owned newspapers, broadcasting houses are much less independent in their reportage and commentary. To begin with, most are still government-owned, as summarized earlier. The news programs on these stations consist largely of reports on the activities of top government officials—their visits, ribbon-cuttings, speeches, announcements, and the like. Flattering stories about the officials' families are routinely thrown in for good measure. Few stories reflect the views and activities of the populace.

The emergence of independently owned broadcast houses beginning in the early 1990s promises to change the staleness and predictability of Nigerian broadcast news. However, the economic landscape is not very hospitable to large-scale commercial broadcasting, especially television. Industry utilization remains far below capacity, contributing to a relatively limited commercial support. Of course, by the standards of sub-Saharan Africa, Nigeria is media-rich. In fact, few other sub-Saharan African countries can undertake internally funded and competitive commercial TV broadcasting. That it is viable at all in Nigeria is testimony to the country's large population, which is estimated at between 100 and 120 million.[28]

Nigerian media suffers no lack of entrepreneurial zest. When the government offered several broadcast frequencies for allocation to private broadcasters a few years ago, scores of businesses applied. But several of those who received allocations have been unable to take off, and many of those that did are encountering financial difficulties. Some could not even pay for their license fees, prompting the National Broadcasting Commission, the regulatory agency, to temporarily revoke several licenses in 1999.[29] Some broadcast stations were even forced off the air. The affected broadcasters got a reprieve following intense lobbying by the Independent Broadcasters' Association of Nigeria.

The precarious financial situation of private broadcasters has to hamper their effectiveness as robust venues of open discussion. The mere knowledge that the government can pull the plugs anytime for their failure to meet basic legal financial obligations is bound to compromise the stations' programming, especially regarding news and views. A 1999 newspaper editorial said this of the independent broadcasters during General Abacha's regime: "Many were extremely loud in frivolities and kept mute or at times reported stories so skewed that it outshone the best efforts of the Abuja goons."[30] They are less timid now that the prospects for repression have diminished. But their financial vulnerability is likely to continue to compromise their independence for quite some time.

PARTISANSHIP AND THE TRUTH

The first part of the preceding section discusses the importance of pluralism in keeping the Nigerian press robust, and the second part summarizes factors that have the opposite effect. As suggested in the first part, robust discussion sometimes may also do harm to the truth, at least in the short term. The Nigerian press's traditional partisanship and freewheeling journalism have had this side effect.

When governments and political parties/operatives dominated in the ownership of newspapers and magazines, partisanship was the norm. Though most papers carried diverse opinions, including those that are contrary to their commitments, this practice often diminished or disappeared on the most consequential issues, including especially elections. Opinions not consistent with the publications' political orientation rarely were published on such matters. The recent dominance of independent newspapers, especially those founded by journalists, has led to a lessening of this tendency.

Yet, as recently as 1993, during a presidential election that was subsequently annulled, flagrant instances of politically motivated noncoverage occurred. When one of the two candidates, Mashood K. O. Abiola, campaigned in four states whose governments were under the control of his rival's party, both the print and electronic media in those states—all owned by the state governments—blacked him out.[31] Abiola himself owned a group of newspapers and magazines, and they, too, gave his rival short shrift in their coverage. That the rest of the Nigerian press refrained from such gross ethical transgression and, in fact, condemned Abiola's black out, was indicative of the ethical progress in this regard.

Yet during the political crisis that followed the military government's annulment of the election, press coverage still engaged in considerable partisanship. Even *The Guardian* had to acknowledge that it failed to provide an outlet for the viewpoints of those who supported policies or plans the paper opposed. *The Guardian* has since returned to its relatively even-handed coverage of issues, routinely running opinion pieces reflecting a diversity of views. An issue in November 2000, even carried a lengthy guest column that accused the paper of politically motivated and biased commentary.[32] Several other leading papers are also allowing diverse views on their pages, but partisanship in coverage is by no means a matter of the past.

Perhaps one of the worst manifestations of partisan coverage is the readiness with which Nigerian papers publish unsubstantiated claims and allegations. Obstacles to verification of information is a contributing factor in this regard. Nigerian law does not provide for the right of access to information. Although such a right was included in the 1995 draft constitution—a part of the many transitions to democracy that the military never carried through—the clause was strangely enough excised from the 1999 Constitution that established the current democratic government.[33] Therefore, journalists have limited leverage in pressuring government officials and civil servants to disclose information that does not serve their ends. Even when such information can be obtained, problems with the communication infrastructure—getting through phone lines, for instance—hinder journalists' capacity to verify claims.

Still, there is reason to believe that inaccurate information often gets published because it is consistent with the papers' partisan politics. In the case of the Senate president cited previously, for instance, he believed, probably correctly, that the inaccurate information had political motives. In denying the allegation that he was plotting the fall of the man who succeeded him as Senate president, Chuba Okadigbo said: "I know nothing of any plot to oust Senator Anyim Pius Anyim from his position as President of the Senate. Therefore, I think the alleged plot may only exist in the sordid imagination of *The Comet* and some phobic conspirators, hopefully outside the Senate.... I believe that...distinguished senators and honorable members of the Federal House of Representatives are aware of the democratic disposition of some ethnic section of the Nigerian press."[34]

More recently, the minister of information reprimanded the press after some news media carried stories of a government plan to raise petroleum prices. This is a sensitive matter in Nigeria, given that strikes and riots have attended previous attempts to do so. Even seemingly impervious military governments had had to back down on such attempts. The minister said no plan existed to raise petroleum prices, other than the government's widely debated review of whether and how to privatize the petroleum industry. He suggested that the story may have been planted by opponents of the government or critics of the privatization. Referring to his denial, he said, "All statements to the contrary should be absolutely disregarded as coming from agents of falsehood and destabilization." He added: "Media houses, especially radio and television stations, are strongly advised to cross-check their sources before they carry policy statements purported to have been issued by the federal government. The people of Nigeria are entitled to know the truth and nobody has the right to mislead them."[35]

Another product of partisanship is the vituperative nature of press attacks, which reached a crescendo just before the outbreak of civil war in 1967. Then, news media representing sectional interests attacked their opponents in the coarsest of language. Ethnic groups were derided and insulted and individuals uncharitably branded. During the civil war the practice became muted on the federal side but remained intense within the seceding eastern region. Overall, the practice diminished markedly after the civil war, but underwent a resurgence during the political crisis of the mid-1990s. It never reached the crude levels of the years before the civil war, however, and it has further abated since the end of the recent crisis.

CONCLUSION

In the speech cited earlier, Dan Agbese, one of the Nigeria's leading journalists, said: "If all other national institutions have great responsibilities towards the survival and sustenance of democracy, those of the press are truly grave."[36] The Nigerian press is growing in its reflection of this responsibility. If the military does not again intervene in the political process, the press will be in the position to develop its ethical standards through extended experience with democracy. The pressures for continued improvement in standards and ethics will have to come from within the profession and the consumers of news, as happened in the ethical evolution of the U.S. press, among others. [37] The stature and success of *The Guardian*, Nigeria's yardstick for journalistic probity, for instance, is an inducement to other papers to aspire to high standards.

One measure that has been suggested for the improvement of Nigerian press ethics is the establishment of the ombudsman system of performance review and grievance mediation, either of the U.S. type (within individual news media) or of the Swedish kind (a national, all-media mediator).[38] Of course, a national press council such as that which functioned briefly in the United States in the 1970s or its state variants, such as the one that still exists in Minnesota, would be helpful. The current Nigerian Press Council can, in effect, serve the Swedish type ombudsman role and possibly get the cooperation of the Nigerian press if the government takes a less active role in its formation and operation. Clauses in its establishing laws that empower the NPC to register journalists make it more of a government apparatus than an independent ombudsman. If the NPC's powers are modified and its image improved, the burden of libel awards that saddle some Nigerian papers may be an incentive to cooperate with it.

Finally, a proposal has been made to establish a newspaper ownership structure that would ensure both independence and responsiveness to the need for national cohesion. The proposal was made in connection with the federal government's review of its majority ownership of the *Daily Times* group. After considering the options of continued government ownership or full privatization, a former editor charged with making recommendations to the government strongly proposed the establishment of a National Trust that would distribute much of the government's shares in the company to "statutorily identified interest groups and businesses broadly representing Nigerian society."[39] Among such groups are the Nigerian Union of Journalists, the Federal Housing Corporation, the Supreme Council for Islamic Affairs, the Christian Association of Nigeria, the Nigeria Labour Congress, and the Manufacturers Association of Nigeria. A significant feature of this recommendation is that no one group may have a controlling share. This, according to the recommendation, would discourage partisanship and crass commercialism, while making the paper a credible voice for all Nigerians.

Given Nigeria's fractious politics, which are manifest in all facets of national life, it is improbable that such an ownership structure would yield a harmonious management. But it is an experiment worth exploring, if only because it would bring another dimension to Nigerian media ownership and, one hopes, ethics.

NOTES

1. See, for instance, Dietmar Mieth, "The Basic Norm of Truthfulness: Its Ethical Justification and Universality," in *Communication Ethics and Universal Values*, ed. Clifford Christians and Michael Traber (Thousand Oaks, CA: 1997), 87–104. As applied to the African context, the relevant arguments are summarized in David N. Dixon, "Press Law Debate in Kenya: Ethics as Political Power," *Journal of Mass Media Ethics* 12 (1997), 171–182.
2. For values that affect public communication in African cultures, see, for instance, Andrew Azukaego Moemeka, "Communalistic Societies: Community and Self-Respect as African

Values," in *Communication Ethics and Universal Values*, ed. Clifford Christians and Michael Traber (Thousand Oaks, CA: 1997), 170–193; Louise M. Bourgault, *Mass Media in Sub-Saharan Africa* (Bloomington: Indiana University Press, 1995); For a contrast between Japan and the U.S., see Roichi Okabe, "Cultural Assumptions of East and West: Japan and the United States," in *Intercultural Communication Theory: Current Perspectives*, ed. William B. Gudykunst (Beverly Hills, CA: Sage,1983), 21–44.

3. For a review of issues related to access, see Philip Patterson and Lee Wilkins, *Media Ethics: Issues and Cases* (Dubuque, IA: Wm. C. Brown Publishers, 1991), especially Ch. II. For a review of the ethics of the purpose of the truth, see, Matthew Kieran, *Media Ethics: A Philosophical Approach* (Westport, CT: Praeger, 1997), especially 69–74.

4. See Peter Golding, "Media Professionalism in the Third World: the Transfer of an Ideology," in *Mass Communication and Society*, ed. J. Curan et al. (London: Edward Arnold, 1977), 291–308.

5. Usman Jimada, "Eurocentric Media Training in Nigeria: What Alternative?" *Journal of Black Studies* 22(1992), 366–379.

6. Bosah L. Ebo, "The Ethical Dilemma of African Journalists: A Nigerian Perspective," *Journal of Mass Media Ethics* 9 (1994), 84–93.

7. Narinder K. Aggarwala, "What is Development News? *Journal of Communication* 29, No. 2 (1979): 180–181; Hermant Shah, "Modernization, Marginalization, and Emancipation: Toward a Normative Model of Journalism and National Development," *Communication Theory* 6 (1996), 143–167.

8. See, for instance: Minabere Ibelema, "Professionalism as Risk Management: A Typology of Journalists in Developing Countries," *Journal of Development Communication* 5 (June 1994), 22–33; Cornelius B. Pratt and Gerald W. McLaughlin, "Ethical Dimensions of Nigerian Journalists and Their Newspapers, *Journal of Mass Media Ethics*, 5 (No. 1, 1990), 30–34.

9. Pratt and McLaughlin, "Ethical Dimensions of Nigerian Journalists."

10. Julianne Schultz, *Reviving the Fourth Estate: Democracy, Accountability and the Media* (Cambridge, UK: Cambridge University Press, 1998), 233.

11. Douglas Birkhead, "Should Professional Competence Be Taught as Ethical?" *Journal of Mass Media Ethics* 12 (1997), 211–220.

12. UNDP, *Human Development Report 1999* (New York: Oxford University Press, 1999), 55.

13. Ikechukwu E. Nwosu, "Mass Media Discipline and Control in Contemporary Nigeria: A Contextual Critical Analysis," *Gazette* 39 (1987), 17–29.

14. Nwosu, "Mass Media Discipline and Control," 22.

15. Nwosu, "Mass Media Discipline and Control," 22.

16. "Nigerian Guild of Editors launches fresh war on Nigerian Press Council," *Vanguard*, 11 October 1999.

17. See, for instance, Nwosu, "Mass Media Discipline and Control"; Pratt and McLaughlin, "Ethical Dimensions of Nigerian Journalists."

18. Dan Agbese, "The Fourth Estate in the Fourth Republic: What Prospects?" the Fourth Hadji Saka Fagbo Memorial Lecture, Lagos, Nigeria. Speech distributed by the Independent Journalism Centre, Lagos, Nigeria, http://www. Kilima.com/mediamonitor.

19. Dennis L. Wilcox, *Mass Media in Black Africa: Philosophy and Control* (New York: Praeger, 1975), 68.

20. Ibelema, "Professionalism as Risk Management," 30.

21. Gbolahan Gbadamosi, "How Rogers shot Ibru, Kudirat, by Abacha's driver," *The Guardian Online*, http://ngrguardiannews.com, 24 January 2001.

22. Ibelema, "Professionalism as Risk Management."

23. Agaju Madugba, "Court impounds *New Nigerian*'s vehicles over N3 million libel fine," *This Day*, 27 October 1999.

24. Paul Nwabuikwu, "A lifetime for the *New Nigerian*," *The Guardian Online*, http://ngr-guardiannews.com, Wednesday, 21 March 2001.

25. Madugba, "Court impounds *New Nigerian*'s vehicles."

26. Mudiaga Ofuoku, "Way out for *Daily Times*," *Newswatch*, 27 August 1999.

27. Ofuoku, "Way out for *Daily Times*."

28. The United Nations Development Programme puts Nigeria's population in 1997 at 103.9 million. See, UNDP, *Human Development Report 1999*, 199.

29. Okoh Aihe, Bukola Ojeme, and Chioma Ngwonebo, "AIT, MITV, Ray Power, 17 others lose licences," *Vanguard*, http://www.afbis.com/vanguard. Transmitted 5 October 1999.

30. "The Broadcaster's Invention" *Tempo*, 23 September 1999. The phrase "Abuja goons" is a reference to the generals who wielded power from Nigeria's political capital.

31. "How fair is the press?" *West Africa*, 7–13 June 1993, 947.

32. Abdullahi Ciroma, "Between Arewa Forum and Obasanjo," *The Guardian Online*, http://ngrguardiannews.com, 14 November 2000.

33. Chris W. Ogbondah, "The Press in Shackles," *Newswatch*, 6 April 2000.

34. Abiodun Adeniyi and John-Abba Ogbodo, "Senator orders ethics code for journalists," *The Guardian Online*, http://ngrguardiannews.com, 27 September 2000.

35. Kingsley Nwezeh, "Federal Government Warns Detractors, Media Houses," *This Day*, 4 April 2001.

36. Agbese, "The Fourth Estate in the Fourth Republic."

37. Mary M. Cronin, "Trade Press Roles in Promoting Journalistic Professionalism, 1884–1917," *Journal of Mass Media Ethics* 8 (1993), 227–238.

38. Nwosu, "Mass Media Discipline and Control," 23.

39. Ofuoku, "Way out for *Daily Times*."

PART FIVE

In South and East Asia

This section of *The Mission* takes you to south and east Asia, where ancient cultures come face-to-face with modern-day realities, but where practically any other broad generalization is impossible today.

In Chapter 14, Jayanti Ram-Chandran, a native of Calcutta and free-lance journalist now living in British Columbia, Canada, offers us the results of a four-month journey through India—from New Delhi to Bangalore—where she interviewed editors, reporters, and scholars about Indian journalism. She reports of a vibrant, multi-faceted press that ranges from fiery, native-language tabloids with their front-page tales of murderers, smugglers, and elephant poachers to staid, English-language newspapers that often prefer to look beyond India for front-page stories.

In Chapter 15, Akhilesh Upadhyay , one of Nepal's top journalists, assesses the impact of the dramatic murders of members of the royal family on June 1, 2001, and the accompanying crackdown on the press in Nepal—a press that was just beginning to enjoy Western-style freedom.

In Chapter 16, Takehiko Nomura, a free-lance writer based in Tokyo, writes of the entrenched news culture in Japan that promotes incestuous relationships between the media and political/corporate powers and that works against any true sense of independence or individualism.

Chapter fourteen

The Indian Press

Covering an Enigma

by Jayanti Ram-Chandran
Freelance Writer
Vancouver, Canada

India is an enigma to many, even to its own people, a country estimated to be
more than five thousand years old with a population of one billion, five major
religions, and eighteen constitutionally recognized languages with more than
eighty others that don't have such recognition. Charged with understanding
and explaining this enigma is a press system that dates back only to 1817 but
which is one of the most vibrant, free, and highly democratic in all of Asia. It
is certainly the largest in Asia, including more than 41,700 newspapers and
magazines printed in English and other languages and dialects.

The Hindi press accounts for 36 percent of India's newspapers and English
accounts for 17 percent, with the rest divided among the hundred or more
other languages and dialects. Hindi is the nation's official language, yet the
English publications, many of which have regional language editions, are still
considered the national press. Surveys conducted over the past five years show
a general readership trend toward the so-called "language" press, which has
seen its circulation rise some 20 percent compared to only 2 percent in the
English press.

The Indian press—with print being the dominant medium in the world's
largest democracy and thus the focus of this essay—has survived colonialism,
revolution, independence, war, authoritarian leaders, and the global market.
Prior to independence from English rule in 1947, it was known for its crusading spirit and sense of social commitment. The ranks of journalists working in the country included the likes of religious and political leader Mahatma
Gandhi, writer Rudyard Kipling, and future British Prime Minister Winston
Churchill.

Many journalists today, however, see a betrayal of that spirit as newspapers and other media focus increasingly on profits. Dilip Bobb, executive editor of *India Today Plus*, complains that the Indian press has become too devoted to "fluff" stories in its effort to reach an elite, urban, upwardly mobile audience. In the past, he says, perhaps "there have been too many political stories on political corruption and scandals that have toppled governments, and it was time for the country to have 'feel good' news."

ORIGINS AND PRESS FREEDOM

When India ended 300 years of British rule in 1947, the people retained English as the common language that threads through the labyrinth of diversity in the country, and the English press today remains vitally important and influential in political and economic circles. The English press was born in the nineteenth century around the same time as the language press in India. Most of the early English newspapers were bilingual. The country's first newspaper was the *Bengal Gazette* in Calcutta, which was started by the British East India Company in 1817.

Over the next 130 years, many editors, including Mahatma Gandhi, were imprisoned as a result of incendiary editorials that challenged British rule. After independence and the subsequent adoption of the Indian Constitution in 1947, the press began its development into a healthy and democratic institution. Still, freedom of the press was not included as a separate provision in the Indian constitution. It exists by virtue of the fundamental right to freedom of speech and expression granted all Indian citizens in the constitution, and it has been recognized in subsequent rulings by the nation's courts.

After British rule ended, the adversarial and rebellious role that the press played during the colonial era was replaced by a more collegial attitude. The leaders of newly independent India, after all, had fought alongside the journalists in the struggle for freedom. India's first Prime Minister, Jawaharlal Nehru, enjoyed a special kinship with the press and was generally seen as a true believer in press freedom during most of his seventeen-year rule. Even he bristled, however, when the press targeted him for criticism, such as when he turned to the United Nations to resolve India's problems with Pakistan over the disputed region of Kashmir. The first amendment to the Indian Constitution in 1951 prohibited the press from endangering public order or relations with other nations.

After Nehru's death in 1964, leadership passed to his daughter, Indira Gandhi, who found herself quickly at odds with the press. She accused journalists of being biased and hostile to her economic, socialist, and progressive policies. Her rule as prime minister was characterized by governmental pressure, intimidation, and manipulation, reaching the nadir in 1975 with the declaration of a national emergency and the imposition of total censorship. During the 1975-77 emergency, the government gave the press the option of either abiding by its strict censorship guidelines or volunteering to serve as a self-censor. Several newspapers published blank editorial pages in protest.

Veteran journalist and media analyst Babu Bhaskar remembers when the newspaper he worked for at the time had to send photocopied pages of every section on every page to the government for approval. Often the pages would be detained so long that publication of the issue became meaningless.

Both English and the language newspapers, including some of the oldest in the country, acquiesced. Others, like *The Indian Express* and *The Statesman*, defied the government crackdown and incurred huge financial losses as a result. The government stopped buying advertisements to more than one hundred rebellious newspapers. "We at *The Statesman* do not keep our voices down when there is abuse of power," current editor-in-chief Cushrow Irani says today about the emergency.

More than 250 journalists were arrested. Many had their accreditation rescinded, and foreign correspondents from *The Times* of London, the *London Daily Telegraph*, the *Washington Post*, *Newsweek*, and the BBC were deported. Others were banned from entering India. The government also dissolved the New Delhi-based Press Council of India. Says N. Ram of the *Frontline*, a newsmagazine in the southern Indian city of Chennai (formerly known as Madras): most of "the press was stunned to a paralysis and it put up an unheroic fight."

Prabhas Joshi, editor of *Jansatta*, the Hindi language edition of the *Indian Express*, says journalists learned a lesson, however, and later became much more aggressive and zealous in their defense of press freedom. "The experience taught them to keep fighting the establishment, whether it was the British establishment or its own Indian establishment."

RESTORATION OF PRESS FREEDOM IN THE 1980s

The clouds hanging over the press began to disperse after Indira Gandhi was defeated in the general elections of 1977. The respite was brief, however, because she returned to power in 1980. This time she was more discreet in her handling of the press, manipulating as well as intimidating, making sure that friendly journalists were rewarded. "The government's attitude was, why punish the press when you can reward them and still send a message?" recalls Sam Rajappa, the chief correspondent of *The Statesman* in Chennai.

The 1980s also saw the rise to power of Indira Gandhi's oldest son, Rajiv Gandhi, who reigned from 1984 to 1989 and whose hostility toward the press rivaled his mother's. In 1988, he attempted to win approval of an antipress defamation bill but eventually withdrew the bill when editors and publishers united against him. They had learned their lesson from his mother. Rajiv Gandhi was assassinated in 1991.

THE PRESS IS AN INDUSTRY

At the same time that the press was dealing with Indira and Rajiv Gandhi, it was also undergoing a major transformation that included a huge growth in newspaper circulation, particularly in the language press, and a revolution in communications technology. In this still-evolving transformation, the press has become a formidable industry, increasingly corporate in its nature and outlook and today largely controlled by a handful of family-run companies, such as the Birlas, Jains, Goenkas, and Rahejas. The Rahejas family owns *The Outlook*, a weekly newsmagazine that is the closest rival to the popular weekly newsmagazine *India Today*. The Birlas family owns the *Hindustan Times* and the Jains family owns *Times of India*, two of the dominant newspapers in the country.

Some newspapers incurred huge losses during the early 1990s. An example was the 136-year-old *Pioneer* from New Delhi, which was dumped by its owner, the Thapar Group, in 1998 after failing to reap anticipated returns. However, the newspaper, which has featured the bylines of Churchill, Kipling, and Mahatma Gandhi during its long history, survived under the strong leadership of editor Chandan Mitra and, some say, with significant behind-the-scenes financial backing from the government.

Other newspapers and magazines thrived, such as the newspaper *Asian Age*. From its beginning as a local newspaper in New Delhi, *Asian Age* has expanded to include franchise versions in London, Bombay, Hyderabad, and Bangalore. Its colorful editor, Vijay Mallya, a liquor magnate and one of the wealthiest men in India, tells people he'd rather be known as an editor than as the flamboyant jet-setter that is his reputation. Editors have more political clout than jet-setters, he says.

Another major player in the Indian press is the *Times of India*, which has expanded from its western India origins to become a national force. It is considered a trailblazer—albeit a sometimes ruthless one—in the new global market economy. Its tactics have included setting cover prices at only a fraction of their production costs in an effort to undersell competitors, hiring business managers to take over editors' roles in deciding news content and page displays, and instilling an assembly-line mentality in its newsroom that views stories as products and readers as consumers.

"The price war started by the *Times of India* confirms the newspaper's purpose, and to that effect, their aggressive and innovative management strategies have mustered enough financial muscle to sustain (the newspaper)," says *Pioneer* editor Chandan Mitra, a sharp critic of both methods and content at the *Times of India*. "The *Times* group completely ignores the…ethical elements of journalism. … The *Times* would…have to work very hard to upgrade its quality."

Yet even critics such as Mitra have to concede that the *Times of India* has blazed other trails that are admirable. It was, for example, the first Indian newspaper to set up an office of an ombudsman in 1998. The position was abandoned a year later.

With the increasing corporate interest in the print medium has come a greater focus on business and economic news in newspapers and magazines. Prior to 1991, most newspapers carried only a page or two on business and economic news. Today most of them have entire sections, and India's most popular new publications include titles such as *Economic Times* and *Business India*.

Newspapers and magazines have worked hard to adapt to the new realities of publishing today. Media analysts believe the language press generally has moved more quickly than the English press and some of the older, established newspapers to incorporate new technology. Even old stalwarts such as the venerable *Hindu,* a Chennai-based, family-owned newspaper unrivalled for more than a century in southern India and long praised as one of the world's best newspapers, has felt the pressure and now allows vibrant colors and increasing numbers of photographs to invade its once-bland, colorless pages.

Some critics believe the struggle for survival in the market economy has led to a breakdown in the wall between news and advertisement, and to increasingly tabloid-like content on the news pages. Hari Kumar, managing editor of the family-owned and Bangalore-based *Deccan Herald*, counters that his and other newspapers simply have had to change to meet the new demands of the market. Swapan DasGupta, deputy editor of *India Today* in New Delhi, one of India's leading newsmagazines, says that change was long overdue in the Indian press and that quality journalism ultimately will win out over tabloidism. "The...press had underestimated people's adaptation to the new vibrant economic scenario and was slow to act, and the print media (in general) was left to feed on the crumbs by the television industry."

ENGLISH AND LANGUAGE PRESS

The English and the language press have waged a war of words for a long time in India. The language press calls its English counterparts elitist and socially insensitive. The English press tends to view the language newspapers as too frequently catering to sensationalism and raw emotion.

Even the writing style of the English press has come under criticism, including from within its own ranks. "It would be no exaggeration to say that almost all English language papers in the country use a language that is not of human communication, but the fossil language of power that gained popularity during the British rule," says Jyoti Sanyal, associate editor of *The Statesman*, an English-language publication in Bangalore in the state of Karnataka, and dean of the Asian School of Journalism in Bangalore.

Whereas the English press is still seen as wielding substantial influence in the circles of power in India, the press of the Hindu and other Indian languages is viewed as closer to the pulse of the people. The charge that the language press tries to quicken that pulse unnecessarily has been validated at times. For example, the Hindi daily newspapers, *Daily Jagran* and *Amar Ujala*, and the *Samna*, the propagandistic organ of the ruling party in the state of Maharashtra in western India, were widely accused of aggravating tensions between Hindus and Muslims in their columns and news pages after the religious riots in Bombay and other parts of India in 1992.

Still, the growth of the language press is undeniable. Newspapers such as *Dina Thanthi*, published in the Tamil language in the southern region of Tamil Nadu, have outpaced competitors by publishing different editions in different districts and by emphasizing a writing style that is accessible to a broad-based public. Sensationalistic publications such as *Nakeeran*, a newsmagazine with several editions in the Tamil language, specializes in shock stories and screaming headlines, but its layout-artist-turned-editor, R. Rajgopal, defends it vehemently and points to its many examples of in-depth investigative reporting. Arrested several times and threatened because of his journalistic work, Rajgopal says that he has been "in courtrooms just as many times as I have been in my newsroom. … I don't believe in taking the middle-of-the-road option when it comes to journalism and if I am the odd man out, so be it."

However, media analyst Babu Bhaskar isn't impressed. "What is published in *Nakeeran* may be factual, but the style and language in which it is presented has all the signs of blatant tabloid sensationalism that loses credibility among readers."

Rajgopal critics say that the editor plays favorites in choosing the targets of his newsmagazine's investigations, a claim he rejects. He also raised many eyebrows with his assignment as an emissary of the Tamil Nadu government in 1997 to negotiate with Veerappan, one of the most wanted fugitives in India. Rajgopal's task was to seek the freedom of nine forest service officials whom Veerappan was holding captive. A notorious elephant poacher and tusk smuggler, Veerappan had eluded police for more than fifteen years, hiding out in dense forests that spread across two southern states. The fugitive had allegedly killed as many as 120 people, including police officers and forest rangers. After several journeys into the forest to meet with the outlaw, Rajgopal successfully secured the release of the hostages.

Rajgopal was asked once again to broker a deal with the still-at-large Veerappan in July 2000 after the outlaw kidnapped a veteran actor of south Indian cinema and three others. This time, the editor failed to win the release of the hostages despite three separate attempts.

Despite his high-profile role as government emissary and hostage negotiator, Rajgopal boasts of strong convictions regarding his role as a journalist, and he dismisses any charge that he plays favorites or that he seeks to glorify himself or gangsters such as Veerappan. "We have always gone after anything or anyone who poses a challenge to investigative reporting and we don't spare any efforts to get to the truth," he says.

DIFFERENT CHALLENGES FOR DIFFERENT PUBLICATIONS

Unlike *Nakeeran*, the 112-year-old, family-run *Malayala Manorama* in Kerala generally avoids controversy although the paper played an important role in the shaping of free and independent India and was at one time clearly a tool for social change. The newspaper today enjoys a certain special status in India in the public that it serves. Kerala is the only state in the country with a 100 percent literacy rate. Traditionally, low literacy in India as a whole has been on the rise and stood at 62 percent in 1997, compared to the 52 percent reported in the 1991 census.

In southern India, *Eenadu*, a Telugu language newspaper, is only twenty-five years old but wields considerable political clout with its twelve different editions in both the states of Tamil Nadu and Karnataka. It boasts as many as two thousand contributors. Owner/editor Ramaoji Rao attributes the newspaper's success to its unpretentious language and style. "Our aim is to talk to the simpletons in rural Andhra Pradesh in the best way possible and illiteracy statistics haven't discouraged us from the paper's mission." Illiteracy in the state of Andhra Pradesh in southern India is about 46 percent. Rao says *Eenadu* builds on the tradition of the local educator who reads the news from the local daily to villagers gathered around him in the village square. Rao says his newspaper wants to bring awareness of social and political issues at the local level to rural pockets of the state.

S. Ramanujam, executive editor of an English newsmagazine owned by Rao's *Eenadu* group, agrees with this philosophy. "In a rural setting, reading off richly tailored editorials with high-flown colorful language and style, however well-translated in the local dialect, would only sound like passages from a literary publication and have no impact whatsoever."

JOURNALISM ETHICS IN INDIA

With all the changes in the Indian press has also come a serious erosion of ethics, journalists and media observers say. They point to a number of high-profile examples in recent years.

V.N. Narayanan, an editor of the *Hindustan Times* with more than 30 years in the field, was found in October 1999 to have plagiarized a column by Bryan Appleyard, a columnist of the London-based *The Sunday Times*. After the *Pioneer* of New Delhi exposed the plagiarism, the editor resigned, offering as his defense a photographic memory that tended to reproduce everything he read unconsciously.

Another example came just a month later, in November 1999, in a story in *The Hindu* detailing remarks by the Duke of Edinburgh to the Indian prime minister that seemed to make light of the death and devastation in eastern India caused by a recent cyclone. The remarks were to the effect that the Indian authorities should not be too worried about the deaths of a few thousand in a nation with a population of one billion. The next day, the paper carried a simple apology admitting that the report was a hoax.

An example of blatant and damaging sensationalism occurred during communal riots in December 1992. The emotional, biased coverage not only exacerbated existing tensions between Hindus and Muslims but also resorted to outright lies. The Press Council of India censured the owner of one language newspaper in northern India for adding a zero to the number of deaths in its headlines.

Other stories in recent years include an account in *The Statesman* in Calcutta of flooding in a local village that supposedly had killed thousands of villagers and washed away their bodies. The report was later found to be inaccurate. The reporter had gotten the information from a building doorman. Another major press scandal came in 1992 when the widespread practice of rewarding business journalists preferential shares, expensive gifts, and free trips in exchange for favorable coverage was exposed by the *Times of India*.

Editor-educator Sanyal says these ethical breaches are in part the result of newspapers bending too much to market forces and becoming too fearful of hard-hitting, quality journalism.

In his recent book *Mr. Editor, How Close Are You To The Prime Minister?*, Vinod Mehta, editor-in-chief of the national English magazine *Outlook* and one of the best-known journalists in India, said that a major problem is the coziness between journalists and those in power. "Getting too close to people you have to evaluate impartially and censure frequently leads to unnecessary complications and heartburn," he wrote. "One must never compromise one's right to attack. … I realize that editors are not monks. They love banter, gossip, easy access to those in power, and the hope that the friendship will yield privileged information.

"Indian editors, especially, have a tremendous fondness for entertaining and being entertained by the high and the mighty," he continued. "Lunches, dinners, tea parties with ministers and prime ministers are coveted as badges of honor."

Over the years, several high-profile journalists have themselves become politicians in India. Editors Suman Dubey and H.K. Dua were media advisers to prime ministers, and Kuldip Nayar served for a short period as high commissioner in the United Kingdom and later as a member of Parliament from the Rajya Sabha (Upper House). A more recent example is that of veteran journalist Arun Shourie, a fiery editor recognized in the year 2000 by the Interna-

ber of the Rajya Sabha (equivalent to the U.S. Senate) in the Indian Parliament and is a minister of state.

However, proximity to political power isn't the only potential brake on investigative stories in the Indian press today, says editor-educator Sanyal. Corporate interests pose even greater dangers to quality journalism. Sanyal questions how aggressive liquor magnate Vijay Mallya would allow his *Asian Age* franchise newspaper, the *Bangalore Age* in Bangalore, to be in reporting on health problems and deaths related to alcohol consumption in India. How aggressive would the *Times of India* be in investigating the music and credit card industries that are a part of its own financial interests?

A WATCH OVER THE WATCHDOG

The group charged with monitoring the press in India is the Press Council. Established in 1966 on the recommendations of the First Press Commission to preserve the freedom of the press and to maintain and improve its standards, the council attempts to redress complaints about the media from the public. Its 28 members come from various fields, not just the press, and their leader is a retired chief justice of the Supreme Court, P.B. Sawant, who has also served as president of the World Association of Press Councils.

The relationship between the press and the council has been less than friendly, even though the council has no punitive powers and is essentially toothless. When council chair Sawant suggested ways to restructure media ownership in the country, he was accused of stirring up an unnecessary controversy by interfering in matters that did not concern the council. Even the International Press Institute and the Commonwealth Press Union urged Sawant not to step outside his jurisdiction and not to interfere with the market or the laws that oversee the Indian press. When the council tried to impose a ban on exit polls during elections, the press rose in arms to challenge what it considered an infringement of fundamental rights of freedom of speech and expression. Savant countered that the polls were so unscientific that they caused more confusion than clarification.

Despite its lack of punitive powers, the council has censured several newspapers and settled defamation cases with plaintiffs. Newspapers can defy the censures, however, and have done so at different times.

In all fairness to the Indian press, many newspapers maintain a high standard of ethics and continue to do hard-hitting, socially relevant stories on child labor, women's health, education, and other issues. An example is the coverage in mainstream newspapers of the continuing health problems related to the industrial disaster at the Union Carbide Corporation plant in Bhopal in 1984, an explosion and gas leak that killed more than 16,000 people. Another example is provided by Phalguni Sainath, an award-winning correspondent who has gone to some of the country's most backward and inaccessible regions to show how failed government economic policies have worsened living conditions in rural India.

Still, these are the exceptions, not the rule, says longtime journalist and now politician Arun Shourie. "The press is on the trail for three days only before moving on to something else. It is in great variance with the way journalists used to work in the late seventies until the mid-eighties when the reporter did not rest until the whole story was brought into full view of the readers."

Media analyst Babu Bhaskar agrees. Journalism in India once was a true calling despite its low pay and frequently hazardous conditions, he says. Today, however, it is too often simply the "foot in the door," a transition point between jobs, or "a consolation prize in the race for the choicest jobs in the market."

Chapter fifteen

Palace Intrigue in Katmandu and the Press in Nepal

by Akhilesh Upadhyay
U.S. correspondent for Kantipur Publications
Katmandu, Nepal

This timely account by a leading journalist in Nepal provides insight into an ancient nation steeped in tradition and, to many Western eyes, mystery, a nation that was thrust into the international limelight with the June 1, 2001, slayings of the king, queen, and other royal family members, murders allegedly committed by the crown prince and king-designate. The less-publicized story has been the role of the press in Nepal. At the time of the killings, the Nepalese press was just beginning to enjoy new, Western-style freedom as a result of the pro-democracy movement of 1990 that ended decades of autocratic rule by the monarchy. However, the instability of the subsequent ten years—a decade that included ten different governments, some of which were headed by Marxists, all of which were accused of corruption and inept leadership—and other factors made the press vulnerable to new autocratic measures and to self-censorship during the national crisis of the summer of 2001.

When the Eiffel Tower was built in the mid-nineteenth century, one Parisian angered by the structure was the celebrated writer Guy de Maupassant. He would go around the city telling everyone that the tower was an eyesore, a blot on the Parisian skyline.

Yet he went to the Eiffel Tower every single day and had lunch in the restaurant there. People around him began to wonder why he didn't simply keep away from the structure because it infuriated him so much.

"I go there because being inside it is the only place in Paris where you don't have to look at or even see the Tower," Maupassant replied.

Noted scholar Edward Said has used the Maupassant story in assessing how differently Israel sees its Palestinian situation from the way those outside Israel see it, particularly others in the Middle East. The Maupassant story is also applicable to Nepal, where the view from inside the country is often radically different from the view outside. This is especially true in the aftermath of the June 1, 2001, massacre that wiped out almost the entire royal family and threatened to plunge the country into its most serious political crisis since the restoration of democracy in 1990.

The country's major newspapers failed to break the story the next day, and when they finally did, their news reports failed to relay the confusion on the ground or what actually transpired in the palace that fateful night. The differences between the Western press and the local press were obvious.

Reporters from *The New York Times* and *The Washington Post*, for instance, relying on eyewitness accounts and common sense, were soon able to establish a clear-cut story line in the ensuing confusion. Nepal's press, however, seemed completely baffled by the carnage and sustained a pervasive disbelief over eyewitness claims that held Crown Prince Dipendra responsible for the killings.

Long used to government handouts, most Nepalese journalists thought it was wiser to wait for official confirmation of the massacre, which unfortunately for them came seventeen hours later. One media analyst noted that the press seemed to be waiting for some ephemeral source to simply appear and tell them the story, and that source never came.

Little wonder, then, that newspapers were swamped by conspiracy theories and that editors got carried away by a groundswell of sentimental outpouring for the dead King Birendra and Queen Aishwarya as well as for Crown Prince Dipendra, who, as a probe report later said, had pulled the trigger on himself after gunning down nine members of his family. Rather than come out with the real story behind the whodunit, the press fed the paranoia of the frenzied crowd, and truth became the first casualty.

For nearly two weeks, Katmandu became a global spectacle as newspapers and networks from around the world flocked to the medieval city in a bid to unravel the mystery behind the royal killings. Was it the prince, crazed by his parents' refusal to give consent to his choice of bride? Or was it his uncle, an alleged hardliner, who many believed had strong differences with his slain brother over the handling of the country's military?

A real-life Shakespearean play was enacted, scene by scene, on the high Himalayas. It shook the very foundation of a nation that took pride in its 250-year-old monarchy.

Yet those reading the Nepali press a day after the massacre would have thought it was business as usual in the nation's capital. The country's leading newspapers—*Kantipur* and *The Katmandu Post*—didn't have a word to say on the killings.

Palace officials were as secretive as ever; government officials refused to confirm the nighttime shootouts; and the editors decided that they would be better off staying clear of a highly explosive story without 100 percent confirmation. In their overriding concern to play it safe, they failed to realize that they had missed the biggest story in the country's modern-day history. It was self-censorship of Himalayan proportions.

The incident is instructive of what ails Nepal's ten-year-old free press. But it would be unfair to claim that the country's media has remained stagnant over the years. Far from it.

The first private sector media house, Kantipur Publications, was established in early 1993, and its newspapers—the Nepali-language *Kantipur* and *The Katmandu Post*—have since emerged as market leaders, leaving their state-owned competitors—*Gorkhapatra* (established more than a hundred years ago) and *The Rising Nepal*—far behind in the circulation race.

Kantipur, which started out humbly with fewer than thirty employees, now brings out five major publications, runs an FM radio station, has a staff of more than 700, and bases its correspondents in almost all of Nepal's seventy-five districts. It is one of the biggest success stories of corporate Nepal, and its trail-blazing success is attracting other investors to the media sector.

This corporatization of the news media has paid handsome dividends. Historically, newspapers in Nepal were run to propagate party interests. A parallel can be drawn to the party press of the eighteenth century United States, with its divisions into Federalist and Anti-Federalist camps and their accompanying vituperative attacks on each other. The party press in Nepal continues to exist—and even thrive, especially the left-leaning weeklies—but it is the corporate papers that enjoy wide circulations and high levels of credibility. Because they are not dependent on the party dole-outs, they are free to criticize party policies.

The country now has eight broadsheet dailies; newsrooms are abuzz with excitement over an ever-expanding pool of investors in the media; and reporters are slapping each other's backs with prospects of lucrative careers. In many ways, the media scene has never been so rosy.

A twenty-six-year-old journalist who started his career in 1999 now makes twelve thousand Rupees a month (approximately $160), more than double his initial salary. Editors in corporate houses earn an estimated forty thousand to fifty thousand Rupees a month.

Newspapers are also fast changing into meritocratic institutions, in which each journalist commands his price according to his or her worth in the market. It won't be long before the so-called senior journalists—the vestiges of thirty years of the pre-1990, partyless, autocratic Panchayat system introduced by King Mahenda, father of the slain King Birendra—are phased out from the upper echelons of the corporate media houses and replaced by a younger, better-educated, and more motivated generation. Indeed, the trend is inevitable.

But this assumption factors in a number of determinants. Not the least of these are the overall economic growth and improvements in the rapidly deteriorating law-and-order situation in the country.

The Maoist-led People's War, which started in the remote mountain districts of western Nepal in 1996, now threatens to paralyze the entire country. Fears of a Maoist takeover loom large in every Nepali mind. The insurgents have never attacked a tourist, but the terror of the People's War ultimately threatens to deliver a crippling blow to tourism, Nepal's economic mainstay. Factory shutdowns and labor unrests have become common.

Officials finally seem to be grasping the restive mood of the population. A newly enforced Public Security Act allows police to detain citizens without having to bring them before a court of law. The law was introduced largely to fight the Maoist insurgency, but trigger-happy government officials may use it against any individuals they perceive as threats.

The government in June 2001 turned the clock back to the dark Panchayat days when it arrested the editor-in-chief and two publishers of *Kantipur* on charges of sedition. The publishers, Kailash Sirohiya and Binod Gyawali, were later released following a court order, but the editor, Yubaraj Ghimire, who has been released on bail, still faces a charge of sedition.

Days after the royal massacre, *Kantipur* published an op-ed piece by a Maoist ideologue who claimed that a grand conspiracy existed behind the palace killings. As with most of the other conspiracy theories, this one pointed an accusing finger at the newly enthroned King Gyanendra, a supposed hardliner who many believe wants to engage the military in resolving the insurgency.

Frustrated by worsening law-and-order conditions, a wary public now is ready to give an unprecedented level of license to the government to thwart the insurgency. Many people supported the government when the *Kantipur* journalists were charged with sedition.

Amid all this confusion, the first generation of nonpartisan journalists is struggling to keep its hard-earned reputation and perspective in tact. They realize deep down that an intrusive government may well put a clamp on press freedom someday, but little outcry has been heard against the Public Security Act that gives sweeping power to police and local authorities. If unconditional press freedom, guaranteed by the constitution, were to be put to a popular vote, many believe it would fail.

Is it wise to draw a parallel between press freedom in Nepal and that of established democracies? Does the press need to restrain itself in face of a government crisis? Is the press supposed to keep away from unpopular, even explosive, ideas? The journalists do not have easy answers to such questions. An angry mob tried to burn Kantipur buildings on June 4, 2001, when its newspapers reported that the Crown Prince was behind the killings. A frightening self-censorship followed.

Are journalists supposed to under-report incidents when fallout is possible? Doesn't common sense lead to too many compromises?

Burdened by all these soul-searching questions, the press vacillates between one extreme and the other—from being unusually bold at times and to being disturbingly timid, paranoid, and simply lost at other times, such as during the royal massacre. Press freedom has to be more than a clause in a constitution to be real. Journalists, and the society at large, must carefully nurture and zealously guard it to make sure that it survives.

Chapter sixteen

The Press in Japan

Job Security versus Journalistic Mission

by Takehiko Nomura
Freelance Writer
Tokyo, Japan

News obfuscates social reality instead of revealing it. It confirms the legit-imacy of the state by hiding the state's intimate involvement with, and support of, corporate capitalism.[1]

—Gaye Tuchman

Whereas more and more countries are wired for receiving a flood of information, Japanese major newspapers still boast their unparalleled circulation, thanks to news-hungry readers. *Yomiuri Shimbun* has the world's largest circulation (10.3 million) followed by *Asahi Shimbun* (8.3 million), and fifteen other dailies including sports newspapers were also among the world's top one hundred newspapers by circulation. Thus, every morning, about 53.7 million papers are printed in a country whose number of households is 47.4 million households. The five national dailies—*Yomiuri Shimbun, Asahi Shimbun, Mainichi Shimbun* (3.9 million circulation), *Nihon-Keizai Shimbun* (3.0 million circulation), *Sankei Shimbun* (1.9 million circulation)—especially exert enormous influence in society. Even the circulation of *Sankei* is still larger than that of *The Wall Street Journal* (1.75 million), which is the largest in the United States followed by *USA Today* (1.67 million) and *The New York Times* (1.08 million).[2]

Moreover, the five national commercial networks are owned by each of the five newspapers, and they manifest the respective editorial outlook of the dailies. With that pervasiveness, what role have such large newspapers played in a country in which one party has ruled for most of the last five decades?

First, Japan's mainstream media enjoy a near-monopoly on access to sources and information under the infamous *kisha* (reporters') club systems. The clubs are attached to government ministries, political parties, major institutions, business federations, police, and so forth. This system puts magazines, freelance journalists, and the foreign media out of the loop, making it difficult for them to get daily access to vital information. Despite such difficulties, as journalist Maggie Farley has pointed out, some of the most significant scandals have been uncovered by journalists working outside the *kisha* club system.[3]

"(In) Japan, ironically, the journalists who are best positioned to ferret out truth—the reporters in the cozy press clubs that cover major institutions—have seldom been responsible for exposing the major scandals of the last two decades."[4]

In late October 2000, after a few Japanese magazines revealed a series of embarrassing scandals, the country's chief cabinet secretary, Hidenao Nakagawa, a top aide of Prime Minister Yoshiro Mori, was forced to resign. Nakagawa reportedly had an extramarital affair, connections with right-wing extremists, and was even alleged to have leaked police information concerning a drug bust. The resignation, which came after his repeated and adamant denials, struck a severe blow to the beleaguered Mori administration. The scandals were covered and reported very differently by the major newspapers and by the outside press. This sharp contrast affords us an opportunity to look at what the Japanese press sees as its journalistic mission in this country.

One of the most serious issues in Japanese journalism is that the mainstream media fail to keep those in power accountable. They rarely take initiatives to investigate and reveal large scandals. But they spew out a flood of related information after a scandal is unearthed or if it causes a major political development. Thus they seldom become leaders and are usually followers.

This is true in the case of Nakagawa's scandal, a story broken by popular weekly magazines. On September 25, 2000, *Shukan (Weekly) Post* first reported that Nakagawa had an extramarital affair with a bar hostess, showing pictures of the two flirting with each other at a bar and in her room. The magazine ran embarrassing details of her one-year relationship with the right-hand man of Prime Minister Mori.[5] The story shook the Mori administration and reminded the public of another allegation—that the premier himself was allegedly arrested in a brothel in a 1958 police raid on prostitution rackets in Tokyo's red-light districts, which the magazine *Uwasa no Shinso (Truth in Rumor)* reported in early May.[6] He denied the accusation and filed a libel lawsuit against the magazine.

Although just how much the media should cover a politician's private life or reveal his or her sexual liaisons is debatable, the *Shukan Post* questioned Nakagawa's statesmanship in the alleged extramarital affair.[7] Furthermore, Nakagawa, who, according to the article, betrayed his wife and paid the equivalent of about $5 thousand a month to his lover to maintain the relationship, is ironically a minister in charge of the Council for Gender Equality, which belongs to the Office of the Prime Minister. The council was set up to promote women's status and respect their human rights as being equal to those of men. Virtually no one in the media, which are dominated by men in Japan, publicly discussed this irony or questioned why the premier appointed such a man to lead the council.

After the *Weekly Post* broke the scandal, Nakagawa responded by saying that he didn't want to comment on his relations with the woman and insisted that the matter is "not an issue that should be taken up in the Diet." The Diet is the national legislative assembly in Japan. Nakagawa also vehemently denied connections with a right-wing group. The magazine's article did not prompt the five major newspapers—*Asahi, Yomiuri, Mainichi, Sankei, and Nihon-Keizai*—to go after the scandal. The papers soft-pedaled the story even though opposition parties questioned Nakagawa during a plenary session of the Diet. They published only his brief denial in short articles buried in the papers. *Yomiuri,* a mass-circulation paper, even criticized the opposition, declaring the story a "misfire of (the opposition's) pursuit of…scandals" in an article that went on to say: "Opposition parties attempted to damage the image of the Mori administration by picking up Prime Minister Mori's 'brothel scandal' and Chief Cabinet Secretary Nakagawa's problem with a woman. But they depended on the reports (of) some media (and) the arguments ended up being dodged by Mori and Nakagawa."[8]

Yomiuri, the world's largest newspaper in terms of circulation, reported this as though the scandals were none of its business. The paper did not mention what Nakagawa's scandals might mean to society and to the Mori administration. Instead, it suggested that the opposition didn't have enough evidence to bring him down and that the ruling coalition of the Liberal Democratic Party (LDP) and the two other parties (The New Conservative Party and New Komeito) would manage to overcome the situation.

As the matter rested for a couple of weeks with the help of major newspapers, Nakagawa was gradually regaining political equilibrium. Then another story and pictures by a publication outside the establishment press, the weekly photo magazine *Focus,* sent an additional shock wave through the Mori administration. On October 18, *Focus* shot a report with the screaming headline "The Conclusive Evidence of Nakagawa's 'Crime.'"[9] The magazine carried pictures of his meeting with senior members of a "right-wing" group, showing Nakagawa sitting face to face with them in a restaurant. Another picture showed an alleged medical document with his signature on it for an abortion that his alleged mistress had undergone. It also ran her tale of their relationship and portions of a conversation with him that suggested his alleged drug use and his leaking of police information concerning a drug raid. In the transcription of the conversation, he clearly stated that he received information regarding a secret police investigation on her drug use, and he gave her a warning. In fact, it was later disclosed that the police did search her house soon after the conversation.

The report of *Focus* accelerated the opposition parties' demand for Nakagawa's resignation as they accused the top government spokesman of lying to the Diet. Still, Nakagawa adamantly denied the allegations, saying he didn't recall the meeting. The allegations of leaking police information and of drug use did not prompt much scrutiny from the major papers. Instead, they maintained the role of being his mouthpiece, running his repeated denials at the Diet in the same day's evening papers. Moreover, while downplaying the opposition's moves, all the national dailies focused more on how the LDP was dealing with the scandals. *Yomiuri* maintained that the opposition's call for Nakagawa's resignation "lacks force for now" as it followed the moves of the ruling party's most powerful members and used unnamed sources within the party for an article titled "The Ruling Party Eager for Damage Control."[10]

Focus was still after Nakagawa, however. A week later, on October 25, the photo magazine produced another embarrassing disclosure, firing off a question in the headline, "Dear Mr. Chief Cabinet Minister Nakagawa, Are You Still Saying You Don't Recall?" The magazine carried two pictures with Nakagawa's alleged mistress sitting on the bed in his home and standing in front of the house.[11]

The persistent magazine propelled the LDP to attempt more damage control. And the major papers became more obsessed with how the party's powerful elders and factions were going to tackle the crisis. Nakagawa continued to insist he had no recollection of the pictures, and he even hinted that he would file a lawsuit against the magazine. He never did.

In their coverage, the major papers allowed themselves to be manipulated by the political infighting within the LDP. They quoted unnamed LDP sources, apparently influential figures, saying that they couldn't back Nakagawa any more. Other LDP leaders, many of them unnamed, suggested that his insistence on keeping his post could negatively affect the fate of the Mori administration itself. The scandals finally were a major story even in the major papers.

After repeatedly saying he would not step down, Nakagawa finally bowed to mounting pressure from within his own party as well as the opposition and announced his intention to resign at midnight. He officially resigned the following day. Soon afterward, he indirectly acknowledged his adultery, saying, "It does not mean I had (a lover) while I was a secretary. There may have been a time when I was not exactly a saint. That happened several years ago."

Then reporters asked about the taped conversation, of which Nakagawa insisted he had no recollection. In the tape, he talked about a police investigation into drug abuse. He contradicted his previous statements and acknowledged that the man's voice on the tape "sounds somehow similar to mine." Despite his vague acknowledgement, however, major newspapers did not go after his alleged leaks of police information concerning a drug bust. Instead, most of their coverage was devoted to his relations with the woman. And, apparently, the allegations have never since been investigated.

This is an example of how the mainstream media fail to fulfill their responsibility to keep politicians accountable. Instead, they prefer to play the roles of mouthpieces for factions and influential figures in the ruling party. And as they lean toward the LDP, they downplay any moves by the opposition.

More evidence of this bias can be seen in the coverage of the 2001 LDP presidential race. Eyeing an upcoming July election, the scandal-tainted party decided to elect a new leader in late April to replace gaffe-prone Prime Minister Mori. It was a desperate attempt as his popularity ratings were plummeting to below 10 percent and disapproval ratings were soaring to more than 70 percent. Winning the leadership is tantamount to gaining the seat of prime minister. So this was one of the most important political events in Japan, although only LDP members can vote in the intraparty race.

With the onset of the campaign, virtually every major paper and national network scrambled to follow the LDP candidates and elders and widely cover them. One result of the pervasive coverage was increased popularity for the troubled party. Its four candidates—Junichiro Koizumi, Taro Aso, Shizuka Kamei, and former Prime Minister Ryutaro Hashimoto—got a free ride in newspapers and on nationally televised programs with appearances on more than twenty talk shows. Meanwhile, the opposition was so totally ignored that it was as though no opposition parties existed in Japan. Although some U.S. papers described one televised debate as a "confrontation," the media in Japan seldom push to have the ruling party candidates meet face to face with the opposition.[12] According to some opposition members, LDP politicians usually refuse to do so.

Moreover, despite the ubiquitous presence of the four LDP candidates in the media, they faced very few tough questions from the self-censoring mainstream media. For example, Heo Young Joong, a real estate developer accused of causing $40 million in losses to the defunct trading house Itoman Corporation because of a conspiracy with two former Itoman executives, told a court of LDP candidate Kamei's alleged involvement in the scandal. Of the five major papers, only *Mainichi* and *Nihon-Keizai* reported the allegation, and even they buried their tiny articles on pages 30 and 43, respectively. Another witness also told a different court that he saw Heo give Kamei $250,000. Kamei's office denied both allegations, and no major papers subsequently dealt with them in their coverage of the race.

Many major newspapers were also silent regarding controversial pre-election remarks by Economic Minister Aso, another candidate, during a news conference at the Foreign Correspondents Club in Tokyo. This is what Aso said, according to the Associated Press: "Maybe I'm saying this from my dogmatic prejudice, but the way I see it, the best country in the world would be a country where the richest Jewish people would want to live. Or it could be Armenians, or overseas Chinese, or any group around the world criticized for being rich."[13]

Of the major papers, only *Nihon-Keizai* reported the comments. *Nihon-Keizai's* tiny article, however, was buried on the inside pages.

After Aso's remarks drew criticism from the New York-based Anti-Defamation League, Aso apologized the next day in an interview with Dow Jones Newswires and CNBC Asia.[14] Virtually none of the Japanese media reported his apology.

Despite the massive coverage of the LDP race, a race toward an election in which the public can't vote, a poll taken by the *Kyodo News Agency* during the campaign showed that a majority of voters do not support the LDP. The poll showed only 25 percent supporting the LDP, whereas 35 percent identified themselves as independent. Among the independent voters, 48 percent said they didn't want the LDP to gain seats in the upcoming elections, and 35 percent didn't want New Komeito, another party in the ruling coalition, to do so either. Only 5 percent said the same about the Democratic Party of Japan (DPJ), the largest opposition party. Such popular sentiment was ignored by the mainstream media as they persisted with their coverage of the LDP.[15]

When some five hundred opposition members rallied in the Diet during the LDP race, criticizing the ruling party and declaring that they were going to win in the upcoming election, the mainstream press either treated the event as a footnote or didn't cover it at all. Not surprisingly, Eita Yashiro, an LDP member and the party's PR chief, expressed his gratitude on national television for the media coverage of the race. With a beaming smile, he said, "We appreciate that the media have cooperated with us."[16]

The biased coverage by the Japanese media is nothing new, said Sumiko Shimizu, a member of Social Democratic Party. Reporters may as well be members of the LDP and governing bureaucracy, he said. "They just report whatever the government or the LDP says. They lack background research and investigation before landing onto a new situation. They don't study issues by themselves. They rarely come to ask us why the opposition is against the ruling party's plan."[17]

Media scholar W. Lance Bennett says this kind of press-state relationship grants "public officials a virtual news monopoly (and) restricts diversity in the politically volatile 'marketplace of ideas,' thereby safeguarding the business climate in which media conglomerates operate." The domination of official voices in the news can be regarded as a result of "transactional" or "symbiotic" relations between journalists and officials.[18]

Japanese newspapers rarely create an opportunity to have political discourse, a real exchange of diverse opinions among different political players. Their closeness to those in power reinforces the dominant ideology, making political reform difficult for the country to achieve.

Major newspapers are "the biggest obstacle" to political reform in Japan, says Karel van Wolferen, author of *The Enigma of Japanese Power* and director of the Institute for Comparative Political and Economic Institutions at the University of Amsterdam. Van Wolferen says that major papers team up with bureaucrats to maintain the status quo, and thus they should be seen "not just as an important political factor influencing things, but as a major component of the political system itself."[19]

The major newspapers are very often used as a battleground for political infighting among LDP factions. So, issues are often argued within a small and limited circle. Van Wolferen describes it this way: "The newspapers are not expected to reveal the true nature of the Japanese political system. So they obfuscate it."[20]

Many scholars as well as foreign journalists such as van Wolferen have long attributed problems in Japanese journalism to the *kisha* club system, a network of hundreds of exclusive "clubs" of reporters attached to the nation's myriad political and economic organizations. Japan's mainstream press, which is privileged in its access to news sources such as government ministries and political parties, adjusts and controls the flow of information. Van Wolferen, a former Far Eastern correspondent for the Dutch paper *NRC Handelsblad*, says that the major papers do this because they have the same "obsession with social order" that bureaucrats have. "They believe that they are responsible for preventing social chaos, and that they must do so at all cost."[21]

The integration of Japan's major press with the political and economic establishment is achieved through connections made at the nation's exclusive universities. The coziness of the relationship is then reinforced through information cartels such as the *kisha* clubs. In no other democracies around the world is the relationship more cozy.

Says Laurie Anne Freeman, assistant professor of political science at the University of California, Santa Barbara: "Japanese politicians and bureaucrats, together with the mainstream media, have both promoted and benefited from what I call 'information cartels.'"[22]

Freeman says three institutions—the *kisha* clubs, the newspaper industry association, and media business groups—determine the character of this news management process.[23]

As journalists curry favor with those in power, information is easily controlled by sources. Self-imposed restrictions abound in Japan. For example, before an official interview, reporters typically discuss with political or business leaders what can be discussed and what can't.

Ivan P. Hall, a long-time Japan watcher who has spent almost three decades in the country as a correspondent, cultural diplomat, and professor, says: "As an integral part of Japan's powerful administrative state, the clubs, with their mutual back scratching between reporters and sources, serve as a brake on the healthy development of Japanese democracy."[24]

In addition to the *kisha* clubs, journalists' participation in *shingikai* (government advisory bodies) is another example of cozy relations between the media and the state. Along with scholars from well-known universities, leaders of big business, and interest groups, representatives of the Japanese mainstream media are actively involved in policy-making organs in which bureaucrats also participate. There are numerous *shingikai* in government ministries. The invitation to the *shingikai* is considered an honor.

Participants in the *shingikai* gain access to information that might otherwise be inaccessible. It is ironic that journalists sitting in the *shingikai* cannot disclose what they come to learn. Frank Schwartz, a Harvard University professor who has studied the *shingikai,* considers their participation in such government bodies "especially problematic. … Although the duty of reporters is to report, they run the risk of being co-opted when they serve on bodies whose operations are confidential."[25]

Journalists' involvement with the *shingikai* aligns them with the government and forces them to give up their neutral-observer status and responsibility to inform the public.

Through the *shingikai* and the *kisha* clubs, Japanese journalists working for the major press erect walls between the public and those in power, limiting the flow of information. They allow themselves to become a kind of public relations department of the LDP and the bureaucrats, a disservice to the public and an obstacle to a true intellectual discourse among citizens.

HISTORY OF THE JAPANESE PRESS

The close relationship between the press and the state in Japan is rooted in the very arrival of newspapers in the mid-nineteenth century. When learning of Western newspapers and their potential power, the Tokugawa feudal government (1603–1868), which had a national isolation policy and strict censorship, decided to try to use the press as a propaganda tool. Its leaders modeled their first newspaper after a Dutch newspaper. *Kanpan Batabia Shimbun* was the first official paper published at the beginning of 1863.[26]

The Meiji Restoration, the 1868 coup d'état that marked Japan's major shift from feudalism to modernity, enhanced the emergence of newspapers. The Meiji government, which was also aware of their enormous influence, considered newspapers to be "the mouthpiece of a benevolent power."[27] In its effort to keep a tight rein on the press, the government nurtured its press relations by giving reporters and editors financial support.

Like the *Yokohama Mainichi Shimbun*, Japan's first daily subsidized by the local government in the port city of Yokohama, early newspapers were servants of the state: they were intended for the most part as "useful organs in further understanding and acceptance of new government policies." In addition, journalists were to play an important role in spreading the new myth of a divine emperor and the nationalist ideology of a "family state."[28]

In the first three decades of the twentieth century, the press was controlled largely through a self-censorship encouraged by an often-inconsistent official censorship. Many important but unpleasant events—such as the killings of ethnic Koreans following the great Kanto earthquake of 1923—received virtually no attention. The establishment and development of the Communist Party also was a strictly taboo subject.[29]

Most of today's major media corporations were founded in the late nineteenth century and were already dominant in the nation in the period of military ascendancy and strict censorship from the 1930s through the end of World War II. For example, in 1944, Taketora Ogata, vice president of *Asahi Shimbun*, became a cabinet minister, reflecting the virtual merger of media and state in wartime Japan.[30]

As media scholar Susan J. Pharr has written, "Examining Japan's prewar legacy in relation to various interpretations of the media's role today, what stands out are dual traditions. Given the powerful roles exercised by the state with regard to the media over the era from 1868 to 1945, the 'servant' tradition is obviously strong."[31]

MALE-DOMINATED FILTERS

Another critical issue in Japanese journalism is its male-dominated filters. Some female scholars and activists in Japan are aware of the issue and seek information in alternative media or even create them to present women's views. The dominance of the media by men is rarely criticized, however.

Japan itself is a male-dominated society with thick glass ceilings for female employees in most corporations, which are invariably controlled by male bosses and managers. Japanese newspaper companies are no exception. Their newsrooms have very few female editors, and only a small number of women cover politics, the economy, and social and international issues. The so-called women's issues are usually relegated to a lifestyle or family section.

No place in the organization is more male-dominated than foreign bureaus. For example, *Asahi*, a "liberal" paper that identifies itself as Japan's "leading" daily, boasts twenty-nine overseas bureaus with seventy-five editors and reporters. The foreign bureau staff includes only four female reporters. Japan's leading wire service, the *Kyodo News Agency*, to which most Japanese newspapers subscribe, has twenty-three editors and reporters working in the United States. Only two of them—both reporters—are female.[32]

Imagine what kind of "world" the Japanese public is reading about through such male-dominated filters. The press has largely contributed to the public's poor understanding of the world. This is the world's second largest economy, and the nation has long been seeking permanent membership in the United Nations Security Council. Japanese leaders often assert that their nation aspires to regional and global leadership.

In Asia, women's issues are especially acute. One of the most pressing of these issues is the growing commercial sexual exploitation of women and children among international tourists in the region. Many of the customers on so-called sex tours in the region come from the United States, Europe, and Australia as well as from Japan and other Asian countries. During the 1970s and 1980s, Japanese men flocked to Asian destinations such as the Philippines and Thailand to buy young girls.

This is an issue that is not widely covered by the major newspapers. Another is domestic violence. In recent years, the number of victims has skyrocketed, as have the seminars and meetings related to the issue. More and more women have sought refuge and help, aggravating a basic shortage of shelters and counselors. Finally, even the staunchly conservative Mori government took long-awaited action by inviting in outside experts and forming a committee to study the matter. However, such issues just don't interest the mainstream press. An example of their coverage came in early October 2000 when the Asia Women's Center (AWC), one of the region's largest and most active nongovernment organizations, held a two-day international forum on "Violence Against Women" in Fukuoka, the largest city in Kyushu, southernmost of Japan's four main islands. The organization invited experts from the United States, South Korea, and other Japanese cities.

The issue was particularly important in Fukuoka, where the number of women seeking help in situations of domestic violence had been soaring. Many of the victims were Asian immigrants who married Japanese men and lived in the region. *Nishinippon Shimbun*, the region's largest newspaper with a circulation of about 840,000, published an advance article on the conference on page 25 of its lifestyle section.[33] No subsequent articles on the forum came out. Other major papers didn't cover the event, either.

The first day of the forum, held on Saturday night, coincided with the victory of Daiei Hawks, a local professional baseball team. The next day the *Nishinippon Shimbun* devoted thirteen of its forty pages, including its editorial page, to the victory.

Only an estimated 9.9 percent of the newsroom workforce at the *Nishinippon Shimbun* are women. The national average in 1999 was an estimated 10.2 percent, with men holding most of the managerial positions.[34]

Masako Katsuki, a female reporter with *Nishinippon Shimbun*, told participants at the Fukuoka International Women's Forum in October 2000 that sexual biases are commonplace even when her news organization does stories on women. When her desk decided to run a special series of reports featuring "successful" working women, her male colleagues almost invariably picked young, attractive women to profile. They even worked to prevent her from getting any of the assignments because they knew she was likely to choose a middle-aged or older woman, she said.[35]

Major newspapers also betray their biases when reporting government statistics. For example, when the National Tax Administration Agency issued a report on the profile of private-sector employees on September 26, 2000, most newspapers focused on the 0.8 percent decrease of their 1999 average annual income for the second straight year. They also attributed the slide to the slow pace of the country's economic recovery and corporate downsizing.

The same papers, however, downplayed or omitted another, significant part of the report: the income gap between men and women. The average annual income in the same year for female employees was 2.8 million yen, or about $25,800. That was less than half the income of their male counterparts, which totaled 5.67 million yen, or about $52,260.

The Japan Times, one of the country's major English-language dailies, acknowledged the gap but then buried it deep in its story with this accompanying assurance: "The gap underlined by 45,000 yen from 1998."[36]

Mainichi and *Nihon Keizai,* a major economic daily, ran articles on the report, but neither paper highlighted the income gap. Moreover, *Mainichi* noted that male employees had actually seen a slight decrease in average income— 0.8 percent—whereas women employees had seen a slight increase from the previous year: "Male employees have been seen to be more affected by corporate downsizing."[37]

Undeniably, however, it is women who have had to bear the brunt of Japan's protracted recession. According to Keiko Tani, a representative of the Tokyo Women's Union, a female-only labor union, more women have lost their full-time jobs than men have as Japan's economy has stalled. Fewer than 50 percent of female employees work full-time while more and more women have no choice but to take either a part-time or temporary job, according to the group. The number of women who come to the Union due to their troubles at work has surged, Tani said. More than half of them were discharged or forcibly dismissed from their jobs under the name of "corporate downsizing," or were victims of sexual harassment.[38]

A CORPORATE CULTURE

The fact that most major newspapers in Japan tend to walk in lockstep in the issues they choose to cover and to ignore reflects a broader characteristic of Japanese society itself. This is a country in which 99 percent of the population is Japanese. The mainstream press in Japan—as do other elements in Japanese society—places great emphasis on "harmony" and thus downplays different perspectives that might exist in important issues. Furthermore, the fact that the five national commercial networks are owned by the five major dailies reinforces the media's homogeneity. The networks sound the same and the newspapers look the same. As long as they remain this way, no major media outlet loses its share of the pie.

In a tightly controlled newspaper business well grounded in the norms of rigid Japanese corporate culture, reporters are hardly likely to challenge the status quo. In a newsroom in which a vertical power relationship is stressed, reporters write what their boss wants.

Yet, journalism jobs are very popular in Japan. Almost every year, major newspapers and TV networks are at the top of the list of corporations for which prospective university graduates want to work. Students consider the occupation stable, "cool," and well paying. Few of them indicate any sense of journalistic mission as their motivation.

JOURNALISTIC TRAINING

Unlike in the United States, it's a rare case in Japan that a beginning journalist gets hands-on training at a local newspaper and then later steps up to a larger one. When new university graduates in Japan embark on their careers at a major newspaper, many of them are likely to stay until retirement. As the Japanese saying goes, "Nagaimono ni makarero," or "Yield to the power." Many Japanese feel comfortable being part of a big corporation or institution.

Journalists themselves place their priority on job security rather than journalistic mission. They see themselves as members of a specific media corporation rather than as journalists. Said Shimizu, a Social Democratic Party member: "What we have now is spineless journalism. We no longer have journalists who are trying to investigate injustice, risking their lives. What they are concerned with is their business in a company."[39]

Many Japanese journalists begin their careers with little understanding of their profession. They lack journalism education and training; most schools and even universities don't offer journalism classes. And there are virtually no internships offered at newspapers. Yet, despite their lack of experience, training, and education, young journalists, rather than seasoned ones, are typically assigned beats such as the prime minister's office, political parties, and government ministries. This also furthers the likelihood of journalists being manipulated by politicians.

Newspapers, however, very often deplore conditions in Japan's educational system and blame that system on the growing problems of violence and crime among the nation's youth. *Yomiuri*, for example, ran a series of stories and editorials in November 2000 outlining its six-point plan for educational reform that would also restore a sense of morality among Japanese youth: "First, education should provide children with firm principles. Second, when they acquire such principles, an educational environment should be created to help them blossom as individuals."[40]

Yomiuri, praised by *The New York Times* as a "respected" paper, owns newspapers, magazines, a national TV network, a publishing company, a baseball team (Tokyo Giants), amusement parks, travel agencies, and a soccer team. On any given night, viewers can tune in to NTV, the network owned by *Yomiuri,* and get their fill of raunchy sexual commentary. Sex, after all, sells.

As Japanese journalist Katsushi Kuronuma has pointed out, "young people's behavior…is a by-product of Japan's distorted capitalism that was developed rapidly after World War II without ethics and morals."[41]

The same could be said for Japanese media. It is money and power on which the Japanese mainstream press places priority rather than journalistic mission or any other high-sounding ideals. Perhaps with the development of the Internet and commercial satellite television, more and more citizens will be exposed to quality journalism, and they will begin to demand it from Japanese journalists. Real reform will never be accomplished, however, without the establishment of a sound watchdog role for the Japanese press.

NOTES

1. Gaye Tuchman, *Making News* (New York: The Free Press, 1978), 210.
2. The average circulations of Japanese morning papers between January and June in 2000, according to Audit Bureau of Circulation. The circulations of the U.S. newspapers were the numbers as of 30 September 1999, according to ABC.
3. Maggie Farley, "Japan's Press and the Politics of Scandal," *Media and Politics in Japan* (Honolulu: University of Hawaii Press, 1996), 144.
4. Farley, "Japan's Press and the Politics of Scandal," 159.
5. *Shukan Post,* "The Confession of Chief Cabinet Minister Nakagawa's Lover," 25 September 2000, 32–36.
6. *Uwasa no Shinso*, "Yoshiro Mori: Scandal That Could Shake the Little Man's Heart," June 2000, 7.
7. *Shukan Post*, "The Confession of Chief Cabinet Minister Nakagawa's Lover," 25 September 2000, 31.
8. *Yomiuri Shimbun*, "The Misfire of [the opposition's] Pursuit of the Scandals," 30 September 2000, 4.
9. *Focus*, "The Conclusive Evidence of Chief Cabinet Minister Nakagawa's Crime," 18 October 2000, 4–7.
10. *Yomiuri Shimbun*, "The Ruling Party Eager for Damage Control," 19 October 2000, 4.
11. *Focus*, "Dear Mr. Chief Cabinet Minister Nakagawa, Are You Still Saying You Don't Recall?" 25 October 2000, 4–5.
12. Howard French, "Rare Event in Japan Politics: TV Debate on New Party Boss," *The New York Times*, April 18, 2001.
13. Eric Prideaux, "Japan Pol Seeks Wealthy Immigrants," The Associated Press, April 19, 2001.
14. The Associated Press, "Japanese Politician Apologizes to Jews," 20 April 2001.
15. *The Kyodo News Agency*, "Independent Voters Don't Want LDP and New Komcito to Increase their Seats," 20 April 2001.
16. Eita Yashiro, "Sunday Project," TV *Asahi*, 22 April 2001.
17. Sumiko Shimizu, personal interview, 29 November 2001.
18. W. Lance Bennett, "Toward a Theory of Press-State Relations in the United States," *Journal of Communications*, spring 1990, 103.
19. Maeda, Toshi, "Newspapers Help Bureaucrats Maintain Status Quo," *The Japan Times*, 23 June, 2000, 3.
20. Maeda, "Newspapers Help Bureaucrats Maintain Status Quo," 3.
21. Maeda, "Newspapers Help Bureaucrats Maintain Status Quo," 3.
22. Laurie Anne Freeman, *Closing the Shop* (Princeton: Princeton University Press), 2000, 160.
23. Freeman, *Closing the Shop,* 160.

24. Hall, Ivan P., *Cartels of the Mind* (New York: W.W. Norton & Company, 1998), 73.

25. Frank Schwartz, *Advice & Consent* (New York: Cambridge University Press, 1998), 84.

26. William de Lange, *A History of Japanese Journalism* (Japan Library, 1998), 24. *Javasche Courant,* a weekly newspaper issued by the Dutch Colonial Office, served as the basis for the first paper. According to Lange, however, recent research seems to indicate that *Javasche Courant* was imported to Japan as early as 1860, and already widely available in Yokohama.

27. de Lange, *A History of Japanese Journalism*, 35.

28. Richard Mitchell, *Censorship in Japan* (Princeton: Princeton University Press, 1983), 55.

29. Karel van Wolferen, *The Enigma of Japanese Power* (London: Macmillan, 1989), 94.

30. Susan J. Pharr, "Introduction: Media and Politics in Japan: Historical and Contemporary Perspectives," *Media and Politics in Japan*, 11.

31. Pharr, "Introduction: Media and Politics in Japan: Historical and Contemporary Perspectives," 11.

32. According to *Asahi Shimbun* and *the Kyodo News Agency* as of April 27, 2001.

33. According to the Audit Bureau of Circulation, as of from January to 2 June 2,000.

34. Masako Katsuki, at the Fukuoka International Women's Forum, 21 October 2000.

35. Katsuki, at the Fukuoka International Women's Forum.

36. *The Japan Times,* "Private-sector workforce has first fall in 50 years," 27 September, 2000, 2.

37. *Mainichi Shimbun,* "Down in Two Consecutive Years," 26 September 2000, evening, 10.

38. Keiko Tani, Personal interview, 13 September 2000.

39. Shimizu, personal interview.

40. *Yomiuri,* Editorial, "Restoring morality among children," 3 November 2000, 3.

41. Takehiko Nomura, "Moms try to fill service-ethic void," *The Christian Science Monitor*, March 21, 2000, 18.

PART SIX

Three Journalists and Their Missions

In this section you will read about three very different journalists and their personal encounters with questions of mission in their chosen craft.

Chapter 17 presents a story unique in this book. No grand themes here, no world-shattering political upheavals, and yet this is a microcosm of those larger worlds, where power politics and money also seek to overwhelm journalistic mission. Here is the simple tale of Neil White as a young idealist fresh out of college who starts his own newspaper in a small Mississippi town. White sets out to challenge the powers that be, does for a while, but then the bills start coming and, too, the pressure from those powers. He wavers where he once stood strong, and before long he finds himself in bankruptcy court, searching his soul for what journalism's mission truly is.

Chapter 18 tells of Chuck Trapkus, an artist and editor who forsakes mainstream journalism to pursue what for him is a life's calling, a journalism that encompasses more than just the day-to-day demands of a newsroom. Trapkus, who died tragically before completing this essay, preferred to think of himself as a craftsman, his work as an artist and journalist as a craft. What is a meaningful life but to pursue one's craft with integrity, honesty, and commitment?

Finally, in Chapter 19 you encounter world-famous journalist Ryszard Kapuscinski. In this essay about his life and work, you learn of a man who indeed sees journalism as a mission, one that demands the faithful telling of the human story however it may manifest itself. Kapuscinski believes journalists and other storytellers really cannot succeed unless they have empathy, that special sense of connectedness that recognizes our shared humanity, no matter how different we may seem to be.

Chapter seventeen

A Journey in Journalism

From Idealism to Bankruptcy

by Neil W. White III
Creative Director and Publisher, *Life 101* magazine
Oxford, Mississippi

Conflict is essential for a good story. For a business, it can be devastating. The journalistic division of church and state—the struggle between editor and publisher, between news values and business values, between defending an underdog and protecting those in power—has been well documented. However, the dilemma facing the individual who serves as editor and publisher, the man or woman who is solely responsible for serving the reader as well as the profit goal, is more difficult to document. The battles fought, internally, within the mind of an editor/publisher are won and lost in solitude—no witnesses, often no discussion, and certainly no explanation. These individuals are reluctant to disclose the stories they chose to ignore. They are even less inclined to discuss the reason.

To report an important story, accurately and fairly, is a noble endeavor. Often, the business of publishing those stories is not. To ask difficult questions, to give voice to those who have been wronged, to participate in real journalism are always considered aggressive acts because we are not leaving well enough alone.

As editors, we are adversaries of power. As publishers, we depend on the powerful to fund the operation of the newspaper. These inherent conflicts are to be worked out between the editor and publisher through deliberation and persuasion. When confined to the psyche of a sole proprietor, however, this deliberation is akin to schizophrenia—the boundaries are unclear and two forceful personalities struggle with little hope of mutual satisfaction.

I understand this struggle. I served as editor and publisher of community newspapers, magazines, and business journals in Mississippi and later in New Orleans, Louisiana. Under my editorship, our stories created uncomfortable situations for readers and advertisers. As the publisher, I continually tried to repair the damage caused by our reports.

Uncompromised journalism and entrepreneurship are ill-suited partners. In regions steeped in tradition, such as the provincial South, the two are mutually exclusive.

In 1985, my first year out of college, I launched a weekly newspaper, *The Oxford Times*, in the Mississippi town immortalized by Faulkner. A complacent, 105-year-old daily newspaper, *The Eagle*, also served the area. *The Times* was a hybrid of sorts. Editorially, we operated much like a metropolitan daily covering the prominent, the powerful, and the notorious. *The Times* was also a "total market coverage" publication with more than ten thousand copies mailed free to residents each week.

Our inaugural editions generated a great deal of enthusiasm. Not because of our experience or professionalism, but because we actually practiced journalism. The town was in dire need of a new voice. Our efforts were greeted with accolades and praise. The applause was motivating as well as intoxicating. The euphoria was brief. Our readers discovered in short order that the subjects of our scrutiny would be their neighbors, friends, and family. Survival in the early days required a hook. I found it in "City Court."

CITY COURT

Our hook was the weekly column called "City Court," a record of the misdemeanor crimes tried before the Oxford Municipal Court. The criminal proceedings were covered in great detail with testimony and dialogue printed verbatim.

Criminal courtrooms are intrinsically interesting, and Oxford's court was no exception. With the promise each week of indecent exposure, simple assault, shoplifting, public drunkenness, disturbing the peace, and voyeurism, demand for *The Times* increased. The presiding judge possessed a sharp tongue and quick wit, traits he utilized in open court that added to *The Times'* popularity. The column seemed ideal for a fledgling newspaper. Readers loved the entertaining details and I was certain it would not offend advertisers.

Hardly a week passed without a defendant pleading with us to exclude his or her name from the report. Our policy on "City Court" was clear: Everyone is treated equally. No names will be excluded.

When the late Willie Morris, a nationally recognized author and local resident, appeared in court for driving under the influence, we reported it. When a top committee chair of the Mississippi legislature was accused of drunk driving, we reported it. When the head football coach at Ole Miss was convicted of littering, we reported it. And when my wife was charged with overdue parking tickets, we reported it. Priests, doctors, and teachers appeared on the docket alongside the town vagrants. Because of the widespread distribution of *The Times*, the threat of a citizen's name being published in the column was often a bigger problem than the penalties issued by the court.

Many of our readers appreciated the column. An acquaintance pulled me aside one day and whispered from the corner of his mouth, "Love the court report"—as if it were a shameful thing to read.

Some readers considered the column cruel and exploitative. A friend recounted a story about a boy who had been suspended from the local high school for fighting. Apparently his classmates called his father "a drunk" after reading his name in the court report.

The personal suffering was troublesome, but the column was too important to tone down or dilute. I justified our action by insisting that it was a matter of public record, that people had a right to know, that it drove readership, and that we did not commit the crimes, we simply reported them.

Then there was the question of $400,000.

A local grocery store manager appeared in court for drunk driving. One of our newly acquired advertisers, the gentleman spent $800 per week with *The Times*.

After the proceedings, the grocer asked that I leave his name out of the report. I explained that our policy was to report every case, no exceptions. He said he understood and that he hoped I understood that he could not continue to support our newspaper if we caused him any further embarrassment.

Prior to our next publication, conflicting internal deliberations ensued. The publisher inside me pointed out that $800 a week translated to $41,600 per year, more than $400,000 over the next decade. "If we were running any other business," the publisher argued, "we would never knowingly act in a manner that would cost us $400,000!"

The editor in me pointed to fairness and integrity. "It's not too high a price for a kid to be beaten in school," the editor contended. "It's only too costly when it comes to money."

My arguments as editor were beyond reproach. We printed the piece and lost the advertising. Reporting the incident was absolutely the right thing to do editorially. It was a terrible business decision.

"City Court" set the editorial tone for *The Times*, but our coverage also extended to good news and human interest stories. Willie Morris, prior to his DUI conviction, submitted several pieces to *The Times*, including an amusing story on his "Ten Favorite Dogs In Oxford". Morris, author of *North Toward Home* and former editor of *Harper's* magazine, also arranged interviews with visiting writers such as George Plimpton and Alex Haley. The long-time mayor of Oxford was widely regarded as one of the best storytellers in the South and was known to make late-night telephone calls after a few drinks (usually in cahoots with Willie Morris) to U.S. senators and other dignitaries in Washington, D.C. Barry Hannah, a short story master and Pulitzer Prize nominee, would stop by the office on his motorcycle waving a pistol in the air wanting to tell stories.

The laissez-faire approach of *The Eagle* left ample opportunity to investigate hard news subjects considered "taboo" by the establishment.

Upon discovering my intent to publish the salaries of the elected officials in Oxford, the town's lanky chancery clerk asked, "Now, why would you want to go and do something like that?" He reluctantly provided the figures. Negligent property owners were shamed into renovation of dilapidated holdings when featured as our "Eyesore of the Week." Hospital administrators were enraged over our narrative about a civilian who drove their ambulance during an emergency. Auto mechanics in the area organized a boycott of *The Times* over an editorial that characterized them as shysters. The mall manager was fuming over our account of her Santa Claus being arrested for shoplifting (he was concealing merchandise in his big red bag).

Our stories seemed psychologically and socially disruptive to those in power. *The Eagle*'s deferential coverage had lulled the prominent of Oxford into a sense of impregnability. Our reports were regarded as scandalous, intrusive, and inappropriate—a blight on this genteel town. Southerners take great pride in refinement and obliging behavior. But a few of the powerful had plans to retaliate.

While researching the city budget, I noticed large sums of public money that had been paid to a local attorney of great reputation who also held a position of vast influence over university administrators. I published the specific amounts paid to the attorney and wrote an editorial criticizing his outrageous fees. I also implied that his representation of the county presented, in some instances, a conflict of interest. I planned to publish updates on the story as information surfaced.

I was called to the office of an upper-level administrator at the University of Mississippi a few days after the story broke. This university official urged me to drop the story. The powerful attorney, it turned out, had leverage over university policy and hiring. I assured the administrator that I would continue my reporting and that I believed the attorney had possibly acted in a less-than-ethical manner. His urging suddenly took a different, stronger tone.

The administrator insinuated that my mother, a university employee, could lose her job over the piece and he convinced me, subtly, that my immediate family was also vulnerable.

"I know you have a family, a one year-old son," he said. "I'd hate to see you get your legs cut out from under you."

He added that the attorney's wife was so distraught over the accusations and disclosure of income that she had left town "to stay with friends in Vicksburg."

I struggled with my decision, but ultimately I killed the story. It is my biggest regret as a reporter. I had the vehicle and the reach to fight this battle, but I chose silence. I wish, for all the individuals who had experienced this bullying before me, that I had reported everything, even the administrators' threats. I had a rare opportunity to fight back, to expose coercive tactics, but I was afraid.

Another dilemma presented itself on August 11, 1986, when I received a letter to the editor from another prominent author and local resident, Barry Hannah. In the letter, Hannah bitterly attacked the "City Court" report, the judge, and what he considered to be my exploitation of the undefended. The letter was full of venom. It was also filled with truths. Hannah likened the court proceedings to that of taking aim at fish in a barrel. He wrote that I had lost my objectivity completely. He described the judge as an "ugly, stunted racist and bully—an example of the craven little Nazi in all of us." He characterized my friendship with the judge as a new era of cronyism.

Hannah added a handwritten postscript: "I dare you to print this."

Despite the personal attacks, I realized the significance of the letter. A prominent local judge versus Oxford's most celebrated and colorful writer. Two giants, with huge egos, going at it. And I could sell ringside seats.

I planned to print the letter in the next issue. But I wanted to give the judge, a personal friend, advanced warning that it was going to be published. He asked me to read it to him, and I did. When I did, the judge warned, "If you print that letter, I'll have no choice but to file suit against your newspaper and Mr. Hannah."

I wanted so bad to print the letter, perhaps for the wrong reasons, but I didn't want to alienate my most compelling source of news. I was confused and I felt paralyzed.

The letter was never published.

THE BUSINESS OF JOURNALISM

Oxford's daily newspaper was roused from its slumber when the advertising dollars started to flow to *The Times*. *The Eagle* remained listless editorially, but its publisher launched a marketing campaign that was aggressive and quite effective. The same small-town, "good ol' boy" network that hindered *The Eagle*'s ability to practice authentic journalism facilitated its efforts to recoup advertising dollars.

The Eagle cut its advertising rates and instituted an enterprising sales effort. It called in favors and portrayed us as trouble-making outsiders. Our having alienated many of Oxford's prominent advanced their campaign. The advertising dollars flowed back to the daily. It became a capital battle, and I was ill equipped to compete.

The financial momentum shifted back to *The Eagle*. And the enthusiasm for our unconventional voice waned. Expenses grew; revenues declined. I did not stand up well under the financial strain. I mismanaged what little funds we generated, using money earmarked for printing to make payroll. I diverted funds allotted for an advertising campaign to pay operating expenses. I pilfered Peter to pay Paul. And, in a desperate measure, I used overdrafts at two different banks to keep the newspaper limping along.

This frantic maneuvering came to the attention of my investors and bankers. Understandably, they pulled all funding.

In December of 1987, two years after our premiere issue, *The Times* was out of business. I owed more than $100,000 to investors and creditors, with no vehicle for repayment.

REFLECTIONS ON FAILURE

Capitalism not only affords us freedom of the press but also gives us the freedom to put ourselves out of business. As the owner of *The Times*, I can trace my failure to any number of factors: poor market choice, lack of long-term financing, uncontrolled growth and inadequate planning, horrendous money management, unrealistic expectations, a sense of invulnerability, the squaring off against established media, and, certainly, the influence of a powerful few who longed for our silence. Ultimately, newspapers require deep pockets. Mine were anything but.

As an editor and publisher, my internal deliberations rarely ended in compromise. I liken my dual role to a light switch: completely on or completely off. Perhaps a rheostat-like approach—with the ability to adjust the illumination of an issue to a degree that was accurate, but not damaging—would have extended my publishing longevity.

Community newspapers cover ordinary people and ordinary lives. I was not fully aware of the impact our unsparing stories would have on a small community, especially the entrenched elite. I was ignorant of the consequences that came along with freedom of the press. My boundaries were good sense and money. I paid attention to neither.

H. L. Mencken noted that as journalists we are "unable, as yet, to control admission to our craft." Our unregulated profession allows for a great range of experience, prejudices, views, and judgments. As a reporter, I expected public trust, though I had little experience. I embraced editorial responsibility without the benefit of dialogue from colleagues. I was a pundit with no real editor, an editor with no sensible publisher, and a publisher with an inadequate understanding of my environment.

Financially successful publishing is a balancing act, one that demands accuracy and judiciousness, accountability and fairness, confirmation and reflection, temperance and discretion. I never quite got the hang of it.

In the spring of 1988, at age twenty-seven, I found myself in a United States Bankruptcy Court. With an attorney at my side and creditors to my back, this was the time to face those I owed but could not pay.

Failure is always costly. My investors lost $60,000. Local vendors lost more than $50,000. My losses came in a different form, a very public loss of trust and voice and reputation. Friends avoided eye contact. Their whispers chipped away at my battered esteem.

I had many regrets: that I'd not asked for help, that I'd presumed such right-eousness in my editorials, that I'd been such a poor steward of others' money, and that I hadn't better understood the virtues of restraint. I also had regrets about not going further with certain stories.

But I did not regret my efforts. I knew, even as I stood in bankruptcy, that I would try again—in another town, in a larger, less provincial, market, with the benefit of this experience, and heeding more to my "publisher."

As I turned toward those I had hurt, I noticed a singular absence in the courtroom: reporters. *The Eagle*'s indolence extended even to our demise. I started this whole ordeal precisely because *The Eagle* was unresponsive to situations such as mine. Now, I was the beneficiary of their lethargy.

There would be no detailed account of my debts, no questions about shuffling funds, no printed opinions surrounding my failure, and no quotations from local merchants who had lost money.

No one was there to tell the story. And I was grateful.

Chapter eighteen

Reclaiming Responsibility

A Journalist and Artist in the Catholic Worker Movement

by Chuck Trapkus
Illustrator, Editor, and Publisher, *The Catholic Radical*
Rock Island, Illinois

I cut my journalistic teeth at a small, editorially conservative daily newspaper in my midwestern hometown. At eighteen, I was not only the youngest editorial illustrator they had ever employed, but, I imagine, also the oldest. After several years of both inventing and learning my job, I had become increasingly conscious that I was somehow in the wrong place. To begin with, I sat through marathon sessions in the publisher's office as the editorial facts of life were patiently explained to me. I'm sure there was every expectation that this naïve but promising young illustrator would someday make a great editorial cartoonist if only he could get the proper (politically conservative) indoctrination. Perhaps unfortunately for the publisher and various editors, this period coincided with the beginning of my political enlightenment. I eventually concluded that they were about as likely to run my editorial cartoons critical of U.S. foreign policy in Central America as I was to enlist with the Marines. I got out before it got ugly.

Among the lessons of my four-and-a-half years with the mainstream press was the shattering of my notions that commercial media is both free and objective. Press freedom is compromised by its dependence on advertisers and ratings; its objectivity is compromised by all sorts of alliances, affiliations, and editorial viewpoints. These compromises are exhibited in daily decisions that every news organization makes: what to cover, and where and when and how to run it. The organization deals with the obvious decisions about what "slant" or "spin" to give a story, and the much more subtle, even unconscious, decisions such as how long a story should be. There may be degrees of press freedom—it seems clear that National Public Radio, for example, can report more freely than, say, CBS news, and that *Z Magazine* makes them both look like TASS, the old Soviet news agency, on a bad day. But I don't think this applies to objectivity. To speak of degrees of objectivity sounds to me like degrees of truth. Either something is or it isn't objective. I say the press isn't—there's just no such thing, or at least *objectivity* badly needs redefining. All journalists bring a bias to stories they cover, no matter how hard they try to avoid it. When the bias seems too obvious, we call it propaganda. And that's where I'm at today: publishing unabashed propaganda with a tiny Christian anarchist quarterly, *The Catholic Radical.* It's as free as a newspaper ought to be; as biased as any. The difference, which makes all the difference in the world to me, is that our paper admits its bias up front. The Catholic Worker (CW) movement began as a newspaper, a fact that is recognized in the several dozens of newspapers and journals that are published to this day from many of the couple of hundred CW houses scattered across the U.S. and elsewhere. But in 1933, there was just the *Catholic Worker* monthly, a penny a copy (still is), and the two people who started it all: Peter Maurin and Dorothy Day. Dorothy took up writing while at the University of Illinois, although she left in 1916 after two undistinguished years, with no degree and no prospects. Her father, John Day, was a writer for *The New York Telegraph* at the time. Dorothy eventually found work as a reporter for a Socialist daily newspaper, *The Call*, in lower Manhattan. She worked for several other left-wing journals over the next ten years: *The Masses*, *The Liberator*, *New Masses*. And after her conversion to Catholicism in 1927, she wrote for the substantially less radical Catholic publications *America* and *Commonweal*, the latter of which brought her into contact with Peter Maurin, a French immigrant, day laborer, and street philosopher twenty-two years her senior. It was his vision of creating a new society within the shell of the old "through a synthesis of cult, culture, and cultivation" that gave the CW its foundation. He preached the much-neglected social teaching of the Catholic Church and he offered a way for Dorothy to combine radical ideals with her newfound religion. Peter came up with a three-point program: Houses of Hospitality, where the Works of Mercy are performed (feeding the hungry, welcoming the stranger, clothing the naked, and so forth); "Agronomic Universities," or farming communes, where "the workers can become scholars and the scholars can become workers"; and clarification of thought, through round-table discussions and—wouldn't you know it—a radical newspaper.

The hospitality idea was as foreign to Dorothy as Peter's thick Languedocian accent. And being a big-city girl, she could barely spell *farming* or *agronomic* whatever. But a radical newspaper! This was right up her alley. With more ambition than cash, they printed twenty-five hundred copies of an eight-page tabloid and sold them in Union Square in Manhattan. Dorothy was forced to pawn her typewriter to pay the bills, but support was on the way after the first issue was distributed. Within six months, the circulation rose to seventy-five thousand. A movement was born, and the houses of hospitality and farming communes were soon to follow. Some seven decades later, it's still going on.

From the beginning, the CW embraced the term *propaganda*. Dorothy wrote "to protest, to oppose, to complain, to point out abuses, and demand reforms," whereas Peter's more refined angle was a "Green Revolution," a reconstruction of the social order along decentralized, agrarian, personalist lines. Although they disagreed on many things, including the very name of the newspaper (Peter preferred *The Catholic Radical*, but Dorothy prevailed) never did any hint of journalistic objectivity appear in its controversial pages. The newspaper was their mission, a printed crusade against the status quo, part of the "path from where we are to where we ought to be," in Peter's words.

Although I've often wondered how different the CW might have been if Dorothy had been, say, a surgeon or a professional acrobat or a chimney sweep instead of a journalist, the newspaper—and most of the many CW publications from corners all over the planet—still serves to inspire and energize its readers as well as to reflect the thinking and doings of the writers published. The propaganda has become integral to the mission of the CW. It should be noted that this is a movement of amateurs, frustrated would-be's and wanna-be's, the occasional professional, and lots of nonwriters, semiliterates, and socictal misfits. This is not *The New York Times,* but what the CW newspapers may lack in polish, they (most of them) make up for in content, integrity, and passion. The content of the writing often includes stories and presentations ignored by the mainstream, such as the ongoing war against Iraq through regular U.S. bombings and economic sanctions. By integrity, I mean that the writers are living what they're writing; an article about eating out of dumpsters is written by someone who's actually doing it. As for passion, it's hard to miss the heart in much of what's printed. There's commitment, even zeal. How often do you find that in *The New York Times*? They're probably too busy feigning objectivity.

No doubt it's unfair and even a bit silly to compare CW newspapers with mainstream journalism. But a radical critique of all journalism raises a handful of issues I'd like to briefly explore here. Because I share Peter's penchant for triple alliteration ("cult, culture, cultivation"), I offer: truth, trivia, and technology.

TRUTH

If we just toss aside the idea of "objective truth" as a myth or at least an oversimplification, what then can we say about truth? For the likes of such philosophers as Aristotle, Thomas Aquinas, Jacques Maritain, and many others, truth is the object of the intellect. Our minds are made up of the intellect and the will, among other things, and the intellect strives toward Truth just as the will strives toward Good. That is, to the extent to which we are intelligent beings, able to recognize what is true about ourselves and our world, we strive toward truth. To the extent to which we are moral beings, able to recognize right from wrong, we strive toward the good. But how to know this truth, this good, in the first place? It shouldn't take a Ph.D. to see that our society's standards aren't much help. From disposable cameras to "Happy Meals" to the robot pets, we seem as a society to possess a fairly insatiable appetite for the absurd, the stupid, the wasteful, the bad.

Our judgment is deformed by all sorts of unhealthful influences, most of which have to do with Madison Avenue and somebody else's profits. When it comes to "news," we tend to apply the same sort of critical judgment, which is to say, very little. And the usual formality of "balanced" reporting—quoting an opposing viewpoint—will no more lead to the discovery of Truth than will opposing lawyers in a courtroom.

We must go back to first things. After we figure out who we are and what we're all about, the rest follows. It's no use speaking of morality when we can't agree upon the nature of humanity. If we were content to see ourselves as robots, good for little more than fitting into some corporate five-year plan, then robot-made plastic whatnots may be perfectly acceptable, a sound bite masquerading as news might be more than we really care to hear anyway, and everything is suddenly quite simple. But if you accept, as I do, that we are creatures of meaning and purpose, products of unfathomable forces, and capable of knowing, willing, and loving, then it gets a bit more complicated. We know on an instinctive level that our knowing, willing, and loving are directed toward Truth, Goodness, and Beauty, respectively. I would substitute the name God here but it needn't be a stumbling block. If you accept that we draw ourselves toward this Utmost Reality through serving one another, then a picture of what human beings are for takes shape. The means of sustaining life, both material and spiritual, the things that women and men have expended all their care and skill and pride on for millennia, are natural to humans and therefore good. But there is much that doesn't fit, such as lawyering and selling. You probably can come up with your own list. Not that these activities have no justification, but the justification comes from something other than what is natural to humans. Lawyers have a role because governments impose laws that restrict and contradict our natural freedoms. What's important here is not a list of what's in and what's out, but that there is a standard for even discussing it. When we discuss truth, we must have some understanding of the truth about the basic facts and issues involved in the story, in the news report, as well as what's true about ourselves. That is, the more we know ourselves ("self knowledge" of one sort or another being the goal of most of the great mystical religions), the more we'll know how to interpret and digest all the news, information, and clutter coming our way.

We also know ourselves to possess free will. I can choose to do this and not that, or vice versa. With that freedom comes responsibility; whatever choice I make, it is *my* choice, and I must accept the consequences.

Thus, as human beings we are by nature responsible and not irresponsible. Yet responsibility is a distressingly rare commodity nowadays. Journalism is one of the few professions still taking this concept seriously. Every time a by-line appears (editorial revisions notwithstanding), the writer is in effect saying "here I am; it's mine." Love it or hate it or ignore it, I am responsible. But in all likelihood, no one claims responsibility for the paper it's printed on, the computer it was composed on, the chair the reporter sat in, the lunch he or she ate, and so on. In an anonymous, irresponsible world, the byline serves as a reminder of what human beings are all about.

From this perspective, a journalism that serves the common good, recognizes what is basic and natural to humans, and insists on responsibility, is a pretty good idea, regardless of its money-making potential.

TRIVIA

Whether or not the story passes the "truth" test, we must consider its significance. We in the United States today are drowning in trivia, words, "information", nonessentials, just plain silliness. With much to-do, the "information economy" is touted; never mind what we're supposed to be doing with all these billions of bits of information at our electronic fingertips. It appears to justify itself: information for its own sake. Visit our Web site, surf the Net (why?), access, access. How did your grandparents even get along without it all? The result is an amazing glut of nonsense, not unlike Vorhees's fabled library of Babble, an imaginary collection of every possible book in which, for example, one book consists of all *A*'s, another of all *A*'s plus a *B*, and so forth. We do not serve the common good by adding to this information glut, especially now that there is such a desperate need for sense, for helpful words. A major reason for the mindlessness of the status quo is the market-driven media. Giving the people what they want is the thinking. Otherwise, the people look elsewhere and the advertisers pull out. Given our capitalist background, any alternative seems downright unimaginable. You want "public" media? There, too, marketability and ratings play a strong, if somewhat lesser, role. I see a parallel between the trivializing of journalism and trivializing of "art." For much of human history, "art" merely meant skill, as it still does today—"artfully" equals "skillfully." But somewhere along a confused line, a few hundred years ago, the notion of art was split off from all other endeavors and became synonymous with drawing, painting, sculpting, music, and so forth. Other creative enterprises were relegated to a second-class "craft" status. Hence today we speak of "art" as though it is the field specializing in Beauty, whereas "crafts" (you know, basketry, pottery, refrigerator magnets) specialize in Utility. Today the art world is awash in nonsensical claptrap, and all because of how we look at it. There is no good reason a painting should be beautiful, whereas a chair or toothbrush need not be. Therefore, there is no good reason to elevate painting over any other "craft" or creative work whatsoever—omelet making, bricklaying, or article writing. Art, said the British stonemason Eric Gill, is "making well what needs making." A little phrase like that is what separates the very important works from the museum filler and critic fodder that most of us take for granted.

So it is with journalism. Can we call it "writing well what needs writing"? If we have to justify every story and every paragraph before publication, perhaps we will come to weed out some of the verbal crabgrass. What is it that "needs writing"? Lots of unreported or underreported stories exist. They won't hit the mainstream press because the mainstream is busy with its popularity contests, and quixotic dedication often is required even to find the stories conveniently buried by governments and other powers that have interest in suppressing them.

A list of such stories from me or anyone else is not what is wanted here. Just ask first: What needs to be reported? Every journalist should be able to focus better on the things that matter. Of course, most will object that it generally falls to editors and publishers—rarely anyone who actually writes the stories— to decide what "needs" to be printed. And this throws us back to the issue of responsibility. Those who do the work must design the work, or at least have a part in its design, in order to be responsible workers. The more utopian and outlandish this notion sounds, the more inclined I am to opt for our eight-page propaganda tabloid.

TECHNOLOGY

We are told these days that technology is changing everything, and we hardly need to be told. What is it doing to journalism? Many of my journalistic friends would argue that computers have made their lives easier; the mechanics of writing and editing are a breeze compared to the "old days." Although I am not equipped to discuss the specifics of that claim, lacking any firsthand experience of the newly "wired" newsroom, I offer the general observation that computer technology is affecting journalism adversely.

It is here that Chuck Trapkus' essay ends, although he left a few additional scribbled notes, such as, "Let's be honest—a stylus on a clay tablet is technology" and "Work is distorted because the medium is the message (what interests benefit pro-tech bias?)." This essay was left incomplete because Chuck died on December 21, 2000, the victim of a car accident. He was forty-one years old.

Chapter nineteen

Ryszard Kapuscinski

The Empathetic Existentialist

by Joseph B. Atkins
Associate Professor of Journalism, University of Mississippi
and
Bernard Nezmah, *Mladina* magazine, and
Assistant Professor, Faculty of Philosophy, Ljubljana
Ljubljana, Slovenia

Ryszard Kapuscinski eyes his modern-but-spiritless surroundings in the café of the fashionable Hotel Lev in Ljubljana, Slovenia. He looks at the sparse Sunday evening crowd, the hovering photographer snapping picture after picture of him. "Splendid place," he says, a hint of irritation growing in his voice. "When I'm on a journalistic mission, I never stop at five-star hotels. I don't feel well in five-star hotels."[1]

The famous Polish foreign correspondent has just finished an hour-long interview with a novice television reporter and now is sitting with veteran journalist Bernard Nezmah in the latest of a series of promotional stops arranged by his local publisher. Indeed, five-star hotels such as the Hotel Lev have never been the norm for Kapuscinski, who is arguably the world's greatest journalist. His more natural habitat for the past four decades has consisted of the jungles, dust-filled backroads, and dilapidated shack-bars of the Third World.

Certainly even in the backwaters where Kapuscinski performs what he calls his journalistic "mission," the occupational hazard of all foreign correspondents is ever present: the sense of being the outsider, the stranger in a strange land. Note this account, in his book *The Soccer War*, of an anticolonialist, anti-Western media, feverishly pro-Kwame Nkrumah rally he attended some thirty years ago in Ghana: "As I stand there in the crowd, writing, suddenly I notice that I am not feeling quite as stifled as I did moments before; that a space has opened around me; that those closest to me are moving away. I look around, and their eyes are not friendly, their gaze is cold, and a quick chill comes over me, and then I understand. I am the only white there, and I am writing in a notebook. Well, I must be a journalist."[2]

Yet Kapuscinski is more at home among the ragged villagers and peasants of the world than he is among the patrons of Europe's upscale hotels. "My own life was the life of poverty—without shoes and food," he said to Bernard Nezmah in their meeting in November 2000. "So when I come to those people in Africa, I feel myself very much at home. I know how to live there. And I find it sort of my duty to tell something about these poor people of the world."[3]

Kapuscinski, the longtime reporter for the Polish Press Agency (PAP), the weekly *Kultura* and other publications as well as author of such classics as *The Soccer War, The Emperor, The Shah of Shahs*, and *Imperium*, may be "the finest foreign correspondent in the world…a cult figure (with the) résumé of a mercenary or a spy," *International Herald Tribune* writer Michael Zwerin once wrote.[4] It's a résumé that covers more than forty years and dozens of wars, revolutions and coups d'etat, and major scoops, such as his reporting on the famous "soccer war" between Honduras and El Salvador in 1969. He has survived bullets, malaria, a death sentence, imprisonment, banishment, fascism, and communism, all to be a witness and chronicler of what he calls "the mental and political decolonization of the world."[5]

To take such risks requires a certain conviction about one's chosen path in life. "Mine is not a vocation, it's a mission," he once said. "I wouldn't subject myself to these dangers if I didn't feel that there was something overwhelmingly important—about history, about ourselves—that I felt compelled to get across."[6]

Much is made of Kapuscinski the adventurer. In compiling his reports of the disintegrating Soviet Union, he "was instinctively drawn to the blood, to the violence along the empire's southern rim," says Michael Ignatieff in his review of *Imperium* in the *London Review of Books*.[7] "As with Hemingway, his death-wish seems to well up, paradoxically from a longing to feel alive, but unlike Hemingway, he avoids all forms of adolescent bravado."

Kapuscinski, by most accounts, is a modest man who readily concedes his human frailties, such as his fear of heights and of public speaking, his need for human contact and courtesy, his tears when faced with abject human suffering. He is a great lover of books, of poetry and philosophy. Yet danger does hold a special attraction. This is clear in his famous account of the bloody 1966 civil war in Nigeria when marauding soldiers and hooligans at a roadblock doused him with benzene and attempted to set him on fire. "I was driving down a road where they said no white man can come back alive. I was driving to see if a white man could, because I had to experience everything for myself. I know that a man shudders in the forest when he passes close to a lion. I got close to a lion so that I would know how it feels."[8]

Many journalists share this spirit of adventure. What sets Kapuscinski apart is the way he combines risk taking with literary skill and, especially, his deep sense of empathy for others. "Empathy is perhaps the most important quality for a foreign correspondent. If you have it, other deficiencies are forgivable; if you don't, nothing much can help."[9]

Born March 4, 1932, he spent his early years in the town of Pinsk in what is now Byelorussia. Kapuscinski's Pinsk was a poverty-ridden small town full of Gypsies, Jews, Ukrainians, immigrants, refugees, and wanderers of all kinds, people who peddled wares from horse-drawn carts, people so poor they used tree bark for shoes. Those with homes had no indoor plumbing or telephones. Kapuscinski's parents were schoolteachers. His father fought in the Polish underground against the Nazis, only to be taken prisoner later by the Russians and deported.

His first memories are mostly of war, with Pinsk and his family's later home in Warsaw caught between the Nazis to the west and the Russian Red Army to the east. "War is everywhere. Villages are burning; people are taking shelter from air raids in ditches and in forests, seeking salvation wherever they can."[10] In his interview with Bernard Nezmah, he also recalled those times. "I come from the poorest part of Europe in that time. I am from a very humble family, from a very small and poor town, and I suffered terrible hunger and disaster during the world war."[11]

These experiences are central to Kapuscinski's sense of himself as a journalist and as a writer. "What is a 'writer'? In all my years in Africa and Latin America covering one revolution and coup d'état after another, I never met a novelist, not one poet there dealing with the real history of our times. They were back in Europe winning prizes for the same love stories and domestic sagas we have been reading for five hundred years. Incredible. And they look down their noses at 'journalists' as some sort of inferior race."[12]

Kapuscinski's "journalists" aren't all that different from the peasants, workers, and villagers he writes about, people plying their trade in relative anonymity, sometimes risking their lives, fighting against all kinds of odds and frustrations with little tangible compensation for it. "What does a reporter carry around the world? Some dirty shirts and a few newspaper clippings, a toothbrush and a typewriter." "Our job is like a baker's work—his rolls are tasty as long as they're fresh; after two days they're stale; after a week they're covered with mold and fit only to be thrown out."[13]

Still, there is a nobility in the work of the journalist "who must experience everything at his own cost," whose commitment to truth and service to freedom and justice are such that "nowhere in the world do the police believe that such a profession actually exists."[14]

This view of journalism as a high and honorable calling is shared by the Colombian-born novelist and journalist Gabriel Garcia Marquez, a writer to whom Kapuscinski is often compared. "Journalism is an insatiable passion that can only be directed and humanized when it has raw confrontations with reality. Nobody who has not suffered this passion can imagine how this servitude feeds on the unknowns of life. Nobody who has not lived it can conceive the unnatural rush that comes from the news, and the orgasm one has with a news scoop, and the moral demolition one feels when one fails."[15]

The journalist, according to the German existentialist philosopher Karl Jaspers, "is one of peculiar responsibility, which, anonymous though he be, should give him self-confidence and a keen sense of honor. … Without a press, the modern world could not exist."[16]

Kapuscinski's work as a writer, his lonely and restless wandering, his way of assessing mankind as he travels and observes the world put him in a literary tradition that includes journalists and novelists such as Garcia Marquez, V.S. Naipaul, Graham Greene, and George Orwell. It is a tradition that in many ways evokes the image of the "existential journalist" whom media scholar John Merrill has described in such books as *Existential Journalism* and *The Imperative of Freedom*.

Eschewing the corrupting influences of both state and corporation, the existential journalist jealously guards his freedom in pursuit of a journalism that is courageous and honest. To do this requires an intense, self-authenticating struggle, a deep-seated individualism willing to challenge any authority that would enslave the spirit or hide truth. "In a dispirited world where mass order and technical life are destroying that which is human and humane, what is needed is an existential approach to life," Merrill writes in his classic *Existential Journalism*. "This takes freedom, will, and courage. But with these, the existential journalist can become authentic and can change the world—at least a small part of it."[17]

Kapuscinski began facing his own existential challenges soon after he received his master's degree in history from the University of Warsaw. Working for the journal *Sztandar Mlodych*, he did an investigative report on the miserable working conditions at the Nowa Huta steel factory in the south of Poland. The report caused such an uproar that he was fired from his job and forced into hiding. Later, as a foreign correspondent, he was temporarily prohibited from leaving the country by government officials for failing to "understand the Marxist-Leninist processes that are at work in the world."[18] With the imposition of martial law in Poland in 1981, he found himself grounded again, his press credentials stripped because of his involvement with the Solidarity trade union. Kapuscinski rebounded each time. "Traveling and writing is my life…I must be an outsider."[19]

Along with fighting government censors, Kapuscinski also faced the restrictions that bind all wire-service reporters. No journalist is more harried by deadlines, production requirements, and stylistic rules. The emptiness inside that came after filing yet another bare-bones wire-service report, the knowledge that the truth still could remain hidden under an avalanche of facts—these things finally prompted him to reach deeper into the stories, writing the second, more personal accounts that ultimately established his reputation. These were the stories that became his books.

It takes a major act of will for any journalist truly to declare his freedom. Furthermore, the communists still had nearly two decades of rule left in Poland when Kapuscinski started writing his books. So, like many fiction writers in the Soviet bloc, he developed a style that employed the techniques of irony and allegory as well as a subtle, finely tuned sense of absurdity to reach his readers. The result became what writer Adam Hochschild has called "magic journalism," the art of telling the truth that the facts and censors might hide. His Polish readers knew he was describing Poland as well as Ethiopia when he depicted official corruption and absurdity in *The Emperor.*

In Kapuscinski, the personal search for authenticity is always linked to his relationship to those around him. In his writings, he always seeks the universal in the particular, a trait that John Merrill's ideological opposite in U.S. academic circles, University of Illinois media scholar Clifford G. Christians, would applaud. Truth, Christians has written, is "reason radiated by love," thus individual authenticity must be contingent on links to the other, the "I" always defined by its relationship to "Thou."[20]

In their seminal work, *Good News: Social Ethics & the Press,* Christians, John P. Ferré, and P. Mark Fackler offer a sharp critique of what they consider the hyper-individualism of the West and, too, of the modern-day, detached, "objective" journalist who has become too divorced from the passions and emotions of the stories he or she covers. "The central feature of human being is community. To the extent that we know the communal, we understand persons. ... In communitarianism, persons have certain inescapable claims on one another that cannot be renounced except at the cost of their humanity. The supreme value of life (is) an affirmation of unmitigated human dignity. Universal solidarity is the normative core of the social and moral order."[21]

Of all journalists, it is the foreign correspondent who typically least feels this sense of universal solidarity, Christians says. "Foreign correspondents are most vulnerable to what Emile Durkheim called *anomie,* a condition reflecting 'the relaxation of social bonds, a sort of collective anesthesia, or social malaise.' ... The foreign assignment has usually been undertaken by reporters with a strong sense of individualism and an inbred suspicion of community encumbrances."[22]

Christians' foreign correspondent resembles the uprooted immigrant in V.S. Naipaul's story, *Tell Me Who To Kill:* "I come from nothing. I have nothing. I will leave with nothing. All afternoon as I walk I feel like a free man. I scorn everything I see... ."[23]

Kapuscinski, at least in part, fits the description. Although a member of the Communist Youth League as a teenager and later a supporter of the Solidarity movement, he has for most of his life eschewed all organizations and any attempts to recruit him into a political role. He once told writer Stephen Schiff that he operates by three rules: "no functions, no titles, no organizations."[24] Even many of the "encumbrances" that most journalists accept as necessities of the craft are rejected by Kapuscinski. Witness his noteless interviews, indifference to names and dates, willingness to use composites.

Yet, if Kapuscinski suffers from anomie, it is the shared anomie of modern mankind. His is a life of contradiction: rootless freedom coupled with a daily dependency on others' help; devil-may-care risk taking tempered by a long-term intimacy with fear. He is the stranger in a strange land who must look beyond nationalities, race, and class to the common wellspring of humanity that binds us all. Therein lies the wholeness all humans seek, the reach beyond isolation and loneliness.

No war correspondent since Ernie Pyle has better evoked the shared loneliness of soldiers and civilians along the frontlines of battle. And Kapuscinski may be in a class by himself in his evocations of the alienation produced by modern-day despotism with its technological, scientific, and bureaucratic weaponry.

Listen to him describe the city/desert dwellers of Iran in *Shah of Shahs*, uprooted from thousands of years of tradition by a leader who is himself rootless, a leader so blinded by notions of the superiority of Western progress and the need to build cities and asphalt the desert that he has lost touch with the essential values and concerns of his own rural, religion-haunted nation: "'People (now) don't want to work, and they don't give a damn about what they produce. Everywhere there's the same listlessness, some kind of vague, sullen resistance. The whole country is stuck on a sandbar,'" Kapuscinski writes, quoting a longtime Iranian expatriate after his return home. "'For these people the concrete has become an asylum, a hideout, salvation. ... The great thing about the concrete is that it has its own clearly demarcated armed frontiers with warning bells along them. When a mind immersed in the concrete begins to approach that border, the bells warn that just beyond lies the field of treacherous general ideas, undesirable reflections, and syntheses. ... To succeed in making each person close himself within the borders of his concrete existence is to create an atomized society made up of n-number of concrete individuals unable to unite into a harmoniously acting comity.'"[25]

Alienation can exist in a business office as well as in a Middle Eastern desert. Here is Kapuscinski describing an attempt by his superiors at the Polish Press Agency to pull him from the frontlines and put him behind a desk: "I cannot suffer a desk! ... Once plunked down behind one, a man will never learn to tear himself free. The loss of his desk will strike him as a natural disaster, a catastrophe, a fall from the abyss. Notice how many people commit suicide at their desks, how many are carried away from their desks to psychiatric hospitals, how many suffer their heart attacks behind desks."[26]

In these words is a good Polish sense of humor and irony but here also are echoes of Kafka, Camus, Jaspers, and other existentialists who saw the utter loneliness and dispiritedness of the Organization Man, battered by the dehumanizing forces of modern-day bureaucracy, technology, power politics. "You survive not by struggling against nature, or by increasing production, or by relentless labor; instead you survive by expending as little energy as possible, by striving constantly to achieve a state of immobility," Kapuscinski once wrote, describing his native Poland under communism. "And fatalism is your philosophy. Man is not the lord of nature, but its slave, humbly accepting commands, reacting to the world around him. He is a dumb servant of a fate from which he can't escape. Fate is the deity. To oppose it is to commit sacrilege and condemn oneself to hell."[27]

Alienation can also be seen in the self-absorbed, profit-obsessed world of the media today, Kapuscinski told Bernard Nezmah. Foreign correspondents, for example, are rushed from country to country with little knowledge of the history and culture and with no time to understand and be able to put events into any meaningful context. "The media world has become the world itself, separate from reality," he said. "Big media have the monopoly, [so] they are competing within the family. They don't allow any competition from the outside. ... The mentality of the chiefs of media is not a mentality toward penetrating, understanding, covering the real world, but in showing how they are managing among others (in the family). Are we ahead or behind?"[28]

In approaching his "mission" as a journalist, Kapuscinski knows the importance of language. "The struggle for the future of the world—and man's consciousness of it—will take place more and more in the realm of language. Language battles, battles with words, are a part of the whole of human history, but, with the advent of mass media, they have become more intense."[29]

In *The Emperor*, Kapuscinski describes the incredibly corrupt and vain Haile Selassie, emperor of Ethiopia, as a man who never wrote, never read, never signed anything and rarely spoke above a mumbled whisper for fear of the *word* and what it could do. In leading his tattered empire, he depended on the whispered reports of his legions of informers, who themselves feared the power of the word. "The Emperor punished silence. On the other hand, incoherent streams of words tired and irritated the Imperial ear, so nervous loquaciousness was also a poor solution."[30]

Haile Selassie was right. Ultimately, words are what brought down his half-century reign, words from journalists who exposed the starvation in the Ethiopian provinces and the corruption, greed, and fear that permeated Selassie's rule from his palace in Addis Ababa.

The importance of the word—the public's need of it, despots' fear of it—places the journalist in a central role in society. Media scholar James Carey equates journalism with democracy itself. Even though "modern despotic societies…go through the motions of journalism," such as in China or the old Soviet Union, "journalism is another name for democracy or, better, you cannot have journalism without democracy."[31] Thus, even in communist Poland, in Kapuscinski and others like him, there was at least the seed of democracy.

The media's role in toppling late-twentieth century autocracies and empires, from Haile Selassie's Ethiopia to the Soviet Union, was crucial. "Formerly, (coup plotters) would assault presidential palaces, governmental, and parliamentary seats," Kapuscinski has written. "Now they try first and foremost to gain control of the television-station building. Recent battles in Vilno and Tbilisi, in Bucharest and in Lima, were waged over television stations, not the president's palace."[32]

Still, the media are a two-edged sword, a Janus with power for good and ill. Political dictators use the media to distribute propaganda to ensure a compliant, passive public. Politicians and corporations in the West use the media to sell images and products also to a compliant, passive public. In both cases, the attempt is made to alter reality for self-serving purposes with little or no real concern about the public's best interests.

This is where journalism enters. It is the role and responsibility of journalism to seek truth, present reality, serve the best interests of the people—not the powerful. "Every effort to bring order to the image of the world, whether we are right or not, is tremendously important," Kapuscinski once told the Krakow-based Roman Catholic weekly, *Tygodnik Powszechny*. "It directs the thinking of contemporary man. Without this direction, man falls into a state of disorientation, from which he seeks to escape by means of false ideas, nationalism, claustrophobia, rejection of those who are 'different,' illusions, irrational fears—all the things he believes he can escape into… ."[33]

This is a challenge that Kapuscinski finds irresistible. "I am fascinated by the real world," he told Bernard Nezmah. "I can sit down in my study and write the books and write novels. But this is not fun for me. For me, it is the fascination of going there, to be there … I could write the history of the last half of the century as I saw it, not as I read it in books, newspapers, or the Internet."[34]

Kapuscinski's mission may be best described as a journey, one of self-discovery but also one undertaken for the sake of others and their own self-discoveries. In his self-searching, Kapuscinski once said he had to "taste (life's) bitter essence and penetrate its mystery" in order to reach the truth about life. "This belief presupposes that life is ultimately an inferno and fragile. It presupposes that life is truly known only to those who suffer, lose, endure adversity, and stumble from defeat to defeat."[35]

The eternal wanderer, the stranger who has suffered and lost but endured nonetheless, ultimately could be all of us. We are all *Everyman*, a community of wanderers, pilgrims. To tell our story, to penetrate what Kapuscinski once called "the forest of things," requires a journalism that becomes in its essence art.[36] Kapuscinski gives us art as well as journalism. Another famous Polish writer and adventurer, Joseph Conrad, saw art this way: "Art itself may be defined as a single-minded attempt to render the highest kind of justice to the visible universe, by bringing to light the truth, manifold and one, underlying its every aspect."[37]

NOTES

1. Ryszard Kapuscinski, interview with Bernard Nezmah, Llubljana, Slovenia, 5 November 2000.
2. Ryszard Kapuscinski, *The Soccer War* (New York: Vintage International, 1992), 25.
3. Kapuscinski, interview with Bernard Nezmah.
4. Michael Zwerin, "Being There," *Details*, March 1991, 122.
5. Ryszard Kapuscinski, *Imperium* (New York: Vintage International, 1995), 309.
6. Judith Graham, ed., "Ryszard Kapuscinski," *1992 Current Biography Yearbook* (New York: The H.W. Wilson Company, 1992), 311.
7. Michael Ignatieff, "What about Anna Andreyevna?" *London Review of Books*, 6 October 1994, 8.
8. Kapuscinski, *The Soccer War*, 130.
9. "Ryszard Kapuscinski," *1992 Current Biography Yearbook*, 307.
10. Kapuscinski, *Imperium*, 3.
11. Kapuscinski, interview with Bernard Nezmah.
12. Zwerin, "Being There," 125.
13. Kapuscinski, *The Soccer War*, 76, 141.
14. Kapuscinski, *The Soccer War*, 137, 77.
15. Gabriel Garcia Marquez, "Out of the Labyrinth; Back to Creativity," *IPI Report*, first quarter 1997, 28.
16. Karl Jaspers, *Man in the Modern Age* (London: Routledge & Kegan Paul LTD, 1951), 125–126.
17. John C. Merrill, *Existential Journalism* (Ames: Iowa State University Press, 1996), v.
18. Kapuscinski, *The Soccer War*, 84.
19. "Ryszard Kapuscinski," *1992 Current Biography Yearbook*, 310.
20. Christians, Ferré, and Fackler, *Good News: Social Ethics and The Press* (New York: Oxford University Press, 1993), 194.
21. Christians, Ferré, and Fackler, *Good News: Social Ethics and the Press*, 14.
22. Christians, Ferré, and Fackler, *Good News: Social Ethics and the Press,* 154.
23. V.S. Naipaul, *In A Free State* (New York: Vintage International, 1984), 96.
24. "Ryscard Kapuscinski," *1992 Current Biography Yearbook*, 310.
25. Ryszard Kapuscinski, *Shah of Shahs* (New York: Vintage International, 1992), 84–85.
26. Kapuscinski, *The Soccer War*, 145–147.
27. Ryszard Kapuscinski, "A Warsaw Diary," *Granta* 15 (Spring 1985), 217.
28. Kapuscinski, interview with Bernard Nezmah.
29. Kapuscinski, "A Warsaw Diary," 222.
30. Ryszard Kapuscinski, *The Emperor: Downfall of an Autocrat* (New York: Harcourt Brace Jovanovich, 1978), 10.
31. James W. Carey, "Where journalism education went wrong," *Journalism Education, The First Amendment Imperative, and the Changing Media Marketplace* (Murfreesboro, TN: Middle Tennessee State University, 1996), 9.

32. Kapuscinski, *Imperium* 322.
33. Excerpt from an interview of Ryszard Kapuscinski by Witold Beres and Krzysztof Burnetko for *Tygodnik Powszechny,* "A Global 'Crisis' of Imagination," *World Press Review*, December 1994, 23.
34. Kapuscinski, interview with Bernard Nezmah.
35. Kapuscinski, "A Warsaw Diary," 216.
36. Zwerin, "Being There," 125.
37. Joseph Conrad, *The Nigger of the 'Narcissus/Typhoon/and other Stories* (Middlesex, England: Penguin Books, 1971), 11.

The White Rose

On the Martyrdom of Student Pamphleteers in Nazi Germany and Their Legacy

by Joseph B. Atkins
Associate Professor of Journalism
University of Mississippi

The entrance hall of the main building of the University of Munich–Ludwig– Maximilians University is nearly empty. This is a cavernous, gray-green space, quiet except for the echoes and muffled sounds from the classrooms down the corridors, very little to distract the occasional passer-by except perhaps the huge statues of King Ludwig I and Prinzregent Luitpold. Looking like Greek gods with their robes and beards, they watch from their perches beside an imposing stairway that leads to an upper level, where light from unseen windows spreads along rows of columns and arches.

On the marble wall opposite the stairway is a modest plaque with seven long-robed, ghost-like figurines carved in bronze, and below them appear a sculpted white rose and list of names: Willi Graf, Professor Kurt Huber, Hans Leipelt, Christoph Probst, Alexander Schmorell, Hans Scholl, and Sophie Scholl. Someone has placed a real white rose among the figurines.

I passed by this plaque many times as a student here in the mid-1970s, knowing vaguely what it represented: the story of the Scholls and the White Rose, the name for the underground movement that fought Adolf Hitler and the Nazis with leaflets. I don't think I ever really stopped to study it, as I'm doing on this summer day in the year 2000.

I know the story by heart now, of how Hans and his sister Sophie were students here at the university in 1942 when they decided they could not stand in silence before the most brutal dictatorship of the twentieth century. Hans, age twenty-four, a medical student who had seen the war firsthand as a medic in France and later in Poland and Russia, was the ringleader in organizing a secret society, a revolutionary cell committed to passive resistance. Joined by Sophie, age twenty-one, soon after her arrival at the university as a student of biology and philosophy, the group was fired by the idealism of its members and the tenets of their Christian faith, and they opposed Hitler with the only weapon available to them: the truth.

With a ragtag collection of typewriters, stencils, paper, and a mimeograph machine, the group printed the truth in the form of leaflets that they distributed clandestinely across Munich and eventually other cities in Germany and Austria.

In their own way, the words on these pamphlets were as powerful as the evil machinery they exposed.

"Nothing is more unworthy of a people than to allow themselves to be governed without resistance by an irresponsible and dark, power-driven ruling clique. ... Who among us can envision the dimensions of the disgrace that will come over us and our children when the dreadful entirety of this all-encompassing criminality is brought to light? ... Already from its beginning, (National Socialism) was a betrayal of humanity, rotten at its very heart, able to extend its existence only through lies. In our land today there is the dictatorship of evil. Every word from the mouth of Hitler is a lie. His mouth is the stinking maw of hell and his might will be condemned to the bowels of the earth."

Even more than a half-century later, who can fail to be stirred by the passion and conviction in these words, by their courage in the face of a power that allowed no dissension whatsoever? The slightest act of resistance brought down upon it the full power of the Nazi state. I have a personal knowledge of this. My German mother spent months in a Gestapo prison for a simple act of kindness to a group of prison workers at the plant where she worked. Certainly the Scholls paid for their "crime" against Nazi Germany.

After extending their movement to underground cells in Hamburg and other German cities, they printed what was to be their last leaflet in February 1943, one that demanded an end to the "frightful bloodbath" Hitler had unleashed upon the world, and that urged the German people again and again to stand up for "freedom and honor." They were caught distributing the leaflets from the stairway in this very foyer, caught by custodian Jakob Schmid and immediately arrested by the Gestapo. Hitler's "hanging judge," Roland Freisler, came in from Berlin to "try" their case. The scarlet-robed Freisler made short work of the unrepentant rebels, sentencing them to die by guillotine. Moments before Hans was beheaded, he cried out, "Long live freedom!"

This was a resistance effort that must have been particularly insulting to the Nazi executioners. First of all, it took place here at the University of Munich, a place that Sophie Scholl's biographer, Hermann Vinke, described as the "spiritual stronghold of National Socialism." The university president was a high-ranking member of the SS. Its alumni included the notorious Dr. Josef Mengele, the Nazis' savage doctor at Auschwitz. And, of course, Munich itself was the birthplace of the party, the fertile soil from which the evil flowers of Naziism sprung.

Second, the fact that the White Rose—which Austrian poet Ilse Aichinger has called "perhaps…the most successful resistance in the Third Reich…a resistance of life, of truth, of warmth and most of all of the spirit"—was led by German young people must have been especially galling to the Nazis. Hans Scholl himself was a former member of the Hitler Youth. One of Hitler's greatest dreams was to instill his ideas, his goals, *his* spirit into the youth of Germany. "You are flesh of our flesh, blood of our blood, the same spirit that rules us burns in your minds," Hitler told thousands of them in one of the giant rallies featured in Leni Riefenstahl's film *Triumph of the Will.*

A third, more subtle insult lies in the mysterious name of the group. A rose can mean purity or it can possess the ancient Roman symbolism of secrecy, but Hans Scholl told his interrogators that he took the name from a novel, probably B. Traven's *The White Rose*, the account of a peasant uprising in Mexico against tyranny and evil. Traven, author of *The Treasure of the Sierra Madre* and one of world literature's great mysteries, used a variety of pseudonyms and is believed to have been the revolutionary journalist Ret Marut, who took part in the brief socialist takeover in Munich at the end of the World War I. Thus he was one of those "Schwabing decadents" whom Hitler describes with fuming rage in *Mein Kampf*, socialists who tried to turn Germany into a "pig-sty." Schwabing is Munich's bohemian quarter near the university. The Scholls also lived in Schwabing.

The members of the White Rose were not professional journalists—although Hans Scholl contemplated becoming one—but their act was in the best tradition of resistance journalism in its courage and its devotion to truth in the face of tyranny. Theirs was truly a voice in the wilderness, trying to fill the giant void left by Hitler's complete appropriation of the German media.

In the years prior to Hitler's ascension to power in March 1933, the *Munich Post* and a few other publications had bitterly and bravely opposed him. After March 1933, however, they were all shut down, ransacked, their editors sent to Dachau or into exile. Mainstream media criticism of Hitler ceased.

By the summer of 1942, when the first White Rose leaflet appeared, the German media was one collective mouthpiece for Hitler. As Inge Scholl, sister of Hans and Sophie, recounts in her book, *The White Rose: Munich 1942–1943*, front-page headlines such as "Hate Is Our Prayer—And Victory Our Reward" were typical of German newspapers at the time. "The papers were like mine fields. It was dangerous to go through them. … It was their task to aid in the total quenching of the German intellect."

Nowhere in the newspapers were there reports of the daily executions, of the village priests imprisoned because they prayed for prisoners of war, of the destitute mothers clinging to their dead babies near the frontlines, of the real stories behind the endless obituaries of dead soldiers on the back pages.

This silence was an affront to the Scholls, both of whom were steeped in the Germany of Goethe, Schiller, and Heine, the land of poets and thinkers, not the Germany that had become what Vinke called a "country of informers and surveillants." They, like another famous martyr of the German resistance, Dietrich Bonhoeffer, were also driven by their religious convictions, the Christian existentialism forged in the writings of St. Augustine, Blaise Pascal, Søren Kierkegaard, and, of course, in the Bible with its exhortation to "Be ye doers of the word, and not hearers only."

After the capture and execution of the Scholls, a Munich newspaper reported that "the culprits, typical loners, had transgressed shamelessly against the defensive strength and the spirit of the German nation. ... In view of the heroic fight of the German nation, depraved elements of that kind have earned nothing but quick and dishonorable death." With this assessment, the curtain of silence fell again, and it was as if the White Rose had never existed.

Ultimately, however, it was the spirit of the Scholls and the White Rose, not the uniformed tyrants who sought to destroy them, that triumphed and that lives today. It is a spirit that reaches beyond time, place, and nationality to all of us; a spirit of freedom, courage, and hope, a spirit for all of humanity but also for the journalist, whose mission in life has been the focus of this book.

"These were students who stood for the civil rights of citizens, for freedom, who showed courage, and in certain ways what they did was a journalistic task," Silke Oekonomopulos, a twenty-two-year-old student of media and literature at the University of Munich, told me during my visit in the summer of 2000. "Every student in Germany knows them, knows what they represent in terms of the idea of the resistance."

Prior to Hitler's rise, economic chaos, political ineptitude, residual bitterness from the first World War, and a general malaise and loss of values, political and otherwise, made the German people desperate for a "Heiland", or savior, as writer Ron Rosenbaum recounts in his book, *Explaining Hitler*. What they got was Adolf Hitler. Today, Germans aren't necessarily looking for a savior but they do need heroes. A recent article in the Germany publication, *Die Woche*, described at length how Germans today have to look back to people such as Hans and Sophie Scholl to find real heroes worthy of emulation.

What is a hero? Someone who lives and acts by convictions? Who has a moral core that won't be compromised? Someone who stands for truth? Dietrich Bonhoeffer once warned that deification even of truth is wrong if it's not in service of humanity. The poet Schiller agreed. Make yourselves freer to be more humane, he urged.

The journalists depicted in the pages of this book—from crusaders to lonely itinerants—are made of flesh and blood. As journalists, they know that their service to truth can never be separate from their service to humanity.

However differently they may describe it, that is their mission. How grievous it is to society when that mission is not served. Consider Nazi Germany, where young medical and philosophy students had to step forward to do what the professional journalists could or would not. Consider how important it is for young, would-be journalists in Germany such as Silke Oekonomopulos to know about the Scholls and their astonishing resistance to tyranny, for which they paid the ultimate price.

Every writer in this book has his or her own views about the mission of journalism. Yet they would agree that good journalism involves reaching beyond oneself in a way that serves and benefits others as well as oneself. It involves a personal sense of integrity, more than a little courage, and an inner resolve. To borrow here again from the late Chuck Trapkus, "We must go back to first things. Once we figure out who we are and what we're all about, the rest follows."

Near the beginning of *The Mission*, John Merrill rather pessimistically predicts a decline of individuality and freedom among journalists as they adapt to the order-loving, corporatized media world that exists today. Indeed, we see in these pages how a lack or a loss of an individual sense of mission can cause journalists to fail significantly, whether it happens in postcommunist Hungary, the emerging democracies of Southern Africa, or a small town in the U.S. South. Certainly it's easy to lose sight of one's mission. The conformist-minded culture in Japan discourages any vision that isn't the corporate point of view. The fiercely partisan editors of Zambia have difficulty seeing beyond the immediate political battle. In Lebanon, the self-serving interests of government and the private sector have undermined the all-important role of television. Despite its comparative freedom, the postwar press in Germany has often failed to see its own narrowness and xenophobia in dealing with immigrants and other minorities.

Yet the overwhelming message of *The Mission* is that the best journalists are still valiantly willing to challenge stultifying order and authority—whether the challenger is Jerry Mitchell breaking the code of silence in search of long-overdue justice in the Deep South of the United States, or *El Espectador*'s defiance of the Colombian drug lords, or Pavol Mudry's challenge to Slovakian strongman Vladimir Meciar.

Good journalists don't undertake the risks of challenging authority just for the sake of doing it. Jerry Mitchell sees himself in the tradition of the early twentieth century muckrakers who exposed injustice in order to make society better. Ryszard Kapuscinski feels compelled to tell the unknown stories of the world's forgotten and marginalized. Bernard Nezmah uses his pen to make sure that politicians in postcommunist Slovenia mean what they say and say what they mean.

Nietzsche once wrote, "He who has a *why* to live for can bear almost any *how*," a view echoed by the famous psychiatrist and Auschwitz survivor Viktor

E. Frankl. Frankl believed that the search for meaning is the central struggle of all human life. To find that meaning and then to try and live it is the path to the worthy life, the goal we all seek. Journalists, too, of course, seek that path, but what is so especially human and even noble about their work is that, when done well and with commitment, honesty, and integrity, it helps others find their way as well. Journalists have done this in Eastern Europe, the U.S. South, in India, and in Colombia and Mexico. They are doing it this very day in other parts of the world that we'll read about tomorrow.

References

Adeniyi, A. and J. A. Ogbodo. (2000) "Senator orders ethics code for journalists." *The Guardian Online*, http://ngrguardiannews.com, 27 September.

Aggarwala, N.K. (1979) "What is Development News?" *Journal of Communication* 29, No. 2: 180–181.

Albrecht, M.C. (1956) "Does literature reflect common values?" *American Journal of Sociology* 21: 722–729.

Alterman, J. B. (1998) *New Media, New Politics? From Satellite Television to The Internet in the Arab World*. Washington Institute for Near East Policy, Washington D.C.

Alterman, E. (1997) "Lionizing Journalism." *The Nation* 24: 6.

Al-Hasan, H. (no date) *Public opinion, information and public relations* (in Arabic). Ad-Dar al-Lubnaniyah lil-Nashr, Beirut.

Badran, A.R. (1991) "Christian Broadcasting in the Eastern Mediterranean: the case of the Middle East Television." *Gazette* 47 (1).

Bagdikian, B.H. (2000) *The Media Monopoly*. Beacon Press, Boston: 4.

Barron, J.A. (1973) *Freedom of the press: For whom?* University of Indiana Press, Bloomington.

Beck, K and G. Vowe. (1998) "Zwischen Anarchie und Zensur—Zur Regulierung internationaler computervermittelter Kommunikation." In *Deutschland im Dialog der Kulturen. Medien, Images, Verständigung*, Siegfried, Q. and G. Wolfgang (Hg.) UVK Medien, Konstanz: 349–366.

Bertrand, C.J. (1993) "Foreword." In *Good News: Social Ethics & the Press*, C.G. Christians, J.P. Ferré and P.M. Fackler, Oxford University Press, New York: 6–7.

Binder, L. (1966) *Politics in Lebanon*. John Wiley and Sons, New York.

Birkhead, D. (1997) "Should Professional Competence Be Taught as Ethical?" *Journal of Mass Media Ethics* 12: 211–220.

Bonhoeffer, D. (1975) *Ethics*. MacMillan Publishing Co., Inc, New York.

Boulos, J.C. (1995) *Television: History and Stories* (in Arabic, French translation, *La Tele: Quelle Histoire?* J. Saadeh). Fiches du Monde Arabe, Beirut.

Bourgault,L. M. (1995) *Mass Media in Sub-Saharan Africa*. Indiana University Press, Bloomington.

Boyce, J. "'Exotenbonus' als persönliches Unwort." *Sage and Schreibe* 3/4 (1999): 18.

Boyd, D. (1991) "Lebanese broadcasting: Unofficial electronic media during a prolonged civil war." *Journal of Broadcasting and Electronic Media* 35(3): 269–287.

Boyd, D. (1999) *Broadcasting in the Arab World*. Iowa State University Press, Ames.

Brosius, H. B. and F. Esser. (1995) "Eskalation durch Berichterstattung?" *Massenmedien und fremdenfeindliche Gewalt,* Westdeutscher Verlag, Opladen.

Browne, D. R. (1975) "Television as an instrument of national stabilization: The Lebanese experience." *Journalism Quarterly* 52: 692–698

Bruns, T., F. Marcinkowski, J. U. Nieland, G. Ruhrmann, and T. Schierl (1996) "Das analytische Modell." In *Fernsehen als Objekt und Moment des sozialen Wandels. Faktoren und Folgen der aktuellen Veränderung des Fernsehens*, Schatz and Heribert (Hg.). Westdeutscher Verlag, Opladen: 19–56.

Burkhart, R. (1994) "Was ist eigentlich ein Medium?" In *Die Zukunft der Kommunikation. Phänomene und Trends in der Informationsgesellschaft.* Latzer, M., M.Rabler, U.Siegert, G. Steinmaurer (Hg.), Studienverlag, Wien: 61–72.

Carey, J.W. (1996) "Where journalism education went wrong." In *Journalism Education, The First Amendment Imperative, and the Changing Media Marketplace*, Middle Tennessee State University, Murfreesboro: 5–9.

Carey, J.W. (1998) *Communication in Culture*. Unwin Hyman, Winchester.

Christians, C. G., J. P. Ferré, and P. M. Fackler. (1993) *Good News: Social Ethics & The Press*. Oxford University Press, New York.

Ciroma, A. (2000) "Between Arewa Forum and Obasanjo." *The Guardian Online*, http://ngrguardiannews.com, Nov. 14.

Conrad, J. (1971) *The Nigger of the 'Narcissus'/Typhoon/and other Stories*. Penguin Books, Middlesex, England: 11.

Cranston, M. (1998) *Political Dialogues*. Basic Books, New York: 148–149.

Cronin, M.M. (1993) "Trade Press Roles in Promoting Journalistic Professionalism, 1884–1917." *Journal of Mass Media Ethics* 8: 227–238.

Dagher, C. H. (2000) *Bring Down the Walls: Lebanon's Postwar Challenge*. St. Martins Press, New York.

Dajani, N. (1979) *Lebanon: Studies in Broadcasting*. International Institute of Communications, London.

Dajani, N. (1989). "An analysis of the press in four Arab countries." In *UNESCO Reports and Papers on Mass Communication*, The Vigilant Press, Paris, No. 103, 75–88.

Dajani, N. (1991) "Managing the crisis of public services in West Beirut." In *Reconstruire Beyrouth*, Beyhum, N., Etudes Sur LeMonde Arabe, Paris.

Dajani, N. (1992) *Disoriented media in a fragmented society: The Lebanese experience*. American University Press, Beirut.

Dajani, N. (1999) "Disparity between Public Interest and Money and Power." (in Arabic) *Al-Mustakbal al-Arabi* 22, No. 250, 83–106.

De Lange, W. (1998) *A History of Japanese Journalism*. Javasche Courant Japan Library, Yokohama: 24.

Delgado, J.M. (1972) "Die 'Gastarbeiter' in der Presse." *Eine inhaltsanalytische Studie,* Westdeutscher Verlag, Opladen .

De Uriarte, M. L. (1996) "Where has the free press gone?" *Quill*, December: 21.

Dorsher, M. (1996) "Whither the Public Sphere: Prospects for Cybersphere." *Conference of the Mass Communication & Society Division of AEJMC,* University of North Dakota, Grand Forks, ND.

Ebo, B.L. (1994) "The Ethical Dilemma of African Journalists: A Nigerian Perspective." *Journal of Mass Media Ethics* 9: 84–93

Etzioni, A. (1996) *The New Golden Rule: Community and Morality in a Democratic Society.* Harper Collins—Basic Books, New York.

Etzioni, A. (1995) "The Need for a New Paradigm." *Responsive Community* 5: I.

Farley, M. (1996) "Japan's Press and the Politics of Scandal." *Media and Politics in Japan*, University of Hawaii Press, Honolulu.

Frankl, V.F. (1965) *Man's Search for Meaning.* Washington Square Press, New York.

Freeman, L.A. (2000) *Closing the Shop*. Princeton University Press, Princeton.

French, H. (2001) "Rare Event in Japan Politics: TV Debate on New Party Boss." *The New York Times*, April 18.

Friedland, L.A. and Z. Mengbai. (1996) "International Television Coverage of Beijing Spring 1989: A Comparative Approach." *Journalism & Mass Communication Monographs* 156: 11–12.

Fromm, E. (1941) *Escape from Freedom*. Holt, Rinehart & Winston, New York.

Gaunt, P. (1992) *Making the Newsmakers: International Handbook on Journalism Training*. Greenwood Press, Westport: 113–161.

Gbadamosi, G. (2001) "How Rogers shot Ibru, Kudirat, by Abacha's driver." *The Guardian Online*, http://ngrguardiannews.com, January 24.

Giegler, H and G. Ruhrmann (1990) "Remembering the News. A LISREL Model." *European Journal of Communication* 5, 4: 463–488.

Gill, A. (1994) *An Honourable Defeat. A History of German Resistance to Hitler, 1933–1945*. Hery Holt and Co. Inc., New York.

Golding, P. (1977) "Media Professionalism in the Third World: the Transfer of an Ideology." in *Mass Communication and Society*, ed. J. Curan et al. Edward Arnold, London: 291–308.

Gourevitch, P. (1997) "Letter from the Congo: Continental Shift." *The New Yorker*, August 4: 42.

Graham,J., ed. (1992) "R. Kapuscinski." *Current Biography Yearbook*, The H.W. Wilson Company, New York: 307–311.

Hachten, W. A. (1996) *The World News Prism*. Iowa State University Press, Ames: 127–128.

Hall, I. P. (1998) *Cartels of the Mind*. W.W Norton & Company, New York: 73.

Heuvel, J.V. and E.E. Dennis (1993) *The Unfolding Lotus: East Asia's Changing Media*. The Freedom Forum Media Studies Center, New York: 31.

Hitler, A. (1971) *Mein Kampf.* (English translation R. Manheim), Houghton Mifflin, Boston.

Hocking. W.E. (1947) *Freedom of the Press*. University of Chicago Press, Chicago.

Hömberg, W. and S. Schlemmer (1995) "Fremde als Objekt. Asylberichterstattung in deutschen Tageszeitungen." *Media Perspektiven* 1: 11–20.

Hughes. F. (1950) *Prejudice and the Press*. Devin-Adair Company, New York.

Ibelema, M. (1994) "Professionalism as Risk Management: A Typology of Journalists in Developing Countries." *Journal of Development Communication* 5: 22–33.

Ignatieff, M.(1994) "What about Anna Andreyevna?" *London Review of Books*, London.

Jäger, M. G. Cleve, I. Ruth and S. Jäger. (1998) "Von deutschen Einzeltätern und ausländischen Banden. Medien und Straftaten." *Mit Vorschlägen zur Vermeidung diskriminierender Berichterstattung*, Duisburg.

Jaspers, K. (1951) *Man in the Modern Age*. Routledge and Kegan Paul LTD, London: 125–126.

Jimada, U. (1992) "Eurocentric Media Training in Nigeria: What Alternative?" *Journal of Black Studies* 22: 366–379.

Johnson, E. (1990) *Mississippi's Defiant Years 1953–1973*. Lake Harbor, Forest, Mississippi.

Johnson, M. (1977) "Political bosses and their gangs: *Zu'ama* and *Qabadayat* in the Sunni quarters of Beirut." in *Patrons and clients in Mediterranean societies*, Gellner, E. and J. Waterbury (eds.), Duckworth, London.

Jung, M., M. Wengeler and K. Böke. (1997) "Die Sprache des Migrationsdiskurses." *Das Reden über "Ausländer" in Medien, Politik und Alltag*, Westdeutscher Verlag, Opland.

Kaplan, R. (1997) "Was Democracy Just a Moment?" *The Atlantic Monthly*, December: 55–80.

Kapuscinski, R. (1978) *The Emperor: Downfall of an Autocrat*. Harcourt Brace Jovanovich, New York: 10.

Kapuscinski, R. (1985) "A Warsaw Diary." *Granta* 15: 217.

Kapuscinski, R. (1992) *The Soccer War*. Vintage International, New York: 84–147.

Kapuscinski, R. (1992) *Shah of Shahs*. Vintage International, New York: 84–85.

Kapuscinski, R. (1995) *Imperium*. Vintage International, New York: 19–21.

Kempt, H. (1994) "Media Ethics Education in the '90s: Status and Trends." Master's Thesis, University of Mississippi: 67.

Kieran, M. (1997) *Media Ethics: A Philosophical Approach*. Praeger, Westport: 69–74.

Klingler, W., P. Zoche, M. Harnischfeger, and C. Kolo. (1998) "Mediennutzung der Zukunft. Ergebnisse einer Expertenbefragung zur Medienentwicklung bis zum Jahr 2005/2015." *Media Perspektiven* 10/98: 490–497.

Knieper, T. (1998) "Der 'Ausländer' im Spiegel der politischen Karrikatur Deutschlands." in *Deutschland im Dialog der Kulturen. Medien, Images, Verständigung*, Q. Siegfried/G. Wolfgang (Hg.) UVK Medien, Konstanz: 101–114.

Kohring, M. A. Görke and G. Ruhrmann (1996) "Konflikte, Kriege, Katastrophen." in *Internationale Kommunikation. Eine Einführung* Meckel, M./ M.Kriener (Hg.): Westdeutscher Verlag, Opladen: 283–298.

Korzybski, A. (1993) *Science and Sanity*. Science Press, Lancaster

Kowalsky, W. and W. Schroeder (1994) "Rechtsextremismus." *Einführung und Forschungsbilanz*, Westdeutscher Verlag, Opladen.

Kraidy, M. (1998) "Broadcasting regulation and civil society in postwar Lebanon." *Journal of Broadcasting and Electronic Media*. 42 (3), 387–400.

Kraidy, M. (1999) "State control of television news in 1990s Lebanon." *Journalism and Mass Communication Quarterly* 76(3): 485–498

Levy, L.W. (1960) *Legacy of suppression*. Harvard University Press, Cambridge

Lewis, A. (1997) "Rally for Latin Journalists." *Commercial-Appeal* of Memphis, TN, 6 August, sec. A, 10.

Madugba, A. (1999) "Court impounds *New Nigerian*'s vehicles over N3 million libel fine." *This Day*, 27 October.

Maeda, T. (2000) "Newspapers Help Bureaucrats Maintain Status Quo." *The Japan Times*, June 23: 3.

Makdisi, Samir, (1977) "An Appraisal of Lebanon's Post War Economic Development and a Look to the Future." *The Middle East Journal*, 267–280.

Mander, J. (1996) "The Dark Side of Globalization." *The Nation*, 15/22: 10–13.

Marquez, G.G. (1997) "Out of the Labyrinth; Back to Creativity." *IPI Report*, First Quarter: 26–28.

Marquez, G.G. (1962) *Man Against Mass Society.* Henry Regnery Co., Chicago.

Merrill, J.C. and S. J. Odell. (1983) *Philosophy and Journalism.* Longman Inc., New York: 172.

Merrill, J. C. (1996) *Existential Journalism.* Iowa State University Press, Ames: 124.

Merrill, J.C. (1998) *The Princely Press: Machiavelli on American Journalism.* University Press of America, Lanharn.

McChesney, R.W. (1999) *Rich Media, Poor Democracy.* Urbana and Chicago, University of Illinois Press, Urbana: 79.

McLean, D. (1998) "Development Redefined: An examination of Malaysian politicians' rhetorical efforts to explain full development to citizens." *The 15th Annual Intercultural Communication Conference,* Miami.

McManus, J.H. (1997) "Who's Responsible for Journalism?" *Journal of Mass Media Ethics* 12/1: 5.

Merten, K. and G. Ruhrmann. (1982) "Die Entwicklung der inhaltsanalytis-chen Methode." *Kölner Zeitschrift für Soziologie und Sozialpsychologie* 34, 4: 696–716.

Merten, K and G. Ruhrmann (1986) "Das Bild der Ausländer in der deutschen Presse." *Ergebnisse einer systematischen Inhaltsanalys,* Frankfurt.

Merten, K. (1999) *Gewalt durch Gewalt im Fernsehen?* Westdeutscher Verlag, Opladen.

Mieth, D. (1997) "The Basic Norm of Truthfulness: Its Ethical Justification and Universality." in *Communication Ethics and Universal Values,* ed. C. Christians and M. Traber, Thousand Oaks: 87–104.

Ministry of Information, Lebanon. (1991) *Proceedings of the seminar on the re-organization of communication in Lebanon* (in Arabic). Beirut.

Mitchell, R. (1983) *Censorship in Japan.* Princeton University Press, Princeton: 55.

Moemeka, A.A. (1997) "Communalistic Societies: Community and Self-Respect as African Values." in *Communication Ethics and Universal Values,* ed. C. Christians and M. Traber, Thousand Oaks: 170–193.

Morrison, J. (1997) "The Changing Model of Russian Media and Journalism Education." *Journalism & Mass Communication Educator* 52: 31.

Moussalem, A. (1977) *La presses Libanaise.* Librairie de droit et de jurisprudence, Paris.

Murphy, D.A. (1997) "A Slow Transition In Eastern Europe." *IPI Report,* first quarter: 13.

Naipaul V.S. (1984) *In A Free State.* Vintage International, New York: 96.

Neuwöhner, U and G. Ruhrmann. (1998) "Das Interesse der Radiohörer an Ausländerthemen. Ergebnisse einer repräsentativen Studie in Baden-Württemberg." In *Migration 2000—Perspektiven für das 21. Jahrhundert. 5. Radioforum Ausländer bei uns,* M.B. Karl-Heinz/K. Martin, Nomos, Baden-Baden: 109–132.

Nixon, R. and J. Green. (1997) "Who owns the Southern Media?" *Southern Exposure*, XXV/1 & 2: 12.

Nuheler, F. (1998), "Migration und Konflikpotentiale im Jahr 2000." Braun, M, Heinz, K./Kilgus, M. (Hg.): *Migration 2000—Perspektiven für das 21. Jahrhundert. 5. Radioforum Ausländer bei uns*, Nomos, Baden-Baden: 29–38.

Nwabuikwu, P. (2001) "A lifetime for the *New Nigerian*." *The Guardian Online*, http://ngrguardiannews.com, Wednesday, 21 March.

Nwezeh, K. (2001) "Federal Government Warns Detractors, Media Houses." *This Day*, April 4.

Nwosu, I.E. (1987) "Mass Media Discipline and Control in Contemporary Nigeria: A Contextual Critical Analysis." *Gazette* 39: 17–29.

Ofuoku, M. (1999) "Way out for Daily Times." *Newswatch*, August 27.

Ogbondah, C.W. (2000) "The Press in Shackles." *Newswatch*, 6 April.

Ognianova, E.V. (1993) "On Forgiving Bulgarian Journalists/Spies." *Journal of Mass Media Ethics* 8: 156–157.

Ognianova, E.V. (1997) "The Transitional Media System of Post-Communist Bulgaria." *Journalism & Mass Communication Monographs* 162: 27.

Okabe, R. (1983) "Cultural Assumptions of East and West: Japan and the United States." in *Intercultural Communication Theory: Current Perspectives*, ed. W.B. Gudykunst, Sage, Beverly Hills: 21–44.

Okoh, A., B. Ojeme, and C. Ngwoneho. (1999) "AIT, MITV, Ray Power, 17 others lose licences." *Vanguard*, http://www.afbis.com/vanguard. Transmitted October 5.

Owen, F. (1996) "Let Them Eat Software." *Village Voice* 6: 30.

Peikoff, L. (1983) *Ominous Parallels*. New American Library, New York: 91.

Pharr, S.J. (1996) "Introduction: Media and Politics in Japan: Historical and Contemporary Perspectives." *Media and Politics in Japan*, 11.

Pinsky, M.I. (1997) "Living Dangerously: Journalism in Mexico can be a deadly business." *Quill*, May: 18.

Pratt, C,B. and G. W. McLaughlin. (1990) "Ethical Dimensions of Nigerian Journalists and Their Newspapers." *Journal of Mass Media Ethics*, 5, No. 1: 30–34.

Prideaux, F. (2001) "Japan Pol Seeks Wealthy Immigrants." *The Associated Press*, April 19.

Rantanen, T. (1996) "What Is to Be Done? Media in Post-socialist Countries." *Journal of Communication* 46: 171.

Revel, J.F. (1997) *The Totalitarian Temptation*. Penguin Books, New York.

Richani, N. (1998) *Dilemmas of Democracy and Political Parties in Sectarian Societies: The Case of the Progressive Socialist Party of Lebanon 1949–1996*. St. Martins Press, New York.

Rosenbaum, R. (1999) *Explaining Hitler*. Harper Perennial, New York.

Rössler, P. (1998) "Wirkungsmodelle: die digitale Herausforderung. Überlegungen zu einer Inventur bestehender Erklärungsansätzen der Medienwirkungsforschung." In *Online Kommunikation. Beiträge zur Nutzung und Wirkung*, Westdeutscher Verlag, Opladen: 17–46.

Rugh, W. A. (1979) *The Arab Press*. Syracuse University Press, Syracuse.

Ruhrmann G. and J. Kollmer. (1987) "Ausländerberichterstattung in der Kommune." *Inhaltsanalyse Bielefelder Tageszeitungen unter besonderer Berücksichtigung ausländerfeindlicher Alltagstheorien*, Westdeutscher Verlag, Opladen.

Ruhrmann, G. (1993) "Ist Aktualität noch aktuell? Journalistische Selektivität und ihre Folgen." in *Krieg als Medienereignis. Grundlagen und Perspektiven der Krisenkommunikation*, L. Martin Hg., Westdeutscher Verlag, Opladen: 81–96

Ruhrmann G. and H. Sievert. (1994) "Bewußtseinswandel durch Kampagnen gegen Ausländerfeindlichkeit? Zur Effektivität von Anzeigen und TV-Spots." *pr magazin* 25, 12: 35–42.

Ruhrmann, G, J. Kollbeck and W. Möltgen. (1996) "'Fremdverstehen', Medien, Fremdenfeindlichkeit und die Möglichkeit von Toleranzkampagnen." *Publizistik* 41, 1: 32–50.

Ruhrmann, G. (1996) "Risikokommunikation zwischen Experten und Laien." *Universitas* 51, 603: 955–964.

Ruhrmann, G. and J. U. Nieland. (1997) *Interaktives Fernsehen. Entwicklung, Dimensionen, Fragen, Thesen*. Westdeutscher Verlag, Opladen.

Ruhrmann, G. (1998) "Mediendarstellung von Fremden. Images, Resonanzen und Probleme." In *Deutschland im Dialog der Kulturen. Medien—Images—Verständigung* Q. Siegfried, G. Wolfgang (Hg.), Konstanz: 35–50.

Ruhrmann, G. and J.Woelke (1998) "Rezeption von Fernsehnachrichten im Wandel. Desiderate und Perspektiven der Forschung." In *Fernsehnachrichten. Prozesse, Strukturen, Funktionen*, Kamps, K./Meckel, M. (Hg.), Westdeutscher Verlag, Opladen: 103–110.

Ruhrmann, G. (1998) "Interkulturelle Kommunikation." In *Politische Kommunikation in der demokratischen Gesellschaft*, J. Ottfried, U. Sarcinelli, U. Saxer (Hg.): Westdeutscher Verlag, Opladen: 663–664.

Ruhrmann, G. (1999) "Medyanin Yabvancilara Iliskin Haberli Veris Sekli - Alamanya´daki Türk Kadinlari Imajminin Olusumuna Etkileri." In *Alman Medyasinda Türk Kadinlari*, Goethe Institut (Hg.), Ankara: 14–28.

Ruhrmann, G. (1999) "Digitales Fernsehen und Individualisierung. Perspektiven für die Mediennutzungsforschung." In *Die Zukunft der Kommunikation. Phänomene und Trends in der Informationsgesellschaft* U. Siegert and G. Steinmaurer, Thomas (Hg.), Studienverlag,) Wien: 329–346.

Salibi, K. (1988) *A House of Many Mansions: The History of Lebanon Reconsidered*. I.B., Tauris, London.

Scheffer B. (1997) *Medien und Fremdenfeindlichkeit. Alltägliche Paradoxien, Dilemmata, Absurditäten und Zynismen*. Leske + Budrich, Opland.

Schillinger, E. (1988) "Journalism at Moscow State: The Impact of Glasnost." *Journalism Educator* 43: 52–56.

Scholl, I. (1970) *Students Against Tyranny* (English translation A. R. Schultz). Wesleyan University Press, Middletown.

Scholl, I. (1983) *The White Rose, Munich 1942–1943* (English translation A. R. Schultz), Wesleyan University Press, Middletown.

Schultz, J. (1998) *Reviving the Fourth Estate: Democracy, Accountability and the Media*. Cambridge University Press, Cambridge: 233.

Schwartz, F. (1998) *Advice & Consent*. Cambridge University Press, Cambridge: 84

Shah, H. (1996) "Modernization, Marginalization, and Emancipation: Toward a Normative Model of Journalism and National Development." *Communication Theory* 6: 143–167.

Stakhanov. O and C. Bowman. (1996) "Russia at the Crossroads." *Nieman Reports* 4: 50.

Trapkus, C. (1999). "Reclaiming Responsibility: A Catholic Worker Take on Art." *The Catholic Radical*, Rock Island, Illinois: 7.

UNDP (1999) *Human Development Report 1999*. Oxford University Press, New York: 55.

van Wolferen, K. (1989) *The Enigma of Japanese Power*. Macmillan Publishing Co., Inc., London: 94.

Vinke, H. (1984) *The Short Life of Sophie Scholl* (English translation by H. Pachter). Harper & Row, New York.

Vinke, H., F. Voss, W. Pohl, G. Zambonini, U.Wagner-Grey and G. Schneider. (1998) "Vom Funkhaus Europa, SFB 4 Mulitkulti über DAB und Internet zu neuen ARD-Ausländerprogrammen—Perspektiven für neue Programmangebote für Migranten und Einheimische." In *Migration 2000—Perspektiven für das 21. Jahrhundert. 5. Radioforum Ausländer bei uns*, M.Braun; K.einz andK. Martin (Hg.), Nomos, Baden-Baden: 133–147.

Weischenberg, S. (1995) "Journalistik. Medienkommunikation: Theorie und Praxis 2." *Medientechnik, Medienfunktionen, Medienakteure*, Westdeutscher Verlag, Opladen.

Weschler, L. (1997) "Aristotle in Belgrade." *The New Yorker* 10: 33.

Wilcox, D.L. (1975) *Mass Media in Black Africa: Philosophy and Control*. Praeger, New York: 68.

Zwerin, M. (1991) "Being There." *Details*, March: 122–125.

Index

ISBN 0-8138-2188-6

90000

9 780813 821887